ONE CLEAN SHOT

DANIELLE GIRARD

Your Free Rookie Club Short Story is Waiting

San Francisco Crime Scene Analyst and aspiring Rookie Club member Naomi Muir is passionate about her work, especially the cases where she works alongside seasoned inspectors, like Jamie Vail. But this latest case has her unnerved. A serial sex offender is growing more aggressive. He attacks in the dirty underbelly of the San Francisco streets… and eerily close to Naomi's inexpensive apartment. Each crime is more violent than the last and also nearer to where Naomi herself lives.

To solve the case, Naomi will have to rely on her own wit and an unexpected new partner as the attacker gets too close to home…

Go to

www.daniellegirard.com/newsletter to claim your copy now!

THE ROOKIE CLUB CAST, IN ORDER OF APPEARANCE:

Hailey Wyatt, Homicide Inspector (also in *Dead Center, Dark Passage, Grave Danger,* and *Everything to Lose*)

Hal Harris, Homicide Inspector, partner to Hailey Wyatt (also in *Everything to Lose*)

Cameron Cruz, Special Ops Team/Sharpshooter (featured in *Dark Passage*; also in *Grave Danger*)

Linda James, Precinct Captain (also in *Dark Passage and Everything to Lose*)

Jamie Vail, Sex Crimes Inspector (featured in *Everything to Lose*; also in *One Clean Shot, Dark Passage,* and *Grave Danger*)

Jess Campbell, Immigration and Customs Enforcement (ICE) (also in *Dead Center and Dark Passage*)

Shelby Tate, Medical Examiner (also in *Dead Center*)

Ryaan Berry, Triggerlock Inspector (also in *Dark Passage and Grave Danger*)

Roger Sampers, Head Criminalist, Crime Scene Unit (also in *Dead Center, Grave Danger,* and *Everything to Lose*)

PROLOGUE

STANDING IN HER in-laws' kitchen, Hailey Wyatt removed the red bell pepper from the steamer with a pair of tongs.

Her eyes burned with exhaustion. She just wanted to be home, catching up on her sleep so she could face another day tomorrow. And hopefully make a break in this case—the murder of a couple in San Francisco and a death in Sacramento that had previously been ruled a suicide. There was some connection between the deaths and gun politics. That was as much as they knew. That and the killer liked to leave them strange clues.

One night off and here she was, at the senator's house. She'd be back on the case tomorrow, banging her head against the walls in Homicide. This was supposed to be her night to relax. She'd wanted a quiet evening at home, with her children.

"A family dinner," John had pressed when she balked at the idea of going out. "My parents want to spend time with us and their grandchildren." She'd never known her grandparents. Hell, she had never even met her father. Of course, she wanted Camilla and Ali to be close to John's parents.

But wasn't it fair to want time with *her* family? Just her and the girls and John?

And since they'd arrived, the girls weren't even spending time with their grandparents. Not Ali anyway. And Hailey was alone in her in-laws' kitchen, making chicken parmesan.

Her mother-in-law, Liz, was helping Hailey's older daughter, Camilla, get dressed for their evening out. Liz had bought tickets to take each of the girls to dinner and a show, and tonight was Camilla's turn to see *Wicked*. In a few weeks, Ali would get to see the *Lion King* with her grandmother, but she was already feeling left out. In the last half hour, she'd moped through the kitchen twice, complaining she was bored.

To make matters worse, Hailey's husband and her father-in-law had shut themselves in the den, planning for John's first political campaign. John had been an attorney in the DA's office for almost six years. The time was right.

According to Jim.

Jim had won his bid for senate, and now the focus was to get John on the next ballot for state representative. What was supposed to be a family dinner had turned into a campaign meeting.

That happened a lot these days.

Lately, Hailey's priorities and John's were rarely aligned. He commented more frequently about her retiring from Homicide. Even Jim had started dropping hints.

California state legislators did not have homicide inspectors as wives.

Neither man had asked Hailey what she wanted.

Quitting her job was not an option. She was proud of what she did. Once upon a time, John had been too.

Ali stomped back into the kitchen. "It's not fair that she gets to do everything first."

John walked into the kitchen and gave Hailey a smile—like everything was fine. Everything was exactly how it should be. He didn't see her frustration. Or he didn't care.

"Once Grammie and Cami are gone, we'll make popcorn and watch *Lady and the Tramp*," Hailey promised Ali.

John brought down two crystal highballs from the cupboard. They would be pouring scotch now. How could they have a proper campaign meeting without a little scotch? Tink, tink went the glasses on the concrete countertop. Ice cubes pinged against crystal. Hailey waited for the sound of the cork coming out of the bottle of Glenlivet John had given his father for Christmas, the splash of liquid pouring. Only there was no pop of the cork releasing from the bottle. John wasn't pouring. He held the bottle in one hand, the other on the cork.

"What's wrong?" she asked.

"My dad just gave me a gun," he whispered as though in shock.

"What?" Hailey scanned the kitchen and was grateful that Ali had left the room. The girls knew how they felt about guns. She did not want to try to explain why their grandpa would have one. "A gun—why would he do that?"

"He's worried about the threats."

Over the past few weeks, John had received a series

of death threats at the DA's office. They came mostly via phone message, but only a few days ago, someone had sent a rather grisly package—a sheet soaked in pig's blood.

"The DA's office always gets threats," Hailey said. "You know that." Jim had always been anti-gun too. Why would he arm his son?

John had recently helped put away a high-level drug dealer, and it wasn't uncommon to receive threats after a successful conviction. Some of the more seasoned Assistant DAs took the threats as a badge of honor. Had Jim gotten wind that John was in real danger?

Of course John's father would worry. His mother too. John was their whole world. What different experiences Hailey and her husband had as only children. While she and her mother had taken care of each other, John was protected by his parents.

John uncorked the scotch. "So you don't think we should keep the gun?"

"God, no. I've got my service weapon. One gun in our house is more than enough."

She stared across the room at the man who'd sworn he'd never touch a gun, let alone own one. How many times had she come home with a story of how a gun in the home had killed someone it was meant to protect? How many times had she heard Jim preach about the need for stricter gun laws? What had changed?

John watched her scatter slivered peppers over the layer of breaded chicken. "I wish I could be as calm as you are," he said.

"Look at it rationally," she said. "Why come after

you? If you die, another Assistant DA takes your cases. The guy doesn't get off because you're dead."

He was silent.

"If I were a delusional psychotic who thought murder was the answer, I'd take aim at Scott Palin." She nodded to the oven. "Could you get that?"

John opened the oven door, and she slid the casserole onto the top rack.

"Palin?" he asked.

"Sure. I'd go straight to the top. Why take out an assistant when I could take out the DA?"

"That's sort of dismissive of the work the ADAs do. Palin's not the only one in that office who's a threat to criminals." He rubbed his face. He'd shaved. For a Saturday night at home with his parents. When had he become so much like his father?

Jim called out from the den. "You gonna bring those drinks before I die of old age?"

"I'm coming."

Hailey closed the oven. "Dinner will be ready soon," she said as John lifted the two glasses and turned to leave. "I need to make it an early night. Got a huge week ahead of me."

"Don't worry about it," he said. "It's Saturday night, Hailey."

He used to say that when he wanted to stay out for an extra round of drinks with their friends. Now it was spending time with his father, closed off in their inner sanctum. Man to man. John and Jim could sit in that room for hours. Not tonight. Not her. She was too tired. Dinner and then home.

Liz entered the kitchen in a cloud of Chloe perfume and the musty scent of her fur coat. "Can we help get dinner on the table?" she asked.

"It's almost ready."

Camilla trailed in behind her grandmother, and Hailey leaned down to give her eldest a kiss. The masses of curls Hailey loved were pinned back from her face. Though she had grown leaner recently, her cheeks were still as round and rosy as they had been since her birth.

"You look beautiful," Hailey said.

"The show will be over by ten, and we'll come right home," Liz assured her, grabbing Camilla's hand. "We've got church in the morning."

Camilla made a little face, but Hailey held hers void of expression. Her in-laws had been talking about the girls attending the confirmation program at Saint Mark's, and Camilla was finally old enough.

"Camilla, why don't you finish packing up your clothes and cleaning up so you don't have to do it tomorrow? I'll call you down as soon as dinner is ready." At some point, Hailey would need to talk to Liz about the confirmation. Did she want the girls to be confirmed in the church? They were baptized. Was it any different than that?

They should at least have a say. Hailey wasn't sure Liz had considered her feelings on church. Liz had always gone and simply taken the girls when they were with her on Sunday mornings.

But Hailey was too tired to have that conversation with Liz tonight.

Camilla frowned and headed for her bedroom.

Jim's sister walked into the kitchen. As always, Dee's makeup was flawless, her hair looked like it had just been styled, and her slacks and light pink sweater were pressed—all the signs of a woman without children. Standing in the kitchen now, Dee fingered the gold locket around her neck. She also had a hard time sitting still. "Would it help if I set the table?"

"It would," Hailey told her. "Thanks."

Jim barked from the den. "That's a load of horse manure, and you know it."

Hailey turned toward the door, listening as Jim's voice grew muffled, the volume dropping.

Jim and John rarely fought. Had Jim been drinking before they arrived? Would that explain why he wanted John to have a gun?

She took a couple of steps toward the den and listened, but the room had grown quiet again.

The oven timer buzzed, and she stooped to pull the casserole from the stove. "Dinner," she called. A moment later, "Dinner's ready."

The crack of gunfire. Shattering glass. A window.

She dropped the casserole dish on the floor. Reached for her holster. Her gun was locked in her case in the car.

"Help!" Jim shouted. "Someone help me!"

Hailey sprinted from the kitchen and almost barreled into Dee coming out of the dining room.

Liz came running down the stairs. "What was that noise? What happened?"

Hailey pushed past them, heading for the front of the house. The door to the den opened and Jim stepped into the hall. He held Ali in his arms, his body hunched over hers. Protecting her. Her legs hung over his elbow. Her head against his shoulder. Her eyes closed.

Liz shrieked. "What happened?"

Jim's face was ashen, his lips open, exposing small gray teeth. Hailey touched the thin, pale skin of Ali's neck.

Pulse was quick but strong. "What's wrong with her?"

"Jim!" Liz shouted.

"She's fine," Jim said, gasping silently as though struggling to draw air. He was trembling. His brow and lip sweaty. Shock.

Hailey took her daughter from his arms, laid her down on the hallway rug.

"What happened?"

Jim glanced toward the den. "Shooter."

"John?" she called.

Jim's mouth fell open. Fear.

Something had happened to John.

Liz shrieked.

No.

Jim leaned against the wall and then sank to the floor. His head made a hollow thud against plaster as he began to sob.

Hailey stood and ran for the open doorway. Her shoulder caught the jamb and she fell into the room. A breeze blew in through the broken window. "John!"

Gasping, he opened his eyes. Blood saturated his white collar. Hailey dropped beside him and pushed his tie out of the way, fumbling to unbutton John's shirt. The buttons were stubborn. Her hands shook.

Stop the bleeding. Find the source.

"Call nine-one-one!"

Liz and Dee appeared at the door, Camilla behind them.

"Call an ambulance!" Hailey yelled.

"Mommy?" Camilla asked from the doorway.

Dee took Camilla by the shoulders and led her away.

"Get me a towel," Hailey barked. "Do it now."

John's eyes followed her movements. Skin pale. Sweating. "It's a Façonnable," he said, trying to joke.

Hailey thought of how she always called the shirts "Fassa-snob" for their outrageous price tag. "Liz!" she screamed toward the door. "Ambulance?"

No response.

John's chest stuttered under the strain of breathing. "Liz!"

John's mother ran into the room, clutching a dish towel. Hailey grabbed it and pressed it against the wound. "What about the ambulance?"

"Jim. They're on their way…"

"How long?"

"Eight minutes."

"You're kidding? We're less than a mile from the hospital. I could run in eight minutes."

"Mommy," Camilla called from the doorway.

"I need to help Daddy, Cami. Stay with Aunt Dee."

"Hailey," John whispered, struggling to speak. His hand flinched as though to reach for hers.

Slow the bleeding. Keep the blood in his vital organs. Work. Think.

"The ambulance will be here soon. You're going to be okay. We need to stop the bleeding." She pressed his hand to the towel. "Hold this."

She lunged for the ottoman, dragged it toward him, and lifted his feet. Took hold of the towel again.

Already, it was wet on her fingers.

Eight minutes.

Eight minutes was forever.

"Where's Ali?" he whispered.

"She's okay. She bumped her head. She must've heard the shot. She's fine."

"You're sure?"

"I'm positive. She's going to be fine. You are too."

John's breath was ragged. "Take care of the girls."

"You're not going anywhere," she said, feeling a rise of anger. "Don't you dare, John Wyatt."

"Make sure they're okay." He struggled to breathe. He gasped. He wasn't getting air.

She pushed harder on the towel. So much blood.

"Hailey." The weak, whispery quality of his voice was terrifying. "Give me your hand."

Jim cried out from the doorway. Small and broken.

She pressed her free hand into John's.

John turned toward his father. "You take care of her."

"John!" she shouted. She could take care of herself. She didn't need Jim or Liz. She needed John. "Damn it, John. You stay right here. You fight for us!"

He drew a trembling breath.

"Focus on me," she pleaded. "Fight for me."

His nod was barely perceptible in the shift of his chin. An involuntary shiver twitched in his shoulders.

The towel was saturated. Blood leaked between her fingers.

His eyes fluttered closed as the paramedics pounded on the door.

*

Rain struck John's black coffin like sprays of tiny silver bullets. The air was bitter, the sky a gray so thick it looked like ash spread upon a canvas. The wind stung their skin through coats, threatened to tear their umbrellas from tight fists, and snapped the pages of the priest's Bible.

Behind the damp of the rain were smells of earth, cedar mulch, and a pungent rotting scent that reminded Hailey of tramping to the waterfall in Kauai on their honeymoon, plodding along in the wet mud with the ripe smell of rotting guavas beneath their feet.

The girls clung to her long black coat. She held one under each arm. Hailey pressed her nose to Ali's head, taking in the buttery smell of her scalp before standing straight against the cold.

Even the bitter, angry wind couldn't break through the chill she'd felt since John's death.

The rain slowed, but the air remained heavy. She didn't know most of the faces in the crowd, although many were familiar—politicians and powerful business people who worked with John's father.

The crowd of friends was smaller.

Jamie Vail, an inspector in Sex Crimes, stood with her friend Tony and her adopted son Zephenaya. Captain Linda James and Jess Campbell of the Immigration and Customs Enforcement (ICE) were talking with them. Three of John's closest friends were pallbearers. The other three were Hailey's friends from the station.

They had divided themselves—John's friends carried the right side of the casket, hers the left.

John's friends were polished, their suits dark, finely pressed, and high-end. They seemed to struggle with the coffin's weight.

The others, hers, wore their dress uniforms. There was her partner Hal, Cameron Cruz, who was as tall as two of the men on John's side, and Tim O'Shea from Homicide. The officers were sharp in their dress uniforms and more at ease with the job.

Cops had buried men before. John's friends had not.

In the last five or six years, their marriage had been divided in much the same way.

How much had changed since they were newlyweds, volunteering nights stuffing envelopes for Bill Clinton. Back when Hailey had been new with the department and John had finished law school and taken a job in the DA's office.

At night, they returned to a tiny South San Francisco apartment and drank wine from big jugs of Gallo, using chipped mugs or two glasses that had come free with a bottle of Jameson she had bought him for their first Christmas.

Those were days when John had dreamt of being DA, when he'd been proud of his newly promoted inspector wife, when they had devoured each other's stories.

When they had been on the same side.

Before everything had changed.

Staring at the box that held his body, Hailey struggled between cataloguing those moments, clinging to every memory of that man and, at the same time, feeling overwhelming anger at the man he had become. A facsimile of his father.

When it came time to sprinkle dirt on the coffin, Hailey couldn't step forward. She couldn't let go of the girls who clung to her sides.

Her father-in-law caught her eye. He looked at each of the girls and stepped forward in Hailey's place, the grief in his face palpable. Losing John was something she and Jim shared. In some awful way, it had made her lean on him. That was okay. It was okay to need him right now.

Ali gripped her mother tighter. Her pupils were too wide, her pallor too fair, as though that night was imprinted on her eyelids, visible at every blink. She slept with Hailey most nights, waking her mother with the smallest whimper, while Hailey whispered into her hair that Mommy was there, that Ali was fine. Praying that she was, that she would be.

Camilla was more stoic, quieter.

In some ways, Hailey worried about her more.

The ceremony ended with the blessings of the priest John had known since childhood, the one who had married them ten years before.

Ten years, four months, and three days before, when Hailey and John had stood at the altar and promised to honor and obey, to love and cherish.

Hailey had failed John.

And now he was gone.

As the dirt struck the hard, dark coffin, Hailey pictured her husband in his casket. The starched collar of his favorite Façonnable dress shirt, his best navy suit, the tie Hailey had chosen that brought out the green of his eyes, the one she noticed even on the days when she could hardly stand to look at him.

Liz had suggested a lighter one.

"No," Hailey had said sharply.

Liz had looked surprised.

"This one," Hailey had said, more softly.

Liz had deferred. Maybe she had understood Hailey's need to dress him this last time, or perhaps she thought it had simply been a power play, some attempt to recapture her husband from his parents.

Something Hailey had failed to do when he was alive.

She shivered thinking of him inside that black box. She would never see him again. Never touch his skin.

Hal took hold of her arm then, and she was surprised to see the crowd walking away from the gravesite.

*

Back at her in-laws' home, people Hailey had never met showed up with casseroles, cakes, and trays of food. Tom Rittenberg was there. A short, heavyset man with a cane, he moved slowly, head down. He'd suffered a stroke a few months after his daughter—Abby Dennig—was killed. Now, he seemed so broken, so much smaller than before. She remembered him from Jim's political functions as a bit shy, but happy—almost jolly. She watched Tom shuffle through the crowd and wondered how Jim would change with John's death. And Liz.

Her friends from the department also came to the house after the service. Cameron brought green chili enchiladas, "My favorite comfort food," she'd said. Linda

James brought tiramisu. Jamie and Tony brought a lasagna he'd made, while Hal came with a potted hydrangea.

Hailey was so thankful for them. Thankful that they looked at Liz and Jim's house the same way she did—as though it were a museum where none of them belonged.

They were *her* people.

Even Bruce Daniels came. Hailey thanked him but only briefly, too afraid that Jim would realize that for the six months before his son was shot, Hailey had been in love with another man. A man now standing in his home under the guise of mourning his son.

Until the few final moments of John's life, Hailey had no longer loved her husband, often couldn't find a way to like him. But, in those last moments, Hailey had loved John more than she had ever loved anyone.

And now he was gone.

When the officers left—all but Hal—Hailey had wanted to go too. Hal stayed, letting Camilla and Ali climb over him, turning them upside down and tickling their bellies until Ali got the hiccups from laughing so hard. It was the first time Hailey had heard them laugh since John's death.

Hailey fought not to cry.

When the girls were finally asleep, tucked into the bed they'd all shared those first days, Hal sat with her on the front porch, in the muggy, cold San Francisco air, and drank coffee in silence.

CHAPTER 1

One Year Later

AFTER HER LEAVE of absence, Hailey spent most of the spring readjusting to working beside Hal. For the first few weeks she wondered why she developed an ache in her neck—until she remembered her long-standing rule: never stand closer than two feet from Hal while talking to him. Barefoot, Hal was six-four where Hailey was only five-four in heels. When they'd first started working together, she'd spent so much time looking up during conversations that she'd developed chronic neck pain.

Hailey was a pale white, the color gracious people call alabaster and others might call pasty, while Hal was so dark-skinned black that unless his eyes were open wide enough to catch the whites, they melted into the shadow between his cheeks and nose. Her head was a mound of dark curls while Hal's was shaved bald. Despite the physical differences, Hal had never acted in a way to suggest that he was bigger, stronger, or better than Hailey, even though he was at least two of the three.

More and more, Hailey thought he was three for three.

Monday morning, after working all weekend, Hal announced that they had a lead on the Dennig murders. Several weapons matching ones stolen from Dennig Distribution more than a year before had turned up in the arrest of a local weapons dealer. The Triggerlock group—who handled weapons-related crimes—was putting together a sting.

Hal pushed the DA's office to resubmit their request to exhume the body of Nicholas Fredricks, a lobbyist working against guns and gun manufacturers. His fingerprint had been found on both the NRA buttons found at the murders—both the Dennigs' murder and the killing of Colby Wesson, an heir to the Smith & Wesson company, up in Sacramento.

Monday afternoon, when Hailey was practically asleep on her feet, Hal came bursting into the department like a storm, waving a piece of paper. "They approved the court order."

Hailey inhaled sharply. "They're letting us exhume the body?" They had been waiting a year to get access to Fredricks's corpse.

"Yep."

It had been fourteen months since Abby and Hank Dennig were murdered. The defensive wounds on her and lacerations on him were consistent with a letter opener that Abby Dennig kept in the car. Cause of death for her was strangulation, exsanguination for him. Tox screens showed that both Dennigs had taken some form of sedative in the hours before their deaths. The Crime Scene Unit had ruled out other blood types, but the vehicle had contained no fewer than thirty unidentifiable prints and a dozen hair samples that didn't belong to the victims or their kids.

According to several of the couple's friends, the Dennigs had been in the midst of filing for divorce at the time of their deaths. The scene suggested the two had killed each other.

The Dennigs had two children, both girls. Just like Hailey and John had. Now, those girls had no parents. They had family, but it wasn't the same. Kids needed their parents. It was the kind of case Hailey would have been a bulldog about. Except for the timing ...

When the Dennig case had fallen on Hailey's desk, she was also working a serial rape case alongside Jamie Vail. *And* trying to solve the murder of one of their colleagues.

She never should have caught the Dennig case.

But she did, because Jim had insisted.

Murder by spouse was the right call, based on practical assumptions. Occam's razor—the simplest explanation was usually the right one.

This time, it wasn't.

After Hailey had closed the investigation, a sheriff up near Sacramento linked Colby Wesson's suspected suicide to the Dennigs' murders via a partial fingerprint on a small, round anti-NRA button, identical to a button found in the minivan where Abby and Hank Dennig were killed.

The print matched a man named Nicholas Fredricks who worked for a local organization on gun violence. He was a big lobbyist in DC for stricter gun regulations, and he'd had the ear of some very powerful people.

Fredricks made a decent suspect. He was certainly

outspoken on gun control. And his short temper was well-documented. He'd twice been arrested for assaulting police officers charged with using unnecessary force.

There was just one small problem with Nicholas Fredricks as a suspect—he had been dead for twelve years.

Now, over a year after Hailey had been on the case, they still only had the two partial prints, each on a separate button. And they were no closer to solving the puzzle of who was killing these people. Or why. Anti-gun activists were usually passive. They argued against violence. But this one was different. This killer was using violence against gun supporters.

Which meant, somehow, the fight was personal.

The court approval to disinter the body of Nicholas Fredricks meant the investigation could finally move forward.

Hailey looked at the time on her phone. She was half tempted to go pull him out of the ground now.

"I'll let the cemetery know we're coming tomorrow morning," Hal said as if reading her mind.

*

Parked outside her in-laws' house, Hailey took two puffs of her albuterol inhaler and mounted the steps to the front door. *Her* front door now, she reminded herself.

A few months after John's funeral, she'd sold her house and moved in with Jim and Liz. Her work schedule made living alone with the girls impossible. Not without being able to afford live-in care. Which she could not.

Surprisingly, living with Jim and Liz had been comfortable, enjoyable even, although it took some time to get used to how Liz liked to make every dinner a formal event. The house was easier when Liz wasn't around—more casual. Unfortunately, that often meant that the girls weren't there either. Tonight she was taking Camilla and Ali to Cirque du Soleil, which meant Hailey would be home with Jim and Dee. They'd probably be working, which might give her a chance to get caught up on her paperwork.

She threw her keys on a table in the foyer and made her way to the kitchen, where she found Jim eating a sandwich on a paper plate and drinking a cabernet sauvignon Cinq Cepages from a crystal glass. Hailey sniffed the air. "Tuna?"

He nodded. "You want some?"

"I think I'll pass," she said. "That's quite a combination."

He smiled. "I know. A terrible waste of a good vintage, but I was starving."

She shrugged out of her jacket and hung it on the back of a chair. She and John used to banter this way—casually teasing each another. She had never imagined having this kind of banter with her father-in-law. One on one, he was surprisingly kind. And funny. He had John's quick wit.

She'd been so angry with him for getting her assigned to the Dennig murders. He'd only been looking out for a friend. If she'd had this kind of relationship with him when the Dennigs were killed, she would have offered to take the case. She would have wanted to help him.

John would have loved to see them like this.

"You want me to make you something else, other than tuna I mean?" she asked.

"Oh, no," he said. "This is fine. There's more in the fridge if you want some."

"Thanks." Hailey made herself a sandwich while Jim finished his.

He refilled his wine glass and she wondered if this was the first bottle. Lately, she had noticed Jim was drinking more. Had it started with John's death? She couldn't recall now. "Wine?" he offered.

She set her plate on the table across from him. "No, thanks."

"There's beer in there. The kind you guys like," he added.

You guys. As though John were still alive. She still woke some mornings, expecting him beside her in the bed or to come in from the bathroom.

Sometimes, she still woke up angry about something he'd said or done. Then she remembered he was dead.

"Christ," Jim muttered.

Hailey searched for an excuse to leave the room. But she didn't really want to be alone either, so she accepted the offer for a beer. John would always be in this room. She sat at the table while Jim got her a beer from the refrigerator. Pyramid Hefeweizen, her favorite.

"You want a glass?" he asked.

"No, thanks."

"Didn't think so." He set the bottle in front of her and sat back down, pushing the paper plate with the crumbs to the center of the table and running his thumb along the dark rim of his wine glass until the crystal sang.

Hailey drank from the cold bottle, thinking Jim would bring up John. Over the last few months, the sharp pain of new loss had faded into an ache. Even when she wanted to talk about him, the ache was still there.

With Camilla and Ali around, the subject of John became silently forbidden unless one of them brought him up. When the girls asked about him, his death, heaven, his bones—and the questions sometimes seemed limitless—they didn't hold back. They followed the advice of the child psychologist and told the girls they would always answer their questions.

Over the course of the months, the torrent of questions had dried up. The questions now caught her off guard like ghosts hovering in closets.

"Rittenberg came to see me today."

She was wrong. It wasn't John that Jim wanted to discuss—it was his friend Tom Rittenberg, another man who had lost his child. His daughter, Abby Dennig, was the victim of the killer they were still hunting. Hailey had met Tom Rittenberg a few times. He'd done well in the insurance industry, and since retirement, he'd become involved in supporting local politics. He was short and a little round, with reddish cheeks that made him look a little like Santa Claus—something Camilla had pointed out at a fundraiser once. But since his daughter's death, he was shriveled and frail, all the joy gone.

She took a bite of her sandwich and said nothing.

No question, this was going to be about Nicholas Fredricks.

"He told me about the court order."

Hailey said nothing. The order gave them authority

to disinter Abby as well as her husband if they found the need.

"No one likes to think about their child being dug up."

Hailey drank from the bottle. "I don't imagine anyone likes to think about them being buried."

"Touché."

Hailey pushed her half-eaten sandwich away. "We're not looking at the Dennigs, Jim. Just because we have authority to disinter the Dennigs doesn't mean we will. At the moment, I can't see a reason why we would. We're only interested in Fredricks right now." She would never have shared these details with Jim a year ago. But Tom Rittenberg had lost his daughter, and Jim would be thinking of John. Tom and Jim had each lost their only child—within a month of one another.

It was Jim's turn to be quiet.

"Did he say he was going to try to stop us?" Hailey asked.

"He didn't mention being opposed to it."

Tom Rittenberg was a powerful businessman with close ties to the political heavyweights in town, including Jim and the mayor. He'd also been president of the NRA for a time, something Hailey had held against him when they first met. Now, she wished he were still their president. His gun politics were a lot more reasonable than the guy leading the NRA now, who was practically suggesting they arm kindergartners.

Hailey waited for Jim to say more on the subject, but he was silent. "I'll let you know what we find," she finally said.

Jim looked surprised. "Thank you."

She nodded.

"I also got a call from Inspector O'Shea today," Jim said.

"About John." It wasn't a question.

"They have another suspect," Jim said. "They wanted to come back and look at the den again."

"What did you say?"

"I said they were welcome to come," Jim said.

Jim's sister stood in the doorway. How long had she been standing there?

"Oh, hello, Dee," Jim said. "Come sit. We were just catching up." He rose and pulled a chair out for her. "Can I get you a glass of wine?"

"I didn't mean to interrupt," she said without moving from the doorway.

"You didn't," Hailey told her.

Holding her locket, Dee crossed the room with the slow grace of someone with royal blood and smoothed her slacks as she sat. "I'd love a glass of wine."

Her brother filled a glass for his sister.

Hailey often wondered why Dee lived here. A success in business, she had plenty of resources, but she had never been married and seemed to like being close to her brother. John had mentioned a few times during their marriage that he was surprised she'd stayed away as long as she had.

Dee had moved in with Jim and Liz a few months before Hailey and the girls did. She'd been working back east and decided she needed a change. Now, she occupied the large basement suite of Jim and Liz's house and worked for Jim.

"You were out?"

"Tom took me to dinner." The skin on Dee's neck appeared flushed.

Hailey recalled how grief-stricken Tom Rittenberg had looked at John's service, which had been a cruel reminder of his own daughter's funeral just a few months earlier. She was glad to hear he had someone, though she had a hard time picturing the lively Rittenberg with reserved Dee.

"You've seen a lot of him," Jim commented.

"We enjoy each other's company," Dee said.

"You deserve it," Hailey interjected.

"Agreed," Jim said, raising his glass.

The three clinked their drinks.

Jim paid a strange deference to his younger sister, indulged her. And she him. They were sweet together, sometimes more like an old married couple than Jim and Liz. Hailey had never had a sibling, but the relationship between Jim and Dee seemed unusually close.

A quiet woman, Dee was hard to read. She spoke carefully, as if she expected her every word to be examined and weighed. Except with Camilla and Ali, who adored her. Watching Dee with them, Hailey was sure Dee regretted not having a family of her own.

Nobody talked about that either.

The doorbell rang and Jim frowned, while Dee, who sat closest to the door, made no move to answer it. Jim stood to get it as Hailey's phone buzzed on her hip. She answered the call. "Hal?"

"There are two ways to look at getting called in

again," Hal said, his tone light and playful. Hearing him made her realize he had been like that less often lately.

Hailey felt Dee's gaze on her. "I'm listening."

"One, we've worked our asses off all weekend, we're being called in again before I've finished my first beer, and the game just started."

Hal would be reclined in the worn, navy leather chair that had been his father's, a Bud propped on his lap and the remote within easy reach.

"And the other way to look at it?" she asked.

"This call saves you from dinner at the senator's." He drew out the *s* like a snake's hiss. "You are there, aren't you?"

"I like the glass-is-half-full view," Hailey said, ignoring the dig at Jim. Old habits died hard. She'd have done the same thing a year ago. "Nice touch. So what is it?"

Hailey heard the groan of Hal's chair as he sat forward and pictured the way he perched his elbows on his thick legs when he was serious. "I got the call. Ryaan Berry's informant says a group is being put together to try to move the guns stolen from Dennig Distribution. I'm going to join."

Ryaan Berry was an inspector in the Triggerlock department. Hailey had heard she was also part of the small group of women officers who gathered monthly for dinner at Tommy's Mexican down in the Sunset. The Rookie Club, someone had dubbed the group, although Hailey didn't see herself as a rookie anymore. She also hadn't been to a dinner since John's death.

Hailey scanned the address on her phone. "What time do you need me there?"

"An hour would probably be about right."

"I'll be there in an hour. Call if you need me sooner." Hailey ended the call, dumped her beer into the sink, and tossed out the sandwich.

Dee fingered her locket with one hand and held her wineglass with the other. "Heading back in tonight?"

"Yeah." Hailey reached for a glass in the cabinet. Something pinged in the front hall. She froze, her hand outstretched.

The sound, though soft, was distinct.

Hailey drew her gun. "Get down," she hissed to Dee.

Another ping of the bullet through a silencer cut the air. Then, the sound of shattering glass.

Dee dropped to her knees and crawled around one of the table's legs, huddling in the center of the rug.

Hailey crept to the edge of the kitchen and pressed her back to the thin slice of wall beside the refrigerator. She waited for footsteps. The creak of the front door. Anything.

The big grandfather clock in the hallway ticked out a rhythm. Her heart pulsed in her throat. The refrigerator at her back kicked on. Startling her. She listened for sounds. The house was silent.

She rounded the corner into the hall slowly, barrel first, crouched low. "Jim!"

No answer.

She turned into the dining room, cleared it and continued along the hall.

The window beside the front door was broken, glass scattered across the dark wood floor, confirming that the shots had come from outside. There was no sign of Jim. "Jim!"

The front door stood partially open. She froze, unsure if the suspect was inside or out.

The hallway was the only route to the back of the house. If Dee stayed under the table, she was safe.

Thank God Liz and the girls were out.

At the threshold to the front door, Hailey paused, drew air until her lungs were full, and yanked the door open.

No shots fired.

She ducked low, crept onto the porch. Empty.

Scanned the front hallway again. Clear.

She crossed to the top of the porch stairs, searching the street. Silence penetrated the dark where the scent of rotting leaves filled the wet air.

No tire sounds.

Whoever he was, he was on foot. Or he was inside. She spun back. Where the hell was Jim?

"Jim!" Panic filled her voice. The only reason he wouldn't answer was ... no. This family could not survive another death.

Pausing in the doorway to the living room, Hailey counted to three and hooked around the doorjamb, flipped the light switch, and dropped behind a Windsor chair.

She rounded the couch and checked the fireplace—only a small mound of ashes sat piled in the center, waiting to be discarded.

She thought of John. An intruder. All the unanswered questions around John's death—the intruder who shot him. Now there might have been another intruder in the house.

Fear caught in her throat, burned her eyes. Ali and Camilla could have been home.

A trail of dark spots lined Liz's white Persian rug.

Behind the coffee table, Jim was flat on his back.

He groaned and lifted a hand to cup his ear. Blood seeped between his fingers. She saw John—all that blood—and blinked the image away. "You're okay."

Beside him lay a thin, white FedEx envelope. Pinned to the clear plastic on the outside was a round, white button.

Hailey didn't need to read its anti-gun message. She already had two other pins just like it—one from the Dennigs' murders and one from Wesson's.

But she was only more confused by the attack on Jim. Anti-gun proponents were normally people who argued that violence was not a way to resolve violence. But this anti-gun terrorist had taken aim at her father-in-law with the very weapon he claimed to despise.

A gun.

CHAPTER 2

THE VAN CHUGGING down First Street hardly looked like police transport. If he didn't know where he was going, Hal Harris would've walked right past the white van with green Celtic-styled letters that had once read PJ's Plumbing. The "J" was faded and the "m" in plumbing was chipped off. What was left was P's Plubing.

Finally back from shoulder surgery, he was ready to work. Ready to spend fifteen hours a day. Six weeks of watching TV and eating takeout was enough to convince Hal that he'd never retire. Nearly made him insane. Not to mention he'd put on ten pounds that he didn't need.

He liked to think the department missed him too. At least he knew Hailey had.

He'd known Hailey for most of his police career, had worked with her a few times as a rookie when she'd been called to a case, along with her previous partner, an acerbic chain-smoker named Charlie Foss.

Foss had retired a few months before Hal was promoted to Homicide. After her new partner made one too many overtures, the last one during a department meeting, Hailey had announced she'd need a new partner before she shot the one she had.

With a straight face, as the story went, she'd aimed her finger at the guy and pulled an imaginary trigger. The guy had only lasted a few more weeks in Homicide.

As soon as Hal was in the door, Captain Marshall had assigned Hailey as his partner. "Don't underestimate her," he'd said.

Hal hadn't, and despite the fact that she stood well below his shoulder, or the fact that he could easily lift her in one arm, he knew which of them was the heavyweight.

Then, she'd lost John and something had shifted between them. He kept waiting for her to come back. *She would.*

Hal stepped into the van, his bulk sinking the van a few inches. Inside the van was a metal box with a computer panel along one side. Two chairs were bolted to the floor in front of the panel and three chairs lined the opposite side. It smelled like sweat and wet pennies. He scanned the ceiling for an air vent and moved toward the plastic chair beneath it. He sat lightly, testing it. Heartier ones had broken beneath him before. The plastic groaned and popped, and he rocked it, testing the bolts. Satisfied, he turned the vent above his head to high.

Triggerlock Inspector Ryaan Berry was the last to climb into the van. She dropped into the seat across from Hal. "How's it going?"

Ryaan and Hal had worked plenty of cases together— homicides and guns went hand in hand—but this was the first time he'd been on one of their stings. And there was no guarantee that he'd get anything from being there.

The Triggerlock informant wasn't sure if these gunrunners had stolen the guns from Dennig Distribution. If one of them was the thief, he might also be the Dennigs' killer.

Or this could be a dead end.

Someone had to know something. Hal was counting on it.

The engine revved, and despite the air blowing hard on his face, Hal felt the sweat pool beneath his arms and down his spine.

It was winter, but still warm. Hal preferred the cold; the brisk air made it easier to breathe—especially when he sat in a confined space.

Like a van.

As they bumped across the pitted department parking lot, Hal stared out the window, his stomach twisting and churning. From the outside, the van panels appeared solid. From inside, they looked like regular windows, which should have made him feel better. Behind him, two other vans carried members of the department's task force.

"Uh, Hal?" Ryaan asked. "You okay?"

"Fine," he lied, fighting the nausea.

He'd never suffered from claustrophobia until he was sitting in the back of a black and white a day after his father died. He was twenty-three. The panicked sensation in small spaces had never gone away, like the shadow of his father's death that he couldn't shake.

After one particularly harrowing experience in a basement during a domestic call, he'd gone to see the department shrink, but her endless theories on his condition just seemed like fluff. He'd never been locked in a box or a trunk. His childhood was as normal as childhood could be. His mother was a kind woman who worked as a nurse at Children's Hospital. His father had been a well-adjusted man, despite the horrors he saw on the job as a cop in Oakland. His two older sisters were healthy. No one else suffered from any phobias.

When Hal had applied to the academy, his father had told him to make sure the committee knew Hal was a legacy. So he had used his old man as a stepping-stone, and it had worked. Departments liked legacies. They were proud to foster the notion that the department was a fraternity to which membership could be passed down, generation to generation.

At least, it was like that until his father was killed.

Hal had been in class when it happened. The academy had given him a week to grieve, and two days after the shooting, his father had received a full police burial. Hal and his two sisters—then twenty-six and twenty-nine—had been pallbearers, along with his father's partner and two other patrol officers.

The day his father was buried was so hot that sweat had soaked all the way through Hal's uniform coat, through the pants at the backs of his knees. But it was hotter the next day when he'd gone outside to get the paper, wearing only his shorts and tennis shoes, and had lifted it off the dew-covered grass, unfolded it, and seen the headline.

"Slain cop charged with three counts of felony."

His father's name was in the first line. They claimed his father had been accepting bribes from a few local businessmen. That he was crooked.

Hal had shoved the paper deep into the trash can.

He didn't go back into the house. Instead he started to run. He ran hard, fast, the way they made him run in the academy, but without his sergeant there to drill him. He felt like he could have run forever.

Ryaan flipped on the interior lights, bathing the inside of the van in a ruby haze. Hal put his hand over his mouth. The red light protected their night vision, but it also worsened Hal's nausea.

He felt his pockets and pulled out a piece of gum—his last piece—and wadded it into his mouth.

This was Ryaan's team. Hal had met most of them before. Lopez was the driver, and in back were Erickson and a third guy—Hal couldn't remember his name. Michaels. He had triplets—three boys.

The last man in the van sat at the control panel. A gray-haired white guy, his large girth filled the chair so completely that his sides spilled beneath the metal armrests, and the gray hairs in his reddish beard stuck out like frizzy white sprouts. Hal didn't recognize him, but he wasn't about to open his mouth to make an introduction, for fear of losing his breakfast.

"Inspector Ryaan Berry," she said, offering her hand. "You're new, right?"

"Sam Gibson," he replied, his fingers never leaving the keyboard, eyes fixed on a screen displaying their destination. "Transferred down from Seattle."

Ryaan studied the feed on the screen, which originated from cameras positioned on roofs surrounding their destination. The images had been enhanced to make the details emerge, even in the dark.

"The guys we're going after are moving a big shipment

stolen from Dennig Distributors more than a year ago. Estimates are these kids have fifty to seventy-five guns. That many guns means some big losses when we show up." She scanned their faces. "Expect a fight, you hear?"

Hal felt a jolt of adrenaline. Homicide inspectors rarely dealt with live scenes. It was good to get the blood moving again.

The air shut off above his head, and Hal fiddled with the vent without success.

"Lopez," Ryaan called to the driver without so much as a glance in Hal's direction. "Turn the air up while we can, would you?" Using a whiteboard, Ryaan drew a box to represent the building where the sting was to go down then added two rectangles for the double doors.

Hal kept his gaze in her direction but had to focus out the window, the gas fumes and lack of air making him feel worse.

"Front of the building is glass." She shaded in the windows. "Doors are glass. Windows next to the doors and on the second floor above too."

Glass was easy to shoot through.

She added a line of Xs to the right side of the doors to represent members of the task force. "Special Ops will circle from the back of the building and be here, ready for our call."

The Special Ops group handled anything that required a large, coordinated offense—stings, riots, or hostage situations. Sam adjusted his monitor with a few keystrokes until Hal could pick out the Special Ops sharp-shooters along the roofline.

"Gibson, you show a view of the cars?"

Gibson struck at the keys and the screen displayed a ground-level view of the building Ryaan had drawn. She pointed to a black Lexus and silver BMW parked in front. "These are the suspects' cars. We think there are two guys in each car. Recon believes the weapons are in the Lexus." She turned back to Gibson. "Can we look at the sharpshooters again?"

Gibson changed screens and Ryaan pointed out the silhouettes stationed along the roof.

"As soon as we confirm the merchandise, we go. Get the suspects down on the ground. I'll lead. You—" She pointed to Erickson and Michaels. "You're on my back, so watch your fire." She turned to Hal. "You just hang tight unless all hell breaks loose."

Hal liked watching Ryaan at work. She was intense, focused. Her people respected her and so did he. Every time they worked together, he wondered about her personal life. He'd never heard anything about her personal life. Was she married? Did she date?

One of these days, he was going to gather the courage to find out.

The van stopped at the curb about twenty yards south of the two cars. Lopez cut the engine, lifted his tool belt off the floor, grabbed his toolbox, and exited the van for his post down the street.

As soon as the driver's door clicked closed, the circulating air inside the van slowed until it was like breathing through a straw.

Streetlights on either end of the three central buildings created a glowing box around the cars and the front of the building. The department had probably sent down folks from PG&E earlier in the day to make sure the lights were functional. Unlike almost anywhere else in the city, there wasn't a single light out on the entire block.

The target cars sat quietly at the curb, their windows dark—no sign of action from inside. It was now only a question of when they decided to come out.

"You okay?" Ryaan asked and Hal nodded. She leaned across Gibson anyway and flipped a switch to turn on the generator and low-level fan system.

Hal felt the wind on his back and was grateful.

"You sure you want to do that?" Gibson asked.

"From out there, it just sounds like a cool-down cycle," she answered. "Can't leave it on too long, though."

Despite the fan, the air continued to thicken with the odors of so many people in the cramped space. Gibson gave off the gritty stench of cigarettes, which mixed with the taste of stale chewing gum in Hal's mouth and the bitter scent of sweat.

Mind over matter. Hal shifted slightly in his seat and put his face close to the van's cool metal wall, hoping these guys didn't sit in those fancy cars much longer.

One of the Lexus's doors cracked open.

"Here we go," Ryaan announced.

No motion from the BMW, but four young men eased out of the Lexus. They could've been his sister's kids, in their hooded sweatshirts and low-ride jeans, boxer shorts exposed like the stripe of a flag across their back-sides. Only the bulges at their sides and ankles suggested they weren't just a bunch of harmless punks.

"Shit," Ryaan whispered, pulling the radio to her lips,

her voice low and tense. "We've got four in the first car, not two. Expect as many as eight."

Hal palmed his gun, trying to remember the last time he'd been involved in an active shooting. Not since he was a patrol officer, six years ago. A fleeing suspect had shot at him and his partner, Jimmy Delucca, a kid from New York. They'd lost the perp. When he'd gotten home, Hal had felt battered himself.

Sweat dripped down Hal's spine. The van air had gone completely still again. He released his gun's magazine, checked it, and snapped it in place as the BMW's doors cracked open.

Five more emerged, and the radio crackled to life as officers prepared to move.

"Count is nine, not eight," Ryaan said into the radio. "Hold for my call."

Hal wondered who had done the reconnaissance. So far their numbers were way off. He hoped they had enough backup to cover it.

The guys from the BMW joined the others.

The group milled around the Lexus. Hal shifted his focus back to the suspects in the street.

"Whitie here's got three," Ryaan said, pointing to the guy in the white hooded sweatshirt. "See it?"

"Right pocket and back side," Jefferson added.

"And right ankle. Watch how he turns," Ryaan went on.

The kid stepped back from the car, and the subtle bulge was visible above his shoe. Damn. Three guns.

The jacket on one of the kids flapped open. Hal's eyes

widened as he zeroed in on the weapon stuffed into the low-hanging jeans.

Ryaan had spotted the same thing he had. "Guy in the yellow-striped boxers has got a Norinco SKS."

The van hushed.

The Norinco held armor-piercing rounds.

Beside Hal, Erickson touched his hands to his vest. "That's a cop killer."

"Right. We take the cop killer first," Ryaan announced into the radio. "I'd expect about three weapons on each guy, but be ready for a fourth. Overkill is key here, emphasis on kill. Drop them if you need to. It's them or us."

Hal shifted in his seat. The chance of something going wrong—of someone getting killed—was high. Either one of them, or one of these kids.

After a moment, the driver of the Lexus slapped the top of the car and swaggered down the street, heading north. He displayed maybe five inches of red boxer shorts, his dark hood pulled down, his Afro like a Q-tip coming unraveled.

"Where's he going?" Ryaan asked into the radio. No one answered, and the Q-tip didn't turn back. "Who's got a line on the walker?"

"He's headed for a dead spot," Gibson said. "If he gets beyond the hydrant, the sharpshooters won't have an angle on him."

"Roof's going to lose him in fifteen feet," came the crackled response.

"Just hold as long as you can. I'll go for the loner myself." She clicked off the radio and turned to Erickson and Michaels. "You got that?"

The other kids ignored the walker and paused in front of a cement building, its front windows broken, the gray surface painted white in big patches where someone had attempted to cover graffiti. Next to the white patches were a series of tags, arranged side by side and on top of each other, as though the artists were competing. Cardboard littered the streets and newspapers blew softly down the sidewalk like urban tumbleweed.

"Is the loner still in sight?" Ryaan asked into the radio.

"For about four feet."

"Where the hell's he going?" Erickson asked.

Hal imagined the kid might be meeting another contact, going to take a piss in private, or maybe just getting the hell out of there, which would make him the smartest of the bunch.

The radio crackled. "He's gone."

Ryaan leaned across the van to see the computer screen. "Any way to adjust your position on the roof?" she asked.

"Not without giving ourselves away," came the response.

She shook her head. "Hold your place, then. We'll try to pick him up from the street."

Hal tightened his grip on the gun, felt the slip of sweat, and dried his hand on his pants before returning the gun to it.

The radio crackled with officers shifting, ready to move, but Ryaan thumbed the radio button, gave the order. "No one goes until I call."

Outside, the kids grew louder, more animated, as two black faces appeared through the broken glass of the storefront and scanned the sidewalk before step-ping outside.

The first one to swagger out was clearly in the lead. Probably in his early twenties, he was geriatric compared to his teenage counterparts. The other hovered behind.

"Front one's our buyer," Ryaan said into the radio and then turned to Jefferson. "You keep on him."

The buyer said something and Whitie laughed, his shoulders drooped and relaxed as the buyer led them toward the car.

None of them had a clue that the police were watching.

Standing around the trunk, the cop killer scanned the street slowly, his eyes only grazing over the police van before reaching to open the trunk. Despite the weapon and the bravado in his stance, his small eyes, partially hidden by the hood, narrowed in fear.

Ryaan spoke crisply into the radio. "Hold until the merchandise is confirmed. Then we go. Nobody moves till then."

The cop killer touched the latch on the trunk and the metal popped open.

"Roof unit one has arsenal in sight," came a voice over the radio. "Quick count ... around sixty."

"Go on three," Ryaan said and Hal felt the adrenaline cooking his muscles, revving his heart like a car engine. "One, two, go. Go. Go!"

Erickson slid the van door open.

"Police!" Ryaan shouted across the street. "Get your hands up where we can see them!"

The task force swarmed in, and a bullhorn demanded the guys put their hands in the air.

Whitie dropped to the ground, hands on the back of his head like he knew the drill, but the cop killer reached for his gun.

Hal started to shout when Ryaan aimed and fired, but the kid fell before her bullet reached him—someone on the roof had fired first.

Hal turned to see another kid dig into his pants for a weapon. Before he could draw, his body jerked as another bullet found its mark.

Down the street, the loner was on the run now, out of the sharpshooters' aim.

"On the roof," Ryaan called into the radio. "Make a move so you can cover me. I'm going for the loner." She waved at Michaels to follow.

Hal glanced at Whitie still lying on the ground. One of his hands vanished from view.

"Watch out!" he shouted, jumping from the van.

The gun fired. The bullet caught her.

Ryaan dropped.

Bullets exploded from the roof, taking down Whitie.

Hal ran to her side and kneeled. Panting, she fingered her lower right side. "It's in the vest."

Paramedics rushed in, and Ryaan nodded after the loner, her face tight. "Get him."

Michaels ran. Hal followed, bent at the waist behind the line of parked cars, and halting where the line of cars ended. If he moved forward, he would be exposed.

Sirens howled behind them.

A black and white sped off to block the loner from the next street as he vanished around the corner.

Michaels sprinted down the street, and Hal stayed

close behind until they reached the next car. They crouched behind a maroon Honda Civic, and Hal peered across the car's hood at the corner, where the loner had disappeared.

The screaming sirens shrilled as the black and white rounded the block, coming at the kid from the other direction. The loner would have no choice but to come back toward them.

Hal kept his gun out and waited. His heart drummed a steady beat in his temples. They didn't risk running back for the cover of the patrol cars. They'd have to stay behind the Civic. Damn it. After a beat, Hal rose. Michaels joined him. They watched the corner, waiting for the loner to make a move.

Michaels glanced back at the patrol cars.

His back was turned when Hal spotted the barrel of the loner's gun glinting under the streetlight. Hal grabbed hold of Michaels and dropped to the ground. The bullet struck the windshield of the Honda, passed through, and shattered the building window over their heads. Glass rained down around them.

Michaels cursed.

Shaking the glass from his collar, Hal looked back for direction from Ryaan. She shook her head, pressed her palm down. *Sit tight.* Too much exposure to move.

They had to wait it out.

Michaels emitted a strangled noise.

Hal turned to see his face was pale, his breathing ragged. "Are you hit?"

He shook his head and raised his hand to wipe the sweat off his lip, the Sig trembling in his fingers.

"What is it? What's wrong?" There was no blood. Where had he been hit?

Michaels bucked forward, and Hal lurched to grab him. His shaking reverberated up Hal's arms.

Leaning against the car for support, Hal shouted to the task force, "I've got a 999."

"Shots fired?" Ryaan yelled.

Hal scanned Michaels's face, felt the cold sweat on his cheek. "I think he's having a heart attack."

The trembling crested into violent rocking. Hal struggled to wrap his arm around Michaels's chest. He half stood and tried to inch them toward the safety of the van.

He reached as far as the tail end of the Honda before Michaels kicked out of his arms, knocking the Sig from Hal's fingers. Michaels's head slammed against the pavement as his convulsions continued, the officer's gun hand now clasping his left arm.

Hal scanned the ground for his gun. Gone.

The crackled warning from Michaels's radio was too late.

The loner appeared beside the Honda's rear bumper—only feet from where Michaels lay.

Where the hell was his gun?

"Shit," he cursed and, before he could locate the weapon, the loner reached Michaels and tugged the officer against his torso like a heavy blanket.

A shot blasted from the roof, and the kid's sweatshirt jumped at his shoulder.

Hal spotted his gun and grabbed for it as the kid howled and sank to the ground.

For a second, Hal thought they might escape, but

the loner moved nimbly. Hal gripped the gun in his hand, chambered a round. The kid jammed the barrel to Michaels's temple and released the safety with his thumb. "Lose the gun or I'll pull."

Michaels's face crumpled, red and swollen, his breathing shallow and his grip latched to his limp left arm.

"You're okay," Hal whispered and while Michaels nodded, it was clear to both of them that he was lying. This was probably as far from okay as Michaels had ever been.

"Lose the gun, asshole!" the loner shouted, voice cracking. Hal saw his face—the broad nose, the dark wide eyes. Fear was wet on his cheeks, pain creased in his brow. "Now!"

"Okay," Hal said. "Hang in there, Michaels."

Michaels closed his eyes, shook his head.

The kid grabbed Michaels's collar, using it to hold the officer as a shield in front of him. Hal's arms still felt Michaels shaking, like aftershocks of an earthquake.

Hal released the chambered round into his palm, moving slowly, deliberately. Then he tossed the gun into the middle of the street and prayed someone could get a shot off before this kid killed them both.

CHAPTER 3

HAILEY BUZZED WITH adrenaline and too much albuterol.

Hal wouldn't answer his phone, but Hailey's pager told her that the situation downtown was now a 187-999. The "999" suggested an officer was down, and when she called for an update, they'd told her that the situation had escalated. An officer was being held hostage.

As soon as she was sure Jim was in capable hands, she left the hospital and headed to the scene.

She arrived to find the police had cordoned off three city blocks with bright yellow crime tape. Patrol officers, their hats pulled low against the wind, manned the tape and kept the crowd of curious neighbors and hungry reporters back.

Hailey showed her badge at two separate checkpoints. Hal still wasn't answering his phone as she made the last blocks on foot, wishing she had worn a heavier jacket. Once the sun dropped, the bay cooled the city quickly, and the raincoat Hailey had grabbed from her trunk barely buffeted the rising winds.

The scene looked like the set of a movie.

Freestanding lights had been set up behind the line of black and whites. Cops crouched behind their windows, waiting for a shot. Bruce Daniels stood off to one side, talking on his phone. She veered away from him, heading toward Linda James, patrol captain for the district that included the Tenderloin, one of the roughest neighborhoods in the city.

Linda had been part of the Rookie Club group since before Hailey joined. She had a sharp mind and a wicked sense of humor. She was also among the first of them to be promoted to captain.

"Where's Hal?" Hailey asked Linda, scanning for her partner. She had expected to see him sitting on the sidelines, but he was nowhere in sight.

Linda frowned and pointed toward the hostage. "He's in there."

Hailey froze. "Hal is the hostage?"

"Practically." She pulled a pair of binoculars off her neck and handed them over.

Hailey's stomach tensed at the sight of Hal so close to the shooter.

He sat hunched over, trying to give the impression of being smaller, less intimidating. A guy his size was a big threat to a kid already prepared to kill a cop.

The other officer was leaned back against his captor, legs and arms splayed. Hailey couldn't tell if he was alive or dead.

She scanned carefully for any angles to see the perp, but he was well hidden behind his hostage. She listened to the chatter coming from Linda's radio, something about a wound. "Wait. Who was hit?"

"The perp," Linda said. "An hour ago."

"Can the roof see how he's doing?"

"Last report has him real shaky. Kid's dying and he has to know it." She raised an eyebrow and took back the binoculars Hailey handed her. "Not so good for our guys."

The familiar tightness clenched in her gut. "You think he'll take someone with him?" Not Hal, please not Hal.

Linda shrugged and raised the binoculars to her own eyes. "What's he got to lose? We just need to get him first."

With the officer shielding his chest, a parked car covering his backside, and Hal just feet away, there was no good shot at the kid.

Why hadn't she come with Hal? She should have been there. Would it have made a difference? Could she have kept him away? But what would have happened to Jim if she hadn't been at home?

The sharpshooters might be able to put one in his leg, maybe get a bullet into his pelvis, but his gun was still at the cop's head. An injury like that wouldn't keep him from getting a couple of shots off.

She would not lose Hal.

Linda's radio crackled. "He's getting weak," Cameron Cruz reported from the roof.

Hailey rubbed her chest. Her breathing felt labored. Her albuterol was in the car.

Giving herself some air, she stepped back behind the patrol cars. Bruce approached. Neither spoke but stood side by side, like parents watching over the hospital bed of a child.

"He's going to be okay," Bruce whispered. As he leaned in to nudge her in the shoulder, she stepped away on reflex. He frowned and returned his gaze to the police tape.

Bruce had been pressing to bring their relationship into the open—even if it meant one of them had to leave the department.

Hailey wasn't ready.

In fact, Hailey felt less ready to commit to him than she had when John was alive, and that truth wasn't easy to explain. Recently, Bruce pushed the issue by acting without caution. Her response was to feel less, rather than more, inclined to make the relationship known.

Hailey was about to respond when the perp broke the silence.

"Get me a fucking ambulance," he shouted. "Now. Do it or I'm taking him with me!"

Cameron Cruz's voice crackled through the radio in Hailey's hand. "Easy now. He's antsy," she whispered to the shooters. "Hold tight."

Hailey edged forward.

Down the block, Hal shifted into view.

"Where's the damn ambulance?" the perp shouted, looking away from his hostage.

Hailey gasped as Hal lunged forward and grabbed the officer, pulling him sideways. The sharpshooters fired. The kid's body bucked and twisted against the bullets that struck him.

The street became a flurry of shouting. Hailey pushed forward until she could see Hal stand from the sidewalk. He stepped forward.

He was okay.

Bruce excused himself, and Hailey moved toward Hal.

The paramedics parked the ambulance beside the car and quickly unloaded a gurney from the back, lifting up the officer as Hailey arrived. Tears stung her eyes. She felt foolish and scared. She touched Hal's back.

He was bent over, watching the paramedics at work, his hands on his knees like a football player in a huddle.

"Had a goddamn heart attack," Hal said.

"Bad time for a heart attack," Hailey said.

Hal raised a brow at her.

"What the hell were you doing in there, anyway?"

"Don't ask." He shook his head and stood up straight. "Don't fucking ask."

"We get the guy selling Dennig's guns?"

"Yeah. That guy over there with the white sweatshirt. Dropped to the ground as soon as the cops showed up."

"Can we talk to him now?"

"Mike Neill's bringing him in."

Neill was an inspector in Triggerlock who worked with Ryaan Berry. This was their sting. "He'll call us for the first crack at him when he's ready. They're going to let him sweat overnight."

Perfect. It was amazing how a night in jail could get people talking. Let him sweat awhile. "You ready for that beer?" she asked. After two gun incidents in one night, they deserved it.

"I'm ready for a whole damn case of 'em."

"Well, I'll buy the first one."

"That's the least you can do. I should've sent you down here to deal with that crazy ass motherfucker. Least you might've been smart enough to stay in the van."

Linda James stopped beside them. "Just got the call about the senator. He okay?"

Hal stared at her as Hailey nodded. "He'll be fine."

Linda left them and Hal waited for an explanation.

"Jim got shot tonight. I don't think the shooter entered the house. Bullet caught his earlobe, barely grazed him."

"Another break-in? Like John?"

Hailey turned away as though distracted by the scene. She didn't want to talk about John. "I don't know. This guy left a package."

"Package?"

"A white button. 'Wage peace, not war.'"

"Another anti-NRA pin? Like Dennig's?"

"Exactly the same. That and a weird note. I didn't have time to try to make sense of it."

Hal leaned back against a car, rubbed his face with both palms. "No shit."

Jim and the Dennigs. Abby's father, Tom, and Jim were friends, but that wasn't enough. There had to be another way in which Jim and the Dennigs were tied together. It would naturally lead to questions about John. "It's all hushed up now. No media, no official police report. Just diplomatic services."

"What did Jim say?"

"That he's got no idea."

"And you believe him," Hal said, an edge in his voice.

She said nothing. Why did she believe Jim? Because she knew him.

How could she explain that to Hal? How could she

tell him that her relationship with Jim had changed since John's death, that she'd come to rely on him ... trust him?

Gunfire cracked from inside the building.

Without hesitating, Hal sprinted for the door, gun drawn. Hailey followed, already several paces behind his long stride. He cleared the foyer as she took his back.

They made their way slowly up the stairs.

As they rounded the corner on the landing, a patrol officer spun toward them, gun aimed. His eyes narrowed at Hal, the gun clenched in both fists, the finger edging toward the trigger.

Rookie.

"Whoa," Hal said, raising his hands. "We're cops."

"Homicide," Hailey shouted. "Lower your weapon." When the rookie's gaze shifted to her, he dropped the weapon to his side. They all breathed a moment.

"What happened?" Hailey asked.

The officer's face was pale and moist, his eyes wide and darting in a way that exaggerated the small, mousy features of his face. He moved like someone trying to thaw out frozen feet, as if he couldn't stay still.

"I don't know. I heard shots when I was coming back down." He licked his lips twice and cast a shaky look over one shoulder. "My first live fire," he confessed in a stuttered flurry.

Hailey nodded. "Who else is up here?"

"Lopez, Shakley, I think. I don't really know. It was supposed to be empty. We were just clearing it to make sure we didn't miss anything. There wasn't supposed to be anyone inside."

"Slow down," Hailey said.

The rookie took a shuddering inhale.

"Where did the shots come from?" Hal asked.

"End of the hall, I think." He shook his head, licked his lips again, half trotting in place. "I don't know for sure."

"Head back down to the street," Hal directed, placing a palm on the rookie's shoulder. It looked huge in comparison to the man's slim frame, which had finally stopped bouncing—maybe from the sheer weight of Hal's hand. "Send more officers up and tell them to watch their fire, that we're up here."

When the officer rounded the stairwell, Hailey turned to Hal. "You okay?"

"Twice in one damn day," he said. "I swear if I end up dead, it'll be 'cause I'm shot by some damn rookie."

"You're huge and black," she reminded him. "That's what they see first." They'd had this discussion a dozen times. Life was exponentially more dangerous for a black man than for a white one. When would everyone figure out a way to stop being afraid of someone for his color? "You want me to lead?"

"Sure. At least then I'm safe from the waist down." The joke fell flat, and Hailey knew he was genuinely scared.

Hailey took the front and called out as they rounded the corner. "Inspector Wyatt here. Hold your fire."

No answer. Hailey wondered if there were really other officers in the building, or if the shots they'd heard had taken them out. A moment later, two officers appeared on the stairs behind them—a heavyset black man about her age whose name badge read C. Carlton and a Latina woman who looked to be in her late twenties, A. Mendoza.

"We heard the shots."

Hailey nodded. "No idea who's up here, so be ready for hostile fire."

"Just make sure it's hostile," Hal added.

"He almost got shot by the rookie we sent down," Hailey explained.

"That's Wainwright," Carlton said. "He's a little green."

"Just a little," Hal agreed in a flat voice.

They split the hallway. Hal and Hailey headed toward the end, where the shots had come from, and sent Carlton and Mendoza to clear the other direction.

As they turned the corner, the full length of an empty hallway came into view. Down the right side, wind blew through a series of windows, some opened from the bottom, some closed, and a handful broken, their cracked glass reminding her of Jim.

Faded brown beer bottles, cardboard boxes, and newspapers lay strewn across a splintered avocado-green linoleum floor. On their left were three doors, the first closed completely and the second two partially open.

They paused at the first one.

Hal rapped his gun on the jamb. "Police!"

When no one responded, he kicked the door open. The wood cracked as the door slammed against the wall.

No one behind it.

Hailey watched the familiar bob of Hal's head as he counted silently to three. Then he stooped into the doorway. After a beat, she followed.

The room was empty except for two folding chairs that had been overturned and an old, partially burned brown couch, which stood in the center of the room.

Around it, the linoleum was scorched, and a black circle of ash marred the ceiling.

The stench of smoldered synthetic hung in the air, but when Hailey leaned down to touch the floor, it was cool. The fire wasn't recent.

Nothing else in the room: no closets, no hiding places, and no people.

They backed into the hallway and turned to the next room, but it, too, was empty, except for a handful of newspaper sheets that fluttered in slow circles across muddy brown carpet, like moths circling light.

Something rattled in the next room. Hal nodded toward the wall.

"I guess I'll take door number three, Bob." His voice lacked humor, and Hailey knew he was feeling the same way she was. Unsettled, scared.

Homicide detectives usually showed up when the victims were already dead. It had been a long time since either she or Hal had dealt with a live scene. Only twice before had she experienced two separate shootings in a single day, back when she was a patrol officer.

Never as inspector.

That, on top of the circumstances of Jim's shooting, made her feel shaky, off balance. Hailey radioed for backup—careful to mention that there were multiple officers in the building.

The next room was empty like the others, except for a closet in the far corner. The door was closed.

Hal nodded and Hailey moved toward it.

Guns aimed, they crept toward the door.

She crouched low—ready to fire. Hal swung the door open.

Propped up against the far wall was a cop in uniform. The policeman's eyes were open, his lips parted as though struggling for breath. Beside him was a black kid wearing a hooded sweatshirt. Seated shoulder to shoulder, they might have been friends. Someone had put them there.

Hailey dropped to her knees by the cop while Hal dealt with the kid.

"Dead," Hal said, touching the kid's neck.

Bleeding from the neck, the cop was alive, his pulse thready but discernible, his uniform saturated down the left side. "He's got a pulse."

Hal radioed for an ambulance.

Hailey worked quickly to peel off her windbreaker and then twisted it into a long, thin strip to tie around the cop's neck. The slick material didn't stop the bleeding. There was nothing in the room to help, and Hal's wool sweater was too bulky to do much good. They needed a tight fabric, something to stop the bleeding rather than just absorb the blood.

Moving quickly, Hailey stripped off the white cotton blouse she had over her bulletproof vest and used it as a tourniquet.

The cop's eyes rolled open, his gaze settling on her momentarily.

"Can you hear me?" she asked as his eyes shifted slightly, glassy and yellow, then shut again.

Hal handed her his sweater the way an older brother would, motioning for her to put it on. Without looking at the bare skin around her vest, he turned to stare out the window.

She pulled the sweater over her head and folded the sleeves up until they were giant bulges at her forearms.

Outside the window, something rattled in the wind, and Hal leaned forward to stare out.

She listened for the whir of ambulances to break the silence.

With every passing minute, the pulse in the officer's neck felt slower and weaker. His blood leached through the white cotton, but the slow pace suggested her efforts to staunch the bleeding were working. How quickly John's blood had poured out of him. She couldn't believe how much there had been. It had never slowed.

Hailey stood to adjust her hold on the wound when something clanked against the exterior of the building. She glanced out the window.

One floor down, a figure in black jumped across the fire escape onto the next roof.

"Who the hell is that?" Hal snapped the radio off his belt. "This is five-Henry-one-seven."

"Five-Henry-one-seven, go ahead," came Linda's voice.

"Suspect is on the roof of the building to the—" He glanced around. He had always been hopeless with direction.

"East," Hailey said.

He repeated it then, without hesitation, slid the window open, and climbed over the sill and onto the fire escape, descending each rung of the ladder with a thunderous clatter, something the suspect had accomplished in near silence.

Hal shouted, but the suspect fled across the length of the next roof without turning back.

Hailey stared after him, hoping to get a glimpse of his face. How did this all fit in with their cold case? And Jim's shooting? Hal was almost shot by another cop. She hoped to hell that they weren't chasing this down for nothing.

About the time Hal was halfway down the ladder, the suspect reached a short dividing wall between the two buildings and deftly scrambled over.

"Five-Henry-zero-eight here," Hailey called into her radio. "Suspect is moving east across the roofs. Head him off at Polk."

Hal reached the bottom of the ladder and climbed across the small gap to the next building, way behind the suspect.

Heavy footfall in the hallway accompanied the shouts of paramedics. When they entered, Carlton was with them, as were Mendoza and the rookie, Wainwright.

"Rest of the building is clear," Carlton said. Then he spotted the wounded cop in the closet. "Damn it. Shakley, man."

Carlton took a short step toward the officer. Hailey put her hand out and shook her head. "Let them work."

Wainwright turned to the wall and threw up.

"You can head on down, Wainwright," Hailey told him.

He nodded, gaze darting, his mouth and nose covered by his arm as he turned to leave.

Outside the window, the suspect had already reached the edge of the third building and stopped to peer down. From his hesitation, Hailey guessed there was some sort of gap between the buildings, and for a moment, she thought they had him.

He glanced back and she saw him in the glow of the streetlight. He was a white man with a reddish-brown beard. She waited, hoping for another look, but he turned away again, clambered over the wall and disappeared. Gangs in this part of San Francisco never mixed race. Where did the white guy come from?

She spun to face the others. "Was there a white man down there? On the street?"

Carlton turned to face her. "What do you mean?"

"The kids, the gun sales. Any of them white?"

"No." He came to stand beside her at the window. "Why?"

"That guy, the runner. He was white." Confused, Hailey stared at the dead kid's face. Had that man killed these two? Why? What would he have wanted from this scene? Was he here for the police officer or for the gunrunners?

It had to mean something.

The paramedics wheeled the officer out of the room.

Hailey found a single latex glove tucked in the Velcro pocket of her bulletproof vest and snapped it over her right hand. She peeled back the suspect's hooded sweatshirt to find a spatter of blood against his dark T-shirt.

Someone had closed his jacket after shooting him.

But why?

Hailey pulled the sweatshirt open farther and found the answer—a white circle pinned just above his heart.

She saw the button at Jim's house. Now here. Two buttons in one night after more than a year. Why the long delay? Why now? Why Jim and this black kid?

Damn it, she hoped Hal had caught that guy.

She raised dispatch on the radio, told them to have the hospital search for a button on the cop who'd been shot.

Just then, Hal's breathless voice called on her radio. "Lost him."

Shit. "You better come up here, Hal. He left us a present."

"I hope it's something good."

Hailey glanced at the dead kid's face and reached out to touch his throat again, as though he might come back to life. "It's not." Her finger slipped off the radio, her focus on the dead black kid.

The connection was the guns. It had to be. There was nothing else that linked them. Which meant she was going to have to start pressing Jim for some answers.

With gloved fingers, Hailey closed the kid's eyelids, wishing they'd caught him with a pulse.

Carlton pointed to the button. "What the hell is that?"

She shook her head, too overwhelmed to answer but unable to pull her gaze from the one-inch white pin with blue lettering.

Around the outside it read, "Wage peace, not war."

Inside a circle were the letters "NRA" with a thick blue line through them.

"'Wage peace, not war?' That's no street kid mantra, I'll tell you that. Never seen anything like it."

Hailey wished she hadn't either.

But she'd seen two in that many hours.

CHAPTER 4

THE NEXT MORNING, Hal watched through the observation window as Dwayne Carson scraped under his fingernails with the broken shirt clip from a ballpoint pen.

His white sweatshirt hung off the back of his chair. His shirt was ripped across the neck and partway down one shoulder, but he didn't seem to notice. He was the only kid who'd emerged from the sting without a bullet wound, and yet he was as cool as the bodies already on ice.

Carson had sworn he didn't know where the guns had come from, that he was just along for the ride, and Hal didn't have high expectations for much more.

Shakley, the officer who'd been shot in that room, was their best bet for answers, but he was at the hospital, listed as critical.

No button had been found on him.

Apathy was already etched into the swollen pupils of Carson's narrowed eyes. Resignation tightened the straight line of his mouth and wiped clean any trace of laughter.

Seventeen, and he was already gone.

Hal hated this part, made worse by the fact that he couldn't do anything to change it. The police couldn't protect him from the dangers of the people who lived in his neighborhood. In reality, the police were more likely to tie on the bricks and drop his ass into the swamp, and Carson knew it. They needed answers from Carson. That put him in the power position.

Carson knew that too.

What Hal wanted to know was who was the guy fleeing the scene—the white guy Hailey saw out the window. There was no way to know if Carson knew anything about that guy.

Carson had come out of the BMW, not the building. Aside from those few minutes on the street, there was nothing to tie Carson to the buyers. Nothing to indicate he had any knowledge of who else was inside.

The ruling in Brown vs. Board of Education had done nothing to touch segregation on the streets. Black delinquents dealt with other black delinquents. That's just how it was. The white guy was out of place—way out of place. Which was why Hal needed to find him.

Maybe the guy Hal chased down the fire escape was interracial—but not white. If he really *was* white—and Hal hadn't known Hailey to be wrong yet—then he'd gone into that building not to participate in the purchase of guns but for the sole purpose of shooting two men and leaving a button on one.

The same button found on Jim.

The same one found in three other homicides before today.

No matter how he turned them, those pieces didn't fit.

His phone rang. "Harris."

"Any news?" Hailey asked.

"Waiting for Triggerlock," he told her. "You?"

"I'm with Roger," she said. "Still working on the button, but they finished printing the fire escape."

Hal sat up, hopeful. "And?"

"Nothing. Clean."

"Damn. You see gloves on that guy?"

"It was dark."

"But you saw his face."

"Yeah. Caught under a street light." She paused. "And he was white," she added, an edge to her voice.

"Easy," Hal said, hearing her defensiveness. "I believed you the first time."

"Well, apparently you're the only one. Did you talk to the kid?"

Hal glanced down at the gun box in his hand. "No. I got his gun and I'm going in as soon as the Triggerlock guy shows, but it doesn't look good."

Hailey sighed. "Call me when it's over."

Hal ended the call as Mike Neill stopped in the doorway. Neill could probably have been a businessman as easily as a cop. He was thin, gray-haired, and clean-shaven, the kind of guy who used hair gel. But what did Hal know? Maybe he would have used hair gel too, if he had any hair. "You want to come?" Neill asked.

Hal nodded. "If it's okay."

"Be my guest."

Together, they stepped into the room with Carson. Neill went first.

Carson barely glanced up at them before returning his attention to what must have been some stubborn dirt beneath the nail of his right index finger.

Hal dropped the box from one of the guns stolen from the Dennigs onto the table as Neill walked behind Carson to the far side of the room, just out of Carson's peripheral vision. Carson kept his eyes focused in his lap.

"Let's hear about these guns, Dwayne," Neill said.

Carson averted his gaze from the box on the table and shrugged his shoulders, spreading his hands out to his sides. "I told that other guy I don't know nothin' about them guns."

Hal tapped on the box. "Yeah. I'm not buying that bullshit."

"I swear. Got nothin' to do with that scene. Didn't know what was going down. Saw the cops and shit and got to the ground like you said. Don't know nothin' about guns. Shit, I was afraid they would explode or somethin'."

They'd heard all the stories already. Kids turned on friends, called it police conspiracy, pointed to strangers. They blamed younger siblings, knowing that anyone under sixteen had a better chance of getting off.

Hal flipped open the gun box so the lid clattered to the plastic tabletop.

This particular gun had come off Carson's ankle, but they'd dusted all three of the weapons he'd been carrying, and the only prints they'd found were his.

"What about this? It's a nice piece."

The gun's metal had a bluish tint, and its grip was inlaid wood. SIGs in general were common, standard issue for the department, but this particular gun was more obscure.

A recoil-operated, locked-breech handgun, with a modified Browning HI-Power-style barrel locking.

The P210 was known as an incredibly accurate military handgun.

According to the guys in ballistics, it was not a likely choice for someone on the streets. Too fancy, more show than they needed for what they were doing. Which meant it was stolen. Almost certainly. Now they just needed to tie Carson back to the robbery at Dennig Distribution to find a link to the murders. But they weren't having much luck with that part, either.

"It ain't mine," Carson protested.

Neill stepped forward. "Had your prints all over it."

"So I touched it. Touched the door to that Beamer too. Don't mean I own it."

Hal studied the gun, felt Carson watching him as he turned it in his hands. "You think we can link this gun to murder, Dwayne?"

He didn't answer.

Hal hitched his thumb toward the door. "How about the other two? Because we do that, you know where you're headed?"

Carson tipped his chair back, shook his head. "I told you. Ain't got nothin' to do with guns."

Neill shoved his chair flat again.

Carson jumped up. "Hey, man."

"Sit down," Neill commanded.

Carson moved the chair to the far end of the table and sat.

Hal pulled a holster from the box, the one they'd found strapped on Carson's ankle. "How about this? You just happened to have it?"

"Got it from a friend. A gift."

Hal laughed coarsely, and Carson started slightly from the sound, which echoed in the small room. He knew how to rattle these guys. "Weird gift for a guy with no gun."

"Yeah, my friend, a weird dude," Carson said, his voice dropping, the tone less confident.

"We've got a lot of dead kids, Carson. You don't start talking, you're going upstate."

Carson didn't answer.

"Maybe there was someone else out there, someone we couldn't see."

Carson narrowed his eyes as though sensing a trap. "Yeah. Sure."

"You see anyone else?" Neill asked.

"Nah. No one else."

"Was there a white guy?"

"A white cop?"

Hal shook his head. "With you guys."

"Didn't see no white guy. But what do I know? I didn't know they was gonna pull that shit either."

Hal kept pressing. "How about the guys in the building?"

"Told you I don't know nothin' about them."

"So you didn't see a white guy with them?"

"Didn't see no white guy 'cept the cops."

Watching Carson in silence, Hal tipped his chair back and then forward again, landing with a thwack on the linoleum.

Neill rounded the table to stand beside him. "You're seventeen—means you're an adult in the eyes of the law. You ever been to prison?"

51

Carson didn't answer. Instead, he stared at the ceiling like it was a screen playing a movie he'd never seen.

Neill put his palms on the table. "Nice-looking guy like you. You'd be some fresh meat."

Carson didn't make eye contact. Which meant they were losing him.

"You know what they're going to do with you? Some big guy's going to make you his girlfriend, Dwayne. You go that way? You like being some guy's girlfriend?"

Kid like this, he'd heard these threats before. Most of his friends had probably been to jail. This was Neill's witness, but Hal felt him slipping away. He waited for Neill to give Hal some room to work.

"Ain't no faggot."

"Only thing standing between you and prison is me, Dwayne."

Hal sat back, glanced at his watch and rubbed the face of it gently with his shirtsleeve. His only link to the murders. *Come on, Neill.*

"You got sixty seconds to start talking," Neill said.

Carson patted his pocket and sat up in his chair, something in his expression relaxing as though he realized he'd had the answer the whole time. The spark of fear in his eyes vanished. "I want my lawyer."

Hal watched him draw something from his pocket.

"What bullshit is this?" Neill asked. "A lawyer?"

Carson handed Hal a worn business card. *Martin L. Abbott, Esquire.*

A lawyer. Hal turned away and clenched his jaw. It was over. Abbott was high profile and expensive, not someone this kid would have access to. Not on his own, anyway.

Someone was helping him.

Hal handed it to Neill, who tossed it back at Carson.

"You think that lawyer's going to help you?" Neill barked. "How are you going to pay him, Dwayne? A guy like that costs five hundred bucks an hour."

"I ain't talking without my lawyer."

"You'd be saving yourself a lot of trouble by telling us who hired you to sell those guns," Neill said.

Carson didn't respond.

Hal smacked his palm on the table, making it stutter across the floor. "This isn't a game, Dwayne."

"I ain't playing at nothin', officer."

Hal heard the knock on the door and knew they were done.

Carson had asked for an attorney. No more questions until he made his call. And to Martin Abbott.

That was bad luck.

*

Down in the lab, Hal found Hailey pacing the speckled linoleum floor. One of the techs, Naomi Muir, was working at a station nearby.

"She driving you crazy?" he asked Naomi.

Hailey stopped and scowled at Hal.

"Not at all," Naomi said. "I like the noise."

Across the room, Roger sat hunched over his keyboard. Roger had a condition called alopecia universalis, which left him completely hairless. It had taken Hal some time to get used to the way a person looked without eyebrows or eyelashes. Even after five years, it was still the first thing Hal noticed whenever he saw Roger. Seemed like it shouldn't be that way, but there it was. As a way of an unspoken apology, he had brought Roger a bumper sticker a few months back. It hung on the wall of his workspace.

With a body like this, who needs hair?

"Can you make her stop?" Roger asked.

"No way," Hal said. "She's the boss, man."

Hal and Hailey had both been up most of the night, and while he moved slowly, dragging his limbs like he was underwater, sleep deprivation made Hailey antsy. And the more exhausted she was, the harder it became for her to sit still.

She still had no answers from Jim, who had been given a sedative at the hospital and was sleeping. CSU had spent most of the night processing the house, though they hadn't come up with anything particularly useful in the process.

Hailey finally stopped pacing long enough to ask Hal what had happened with Dwayne Carson.

"Kid's a dead-end with a high-priced attorney." He filled her in on Martin Abbott.

Hailey sank into a chair.

"Martin Abbott," she whispered. Her shoulders tightened, and for a moment, she was completely still.

Hal tried to read her reaction. What was she thinking? "Did Jim know Abbott?"

She shrugged, an awkward jerky motion, without looking at him. The way she averted her gaze, hesitating to answer questions related to her family—that was not new. It had started in the months after John died.

In the weeks after his father's death, he, too, had distanced himself from his friends, creating a safe buffer to see whether they settled on his side or the other. He'd been a kid—only twenty-three. So much about that time was blurry now. He wished he could share it with Hailey, tell her that it had been a mistake not to trust in the people who had always been there for him.

How could he do that without confronting her about how secretive she'd become?

She finally looked up, caught his stare and said, "They're friends, I guess, but I can't see what either would want to do with that gunrunner we found dead in the closet."

"But Jim, Colby Wesson, the Dennigs, the gunrunner—they all got buttons. Then, we've got a kid who lawyers up with *Martin Abbott*, of all people… It's a tight circle. There's got to be some link. The only thing that makes sense is the guns."

Hailey said nothing, so Hal turned to Roger, who was still typing at the computer. "What've you got, baldy?"

Roger smiled, one bald man to another. "Just getting a read on the button now. Letter's still running."

Hal had seen the letter the night before. After the interview with Carson, he had stopped by the lab to talk to Roger. The letter had been inside the FedEx envelope lying beside Jim.

Now, he followed Hailey across the room and looked again at the single page, printed on an HP LaserJet in Times New Roman font.

"Knowing your own darkness is the best method for dealing with the darkness of other people," Hal read out loud. *"I know your darkness, Senator. Yours is a very old special."*

"It's Jung," Roger said.

Hal and Hailey said nothing.

"Carl Jung," Roger added. "The famous—"

"Okay, Doctor Wikipedia," Hailey said.

Roger laughed.

"It sound like anything else you've seen?" Hal asked Hailey.

She shook her head. "I'm sure Jim gets all sorts of weird stuff."

"But usually not with a bullet," he pressed.

"Right," Hailey agreed. She met his gaze and held it, her normal confidence gone, as if she'd just accepted a dare she wasn't sure she could stomach.

Finally, she rubbed her arms, and said, "I don't honestly know," and resumed her pacing.

Hal felt slighted by the response. Though she'd been keeping her distance for more than a year, he still felt the fresh sting when he butted up against the wall Hailey had built between them. What stung more were the lies and omissions. Maybe they weren't important things. Maybe they were none of his business, but he used to think they shared more than other partners did.

He'd thought they were closer than other partners.

Now he wasn't sure.

They'd been together seven years now, since she'd returned from maternity leave after Camilla was born. They'd had only a few periods of separation since—when she gave birth to Ali, the five weeks he spent recovering from a shoulder surgery, and her leave of absence after John's death.

In all that time, he had never felt more distant from her than he did now.

From across the room, Roger asked, "You get philosophy on any of the others?"

"Only to wage peace and not war," Hailey answered, still moving.

"I guess that's philosophy."

"We're not much into philosophy, Roger," Hal said.

"Right, we're more into names," Hailey added and turned to pace the silent lab, her heels clacking on the floor.

As Hailey walked by, Hal took her gently by the shoulders.

"I'm pacing?"

Hal nodded.

Hailey exhaled and sank into a chair.

"Thank you, Hal," Roger said. "Now I can think."

Hailey rolled her eyes at them and turned to her phone. "Got a text from ballistics." She scrolled, reading the message. "They dug a .38 slug out of the wall of Jim's house," she said.

"Like in the note."

"Maybe," she said.

Hal found it hard to believe that Hailey hadn't made the same connection, but he didn't push. *You're going to have to push.* He tried to follow the logic. "So Jim gets this letter yesterday and a button, along with a bullet. A dead gunrunner is found with an identical button. We haven't seen any of these buttons in a year and now we've got two inside two hours."

"That's what it looks like," Roger said.

"Why now? Why these guys?"

Hailey didn't look over at him. "Jim isn't pro-gun. He's more moderate than most Republicans. He actually believes in restrictions."

"He doesn't vote for restrictions, does he?" Hal asked, feeling his own outrage building.

Hailey glanced away. "The party politics make it tough."

"A republican voting for gun control would be outrageous," Roger added.

"Seems like he's in pretty heavy with the gun guys," Hal said. "Can't imagine they would like a vote for restrictions."

Hailey didn't respond.

Hal tried to appreciate that Jim was her family now. She wanted to protect him. But above the truth?

"How long before we get lab results on these?" she asked Roger.

"We're running the button from the senator's house and letter concurrently," Roger explained. "It's faster to run both at once, but we've probably got another five or ten minutes."

Hailey went to sit on the far side of the room, and Hal leaned back, watching her through partially closed eyes, wondering what she was thinking, if she'd considered that Jim might, somehow, be involved in something that would warrant someone wanting to shoot him. He wondered if she'd ever tell him, one way or the other. Wondered if he'd have the guts to ask the question.

He hadn't pushed his mother for the truth either. To this day, she'd never told him whether or not she thought the allegations about his dad were true. Somehow, the real story became like a neighbor she could avoid by not answering the doorbell. Hal was out of the house by then, attending the police academy in Alameda.

The day Hal read the newspaper headline, he ran for four miles before he reached the fancy part of Oakland, where the houses were as large as city blocks, where the lawns were manicured, and flowerbeds were as big as his whole front yard. He ran through the oak-lined streets while white people in fancy cars stared at him. Ran back up under the freeway and into the desolate streets of Oakland, the place where black kids didn't have a fighting chance, where instead of struggling their way toward the top, they simply made themselves at home on the bottom.

He ran through the place where his father had worked, the "war zone."

Ten miles later, soaked and beaten, Hal had arrived at the police station where his father had brought him from the time he was barely old enough to speak, long before he was old enough to understand his father's job.

He never made it inside the heavy glass doors.

They met him on the steps—his father's captain and partner. Before he could get inside for a breath of air-conditioned air, they told him to walk back out, to leave it alone. He wouldn't. Couldn't. He wanted to fight. He started a brawl, but before he could throw a punch, he'd been handcuffed.

As a favor to his mother, his father's partner had put Hal in the back of a squad car, still cuffed, and delivered him home. Sitting in the back of that black and white, the grill separating him and the good guys, Hal had felt a penetrating suffocation, the terrifying sense that he'd never fill his lungs fully again.

By the time he got home, he was wheezing and choking so badly his mother had wanted to take him to the hospital. After the officers had uncuffed him, he'd huddled on the front lawn, fighting to catch his breath. He got down on hands and knees and pressed his face to the grass his father had tended with such pride—the same grass his father had studded with American flags every Fourth of July.

His father's captain had agreed not to record the incident as long as Hal stayed away, to give him a final chance to make it through the academy, if that was what he wanted.

His lungs had settled just fine once those cuffs were off and he was outside the car.

Seeing he was all right, his mother had gone inside, and when he walked into the house, still drenched and hot, she was sitting at the table, the paper he'd stuffed into the garbage can spread in front of her, the torn bits of print smoothed out, her pink fingertips blackened with ink. Without a word, she motioned for him to sit across from her where a tall glass of water waited. He chugged the water, and as soon as it hit his stomach, he stumbled outside to retch. He sat on the front step then, and cried, his tired, tight stomach heaving until his mother finally emerged from the house to join him.

"You're going to upset your sisters, Hal. They've been through enough. We all have."

"It isn't true. It can't be."

She sank onto the stair beside him, using the railing to lower herself down. "It don't matter one way or another now, baby."

"They set him up."

She stared at her stained fingers and ran her palms over them. "Maybe."

"What about his name? What about our name?" He nodded toward the house. "You're going to stay here and just let them print that shit."

"No, son. I ain't. I'm going to go down and stay with David and Becca for a while. They got no kids and plenty of space."

Los Angeles. She was moving across the state, away from their friends and family. "You just going to give up?"

"I don't see it that way, Hal. I see it the opposite. I'm moving on."

"What about his pension?"

She shook her head. "Don't think we'll be getting that, but we'll make do without it."

"What about—"

She stood then, wiped her hands across her sweat-pants where they made little black hash marks like she'd been keeping score. "Your sisters will be back soon. They went to get some boxes. Don't be talking this nonsense to them, you hear?"

He had wanted to ask her what he was supposed to do, where he fit in now with his whole family down south and him up here, him in the academy, setting out to follow in his father's footsteps. He'd always considered it an honor, a legacy to be a cop, but that was all different now.

How could he go back there without knowing the whole truth about his father's death?

What choice did he have but to go back?

Leaving the academy was as good as admitting to his father's guilt. He owed it to the family to go back, hold his head high, and reclaim their family's name. If they would let him.

On the day he returned, his captain had summoned him. In full dress uniform, he'd gone into the office, prepared to leave the academy behind with dignity.

His captain sat behind the desk, hands folded on a leather blotter while his lieutenant leaned against the far wall. "We hope you'll finish the academy, Officer Harris," his lieutenant said.

Hal had never felt such intense relief. He would stay. They wanted him to stay. There, he could prove himself. "Yes, sir," he'd answered.

"Some of the men are going to have heard the news," the captain said. His skin was as dark as Hal's, peppered with tiny moles that you could only make out standing face to face. But his eyes were oddly light for such a dark man. It gave the impression that he held special powers— like he could see past words simply spoken to the truth behind them. "You understand, Officer Harris?"

Hal's stomach went taut, his breathing skittish. "Yes, sir."

"There are plenty of men with stories like this one.

You have to decide how to handle it. Whether you're going to fight his battle or yours," the captain continued.

"Yes, sir."

"I need to know whose battle you're fighting."

It would not be about his father, but about him. "Mine, sir."

"It won't be easy."

"I know, sir."

The captain and lieutenant shared a glance as Hal stared at his lap. He held his chin high, eyes open, and focused on the flag in the corner of the room.

His father had loved that flag.

Every year, in the last days of June, his father would line up flags all along the border of the yard. More than a hundred of them, one right beside the next, with just enough distance between them so that when the wind blew they had the space to stretch out.

If it rained, he'd take them down and put them back up as soon as it dried out again. If he was on patrol when the rain started up, he'd call from the car and tell Hal to do it.

At the end of July, when Mama finally convinced him that the holiday was over, he took them down again. He sat in the living room and rolled them one at a time, fastening each with a rubber band, laying them in a box labeled "Patriot Day" in his narrow print. The box then went up into the attic until the next year.

Hal wondered what would become of his father's flags.

"Dismissed, Harris," his captain said and rose from his chair.

Hal pried his eyes from the flag. "Yes, sir. Thank you, sir."

And with that, he had gone to face his classmates, to wait for one of them to mention his father, steeling himself for the fight. There had never been a single word.

Hal jumped at the sound of his name.

"Wake up!" Roger shouted.

Hal sat up, blinked, then rubbed his eyes.

"That's why I pace," Hailey told Roger. "Otherwise I end up asleep."

Hal stood and stretched. "What is it?"

"Nicholas Fredricks's print is on the button," Roger said.

Of course it was. They'd known it, hadn't they? He rubbed his eyes.

"Again," Hailey said. "We're waiting for results from the letter."

Just then, a bell rang from the computer.

"We've got a match," Roger announced.

"Okay, let's see what we've won," Hal added, trying to shake off the heaviness he always felt thinking about his father.

Hailey made room for him behind Roger's chair, and they stared at the computer screen where a small hourglass emptied and filled and emptied again.

"Come on," Hailey whispered.

The screen went black and a name appeared in bold, white letters.

Roger clapped. "Well, look at that. It's your dead guy again."

Hal stepped back. Hailey cursed.

The screen read "Nicholas A. Fredricks."

Nothing. Again. Hailey was hoping for a new lead. "Guess we're going to be digging up a dead guy today. I better go change my clothes."

Hailey closed her eyes with the look of someone considering the possibility of not opening them again.

Hal knew exactly how she felt.

They needed a break in this case.

CHAPTER 5

HAL DROVE TOWARD the cemetery while Hailey sat beside him, silent. They had reviewed the case that morning, but there was nothing new to go on. Dwayne Carson was still being held at the station. There was no word from his attorney, Martin Abbott—if Abbott was really his attorney.

Officer Shakley remained in critical condition from yesterday's gunshot. The dead gunrunner had been identified as Jeremy Hayden. The records department was running a full background check on known associates.

As Hal turned in through the cemetery gates, Hailey struggled to focus on something that felt so distant, so far in the past. Abby and Hank Dennig had died fourteen months ago. Hailey could still picture Tom Rittenberg with his cane at John's funeral, a gentle giant moving through the services. It was obvious that his grief was still raw. She had interviewed him in the course of the investigation, and he'd been earnest and forthright, anxious to help. More than a year later, they still had nothing. She owed him some answers.

When Hailey thought of the Dennig murders, she

thought of John. Their deaths had happened so close together. Hailey thought about the Dennigs' orphaned girls. Where were those girls now? Who took care of them?

At least Hailey's girls had Liz and Jim. The Dennigs' kids had their grandfather. She hoped Tom Rittenberg would make sure they were cared for.

At their morning department meeting, Captain Marshall had been relatively quiet. That was never good news. Usually, he started meetings with a little banter, shooting the shit about the game the night before.

Not today.

This morning, Marshall made sure to remind the team that closing the case had been Hailey's error, one that he was giving her a chance to fix. He also expressed that the case belonged to her and Hal. At the conclusion of the meeting, Marshall held her and Hal back. "I don't think anyone needs to know about Senator Wyatt."

Hailey and Hal reviewed the case file on Nicholas Fredricks, starting with his emigration from Germany when he was fourteen. He was an average student in Brooklyn and had no formal education past high school. Other than an arrest in 1970 for the use of explosives during a riot against gun maker Smith & Wesson, he had a clean record. When the police couldn't prove the explosive device belonged to Fredricks, the case was dropped.

Fredricks spent his early adult career working in the administrative offices at the New York City Police Department. According to the records, he quit abruptly after about fifteen months, just ten days after a veteran NYPD officer shot a sixteen-year-old black kid on a school playground. The officer claimed he had drawn a weapon, but no weapon was ever found on the scene. He then moved to Washington to work for a liberal senator of New Hampshire.

Fredricks's involvement in the riot against Smith & Wesson linked him loosely to one of the other victims, Colby Wesson, although Wesson didn't join the family business until after Fredricks was killed. But even if Fredricks and Colby Wesson had crossed paths somehow, the two would have been opponents. How did it make sense that they would be victims of the same killer?

As always, that was where both Hal and Hailey got stumped. And the Fredricks case file, after twelve years, was as cold as they came.

The inspectors who had originally handled the case were both retired now, and neither remembered anything noteworthy. They spoke to two witnesses in the days following the shooting, both residents of the street where Fredricks died. One man said he saw a black man shoot the victim. The other said it was a couple of young white kids.

The houses on the street where Fredricks was killed were all set up from the street, like Jim and Liz's. One of the witnesses lived in a house that was twenty-six steps off the sidewalks. She had been looking out her bedroom window on the second floor. The other was working in his study, which was on the third floor of his home. Both were over sixty and admitted to being nearsighted.

In terms of potential eyewitnesses, Fredricks couldn't have met death on a worse street. Not to mention that he died before the days where everything was filmed—no traffic cameras, no bystanders with their cell phones recording.

And the investigators hadn't gotten anywhere with Fredricks's clients either. They had searched his recent correspondence, interviewed a number of the politicians and their staff. There was no evidence that anyone had a beef with Fredricks. One politician, one of his opponents, had been quoted in the murder file. "Nick knew the rules of the game and he played it well. Even if you didn't agree with him, you respected the way he thought."

Hailey had a call into the New York Police Department to ask about the circumstances of Fredricks's abrupt departure from his job, but she wasn't hopeful.

Hal parked against the curb and turned to her. "You ready?"

She nodded, fingering the albuterol inhaler in her pocket. Exhumations were never pretty, but this one was unavoidable. When a corpse left fingerprints at crime scenes, it never hurt to check out the casket. Was the body even in there? Or did the killer have a stash of old anti-NRA buttons with Fredricks's prints on them? They were about to find out.

Through the windshield, a hill in the distance rose like a phantom through the fog, tombstones standing on its rise like little gray soldiers. When she stepped outside the car, the smell of wet grass and musty, turned earth filled her lungs.

Together they crossed the wet cemetery grass to join the three men from the crime scene unit who were disinterring the body. Hailey recognized two of the three, though she didn't know either well. On the far side of the gravesite, Shelby Tate was working at the back of the unit's van, probably readying their kits for evidence collection.

Fredricks's headstone, a simple rectangle made of granite, lay off to the side. Its inscription offered no clue as to who might have paid for it. The etching, in simple, clean script, said only his full name: Nicholas Adam Fredricks, and the dates of his life: November 19, 1951 to April 2, 2004.

He had lived to be fifty-three. John had only made it to thirty-four. What would those nineteen years have brought them? Would John have gone into politics? Would their marriage have survived that?

Hailey picked up one of the shovels from a stack and helped dig. Her efforts were awkward, the shovel nearly as tall as she was, but she didn't stop. There was something soothing about the continuous motion.

For those moments, she could stop thinking. This was why people ran. She needed to get more exercise. John had always run. She hated running.

Beside her, Hal stopped shoveling. "Hailey?"

"What?"

"Uh, we might be quicker if you don't help. No offense—"

She returned the shovel to the stack and stood in the grass, stomping her feet to stay warm. The ME, Shelby Tate, was still occupied at the van.

Hailey's cell phone rang. Bruce. She didn't answer.

A few minutes later, her cell rang, unanswered again.

Surrounded by the cemetery's cold, dank smell, Hailey felt John's presence, the way she sometimes did when the house was perfectly still, the only sound a lonely creak from inside the old walls or a car passing on the road below. She lay in bed silent and unmoving, focusing on the sounds and searching out a rhythm, like a Morse code she could translate if she listened hard enough.

She had promised to call Bruce, but the last twenty-four hours had been nuts, and standing in the cemetery—so close to where John was buried—Hailey couldn't bring herself to phone him.

As the men dug, she felt as though she was holding her breath. The exhumation of Fredricks's body would inevitably cause a renewed media storm around the murders. If this dig didn't lead them to any usable evidence, Tom Rittenberg and his family would have to relive the Dennigs' deaths without the investigation team gaining a damn thing.

The wind lashed its icy hand across her neck. For several minutes, she didn't move, allowing the dampness to seep into her bones. It was oddly comforting, the cold numbness.

Across the lawn, the massive tires of a backhoe dug into the gravesite, while mud squished through the tread like the innards of thousands of earthworms. They were supposed to have help from the cemetery, but the cemetery's workers were busy digging new graves and had no time to help the police dig up an old one.

The men shoveled in rhythm, each digging his corner of the plot, the dirt making whooshing sounds as it slid off the shovels and landed with a crunch, striking the cold grass.

Whoosh crunch, whoosh crunch.

No bodies were buried in San Francisco County—the

land was too valuable to hold the dead, though it still produced them. Instead, the bodies came to Colma. About ten miles south of San Francisco, Colma was a city of cemeteries—one after the other, and new ones going up all the time.

Dead people were a rising commodity in San Francisco.

Hailey was all too aware of the number of murders in her city. So far, this year's homicide rate was the highest in a decade, and gangs were primarily to blame. The increase made life in Homicide busier and more stressful. The spotlight burned hot on them to solve the murders the moment they happened.

The guys on CSI did it, why not SFPD?

There was nothing unusual about the gun dealer they'd found dead in the closet. His rap sheet was standard for guys like him. So Hailey had focused on the white guy who'd gotten away. She sat with a police artist to create a composite, but she didn't think the image would yield any suspects. He was too far away, her glance too quick. All Hailey saw was white skin and a brownish red beard. At best, she was narrowing it down to a white man, but the suspect could have been a woman in disguise.

Her cell phone buzzed and she pulled it from her pocket with stiff, frozen fingers, her teeth chattering slightly as she answered. "Wyatt."

"I want to see you this week. No excuses."

Hailey shoved her hand into her pocket and fingered her inhaler. "Okay. Maybe a drink tonight."

"Promise?"

"Promise."

"At my house?" he asked.

She pictured Bruce's house, as it had been the few times she'd been there since John died. The black leather Danish couch, a steel coffee table, a geometric-patterned rug, and two large pieces of modern art. Everything was always in its place, so totally opposite of her own home. For the first six months, Hailey hadn't allowed herself in. They talked on the phone often—sometimes two or three times a day—but she'd refused to visit. Worse, Hailey was unable to express her worst fear—the one that was ridiculous when she thought of saying it out loud.

Hailey worried John would see them.

Then, two months ago, Jim and Liz had taken the girls to their home in Sea Ranch for a long weekend, and Hailey had stayed to work. Bruce and Hailey had met up for a drink at Bix, a bar not far from his house. It was the first time they'd met in public—ever—though it no longer mattered.

Hailey was a widow. Even if people thought it was early for dating, surely a drink with a man wasn't a cardinal sin. And the chances of running into anyone from the department were close to nil. Bix wasn't a police bar. Too fancy, too far from the department. They had ended up spending the night at his house, two nights in a row, and she hadn't been back since.

"Hailey?" he pressed.

"I don't know. I'll think about it." Just then a shovel struck the casket with a loud thwack. "Hey, I've got to go. I'll call you when I'm back in the department." Hailey paused, about to hang up. "Still there?"

"Yeah."

"I think your house will be okay." As she hung up,

though, she had no idea why she had said that. Lifting the evidence kit off the wet grass, she moved toward the hole as the men cleared the dirt off the coffin.

"Move back, boys," the cemetery guy yelled and Hal and the others stepped away from the hole. He joined her at the periphery as the worker brushed his hands off on gray overalls and climbed back into the forklift. They watched as he maneuvered the machine with ease, lowered it into the ground and after a few jerky motions, returned to the surface with the casket, setting it gently on the damp grass. She stepped forward, snapping latex gloves over her icy hands before pulling the camera from her evidence bag and aiming it at the casket, a solid deep brown box with elegant curves.

Hal whistled. "Look at that beauty."

"You know something about caskets?"

"I know mahogany. We priced it when Dad died. No way I could afford that. I bet not many folks could."

Hailey stared at the wood, picturing John's casket. She'd never considered the cost of it. It was just another thing Jim had managed. "I wonder who paid for this."

"Good question."

Hal reached forward to unlatch the box but stopped when the cemetery worker jumped out of the forklift. "Hang on," he shouted, pulling a cell phone from his pocket and punched. "The director's coming out. He needs to be here when we open it."

"Then he should've been here," Hailey said.

"He's real busy. We've got six burials today."

"We're pretty busy too," Hal said.

A long black town car parked at the curb a few

minutes later. A man in a dark suit stepped out of the driver's side. Though he wasn't much taller than five-ten, he had to weigh north of two-fifty.

"I'm so sorry, Mrs. Dubavich. I truly am," he said, talking into a tiny phone held in his pink, fleshy hand. "I am available for whatever you need." He nodded without looking up. "Yes, absolutely. I think Lipetsky Brothers do a wonderful job. I am certain that's the right choice." He waited, nodded, stopping just feet from them. Hailey started toward him, but he put a hand up to stop her. Hal arrived beside her and the director gave him a quick glance before putting up a single finger and adding a forced smile, as though to plead with Hal not to strike him. "Yes, Mrs. Dubavich. I will call you tomorrow morning to make the final arrangements. Good-bye, then." He slid the phone into his inside coat pocket and looked up, scanning Hal and the other men before settling his gaze on her.

"I'm Inspector Hailey Wyatt. We spoke earlier. This is my partner, Inspector Hal Harris."

"Hailey and Hal," he said, drawing out the words. "Department alliteration. How fun." His lips formed a tight knot, and one brow arched into an unnatural point.

Hal and Hailey exchanged a glance, but the director paid them no attention. He smiled, lips only, a show of politeness from someone studied in the art of dealing with unhappy people, then nodded to his employee. "Go ahead, Miguel."

Miguel hesitated just slightly before reaching for the lid.

"Whoa," Hal interrupted. "We need to do that."

Handing the camera to Hal, Hailey stepped forward and held up her gloved hands. "If I may."

Miguel looked to the director, who nodded. "Of course."

As Hailey lifted the lid of the casket, the hinges keened like a cornered cat.

The director let his breath out, blowing the bitter smell of onions and something spicy, like sausage or pepperoni, over her shoulder. "See," he said. "It's just as I thought. Totally undisturbed." He turned to Miguel. "Let's get it back in the ground."

"Not so fast," Hailey said. From the corner of her eye, she saw Hal give the director a sideways glance that said as plainly as words that he should stay out of Hailey's way. The inside of the mahogany casket was covered in heavily padded walls of off-white satin, small buttons adorning the spots where the fabric was attached to the wood with perfect pleats. Spores of mold covered the surface.

"The mold is all quite normal," the director said.

It was true. In Homicide, Hailey had seen plenty of mold on bodies, buried or not. The casket was still in good condition, as was Fredricks's corpse. Though the layers of fat had deteriorated, Fredricks's skin remained undamaged. The result was that the skull appeared to be covered in thin, tanned leather, and the eyeballs protruded like smooth golf balls, still in their sockets. The almost transparent eyelid lay like a sheet of wax paper molded over them. Bits of greenish-gray mold encircled his mouth and the lower edges of his eyes. Hailey had seen corpses only hours old in much worse condition. The corpse was still there, which meant there was still the question of how Fredricks' fingerprint ended up on those buttons, but seeing the casket and the embalming raised a new set of questions.

"He looks good," Hal said, echoing Hailey's thoughts as he snapped pictures.

"We do wonderful work," the director said, still breathing heavily behind her.

Fredricks had been embalmed, and it had been done well, which brought her back to the question Hal had raised—who paid for his burial? Hal lifted Fredricks's arm, and Hailey noticed the fabric at the elbows was flattened from wear. "Hold that," he said and Hailey did while he photographed.

"Suit doesn't match the casket or the quality of the embalming," Hailey commented.

Hal turned to the director. "You have records on payment?"

The director shrank into his suit. "Payment?"

"Records of who paid for the burial," Hal repeated.

"I can't—"

Hailey frowned. "We can get a warrant."

He nodded. "Yes, you'll have to do that. I'm sorry," he added with the same expression he'd had speaking on the phone to Mrs. Dubavich.

It was no surprise that they'd need a warrant. The days of getting anything easy were long gone. Turning back to Fredricks, Hailey spotted a dried white rose on Fredricks's left lapel, but other than the flower, he was free of adornments: no jewelry and no personal items with him.

Hal and Hailey turned their focus to Fredricks's hands. If his prints were on those other buttons, then he had either touched them a long time ago and somehow the prints had been preserved or … Hailey spotted the white bandage and lifted Fredricks's hand where gauze crisscrossed his palm and wrapped up the index finger of his left hand.

Hal snapped pictures and when he was done, Hailey touched the tip of the bandage, feeling the end shift. Hal leaned forward and using a pair of scissors from the kit, carefully cut off the bandage.

The director, who had stepped away to take another call, charged at them like a rhino. "What are you doing?" Then, when the end of the wrapped finger fell off, he stumbled back. "Oh, my."

Miguel spun from the scene.

Something dropped into Hal's gloved hand and together they stared down at the end of a cork. The index finger of Fredricks's left hand was missing its first joint.

"Now we know where the print came from," Hal said.

Someone broke into a casket and stole the tip of a dead man's finger—all to link Fredricks to a series of buttons planted on the killer's victims. So far Jim was the only one who hadn't been seriously hurt.

Jim. He was being targeted by this mystery shooter.

But for what?

Hailey found an evidence bag from the kit at her feet and opened the Ziploc bag so Hal could put the cork inside. She recorded the time, date, and location on the side with a Sharpie. Marshall had refused their request for an evidence team. There weren't enough cops to go around, so they'd have to process this one themselves.

The director glanced at the cork end, frowning. "He

probably had wishes to be buried with it," he said without conviction.

As Hailey shifted the bag in her hand, she noticed the words "Chateau St. Jean" printed on one side of the cork. The end was stained a dark red. A red Chateau St. Jean made her think of the Chateau St. Jean Cinq Cepages Jim had been drinking last night. It wasn't an uncommon bottle, but it was Jim's favorite.

Hal saw her expression. "What?"

Hailey shook her head. "Later."

"You okay?" he asked.

"What do you think?"

He put an arm over her shoulder and then, in an attempt to make her smile, struck out in a baritone and sang Merle Travis.

"You haul Sixteen Tons, whadaya get?
Another day older and deeper in debt
Saint Peter don't you call me cause I can't go
I owe my soul to the company store."

Hailey forced a smile and seeing it, Hal stopped. "I tried."

On the way out of the cemetery, Hal turned back into the grounds rather than out toward the street. The shadowy form of the fog hung like a ghost above the graceful curves of the hilltops. When the car stopped, Hailey turned to Hal, who rested both wrists on the steering wheel and lightly drummed his fingers on the dashboard.

Outside the window, she recognized John's grave. On the anniversary of his death, Liz and Jim had brought her and the girls, but the rain had been coming down so hard that only Jim had emerged from the car to place flowers on the grave, while the women sat in the back of the town car and made their own rain.

The soft mound that had been there the last time Hailey had come out to see John was now flattened. The dark, wet dirt, whose ripe smell was so pungent in her memory, had been replaced with fall leaves. Even from the car, the marble of John's headstone looked dulled, indistinct from the ones all around it, and she found herself shivering under the scorching blast of the car's heat. "Why are we here?"

Hal stopped drumming. "I thought you'd want to stop. You want me to come with you?"

She didn't look up. "I don't want to stop."

Hal turned in his seat, shut the fan off. "You should."

"I can't."

He waited for her to change her mind or explain her reasons. She didn't.

He pulled away from the curb and paused to stare at John's grave. When he drove forward, he flipped off the radio and the heat, leaving the car silent except for the rattling hum of the engine and the clank of a coin stuck down in a vent somewhere.

He wanted to talk about it.

Every time, she drew back.

They were partners. She trusted him as much as she would ever trust anyone. Maybe even more.

But she didn't trust anyone enough to speak that truth.

CHAPTER 6

FATIGUE PRESSED ON Hailey's shoulders and pinched the small of her back like the weight of another person. She and Hal had brainstormed the entire way back to the station and had come up with nothing. Fredricks had been dead twelve years, which meant either someone took his finger twelve years ago with the idea that they would want to use it in a future crime ... or someone had dug up Fredricks's body recently.

The cemetery had no cameras on the burial plots, so they had no way of knowing when and if the body had been dug up. The director had assured them that the body couldn't have been dug up without someone knowing about it. But he also suggested that Fredricks had wanted to be buried with the cork in the place of his fingertip, so they were having a tough time trusting his insights.

Shelby Tate couldn't say with certainty when the finger had been removed, other than that it had happened postmortem. She had taken some skin samples near the incision to try to do better, but she had warned them that it really was just a guessing game.

Hailey arrived home as the girls were climbing the

steps with Liz, each carrying her small backpack: Camilla's purple with flowers, Ali's a pink Hello Kitty. When Hailey called out, they turned back down the stairs and ran to her. Before they reached the curb, they were chattering about the events of the day in a way that simultaneously relieved the tightness in her back and made her feel all the more exhausted.

Inside, they sat in the kitchen where Hailey made snacks as Liz started dinner. "Jim's gone to the office, if you can believe it."

"He's out of the hospital?"

Liz shook her head the way she did when she was irritated with someone. "Dee spent the morning rifling through his desk, then went to get him at noon time and took him straight to the office. I swear they're insufferable together," she muttered, then caught herself, forcing a smile by carefully creasing each corner of her mouth like her table linen. "Oh, I'm overreacting. Of course it isn't Dee's fault. He should be resting, is all."

"You've got a full house with all of us here," Hailey said, wondering again why Dee lived with her brother and his wife. For Hailey, living with Jim and Liz made sense. She couldn't manage the kid schedules and her job without help. But she didn't see the same logic in Dee's presence at her in-laws' home.

"We love having you guys here," Liz said. "And Dee too."

"She and Jim are close," Hailey said.

"They are. Very," Liz agreed. Hailey didn't read any bitterness in her tone.

"I'm an only child, but it seems unusual to me."

"I'm certainly not that close to my brothers." Liz began to chop a tomato. "Dee had it rough after they went to live with their aunt and uncle. They already had two girls, and their aunt wasn't the kindest woman. At least, that's what I've heard."

Jim would have been a son to them—a bonus probably. Carry on the family name and all that. He'd probably had it much easier.

Liz seemed to deal well with Dee's presence, but maybe that was because they were so different. Dee didn't have any interest in the domestic duties. She was focused on her career and, because of that, on Jim's, while Liz was the matriarch. All household decisions were hers. Hailey helped cook and clean up, but most times Liz ushered her out of the kitchen because she wanted to be there. Dee was more like Hailey. If meals were up to the two of them, they'd probably order takeout and eat off paper plates.

"Here, Mom," Cami said, handing Hailey a stack of math and spelling worksheets. Each was decorated with a rainbow of stars from the teacher.

"Wow. Good work, Cami."

"And I have a new book I'm reading—"

"I did art at school," Ali blurted. "Do you want to see?"

"Of course I do."

Camilla scowled at her sister's interruption.

"It's our whole family," Ali said, unfolding the white page. In its center was a big hill drawn in green marker, and on top were five stick figures, each standing at a different angle along the curve. Ali pointed to the stick figures. "That's Grammie and Poppie and you, Mom, and there's Cami and me."

"That's beautiful, sweetie," Hailey said. It reminded her of a world peace ad of people of different races holding hands along the side of a globe.

Camilla leaned over to look more closely. Hailey stiffened in anticipation of her older daughter's question. "Where's Daddy?"

Ali shrugged. "I didn't have enough room for heaven, so you can't see him."

Desperately, Hailey wanted to open the refrigerator and pretend to pull something out, to hide her face from them, but both girls turned to their mom, and she could feel the steady heat of Liz's gaze as well. "Heaven is a really big place," Liz announced. "Maybe you could draw a picture of it sometime, Ali."

"But isn't Daddy here, with us?" Camilla asked.

Shivers grew tight along her skin.

"I don't know for sure where Daddy is, Cami."

Camilla frowned and Hailey knew they were on awkward territory. Cami was much more logical than her younger sister. For Ali, peace came from knowing that her father was in a better place. That he was happy and okay and that he would be watching over them.

Liz and Jim were Episcopalians who talked about the specifics of heaven the way a doctor could name the specific chambers of the heart. Hailey wanted to know that John was somewhere good, somewhere warm and redeeming, and not just a pile of bones in the earth under the flattened grass.

"If Daddy has any say in it," Hailey said. "He's

right here in this room, watching you guys and thinking about how smart and beautiful you are, and how big you're getting."

"But you can't see him," Ali said, pointing back to the picture. "That's why I didn't draw him." She looked up at Hailey. "Right, Mommy?"

Camilla turned to look up at her mother too, and the pain in Hailey's spine sharpened into an unbearable ache as she winced and sank into a chair. "I don't really know. I haven't ever been to heaven, so I don't know what it's like." Neither girl spoke. "But your picture is really beautiful."

"I'm going to ask Father Dylan on Sunday," Camilla said.

Liz stepped forward and set milk in front of the girls, then put her hand on Hailey's back. Warmth radiated through Hailey's blazer. "I think that's a wonderful idea. Now, why don't you go get changed, Hailey? The girls and I will get dinner going."

"I could use a shower, if there's time."

"Sure, Hailey. We'll be fine."

The tension in her spine dissipated as soon as she had made it to the stairs. With the bedroom door closed, Hailey took a puff of albuterol and sat on the edge of the bed. Dropping onto her side, she shoved her fists into the heavy quilt.

What did it matter where John was? Heaven, hell, underground. He wasn't coming back.

He was never coming back.

So why couldn't she let go of the way their marriage had deteriorated?

On the last anniversary they shared together, John

had taken her to dinner at Boulevard, a fancy spot close to the bay. It was unusual to go someplace so expensive. Celebrations had always involved one of their favorite ethnic take-out places, like Koh Take Thai, which they called "Kentucky Thai," or the little sushi place on the west edge of Golden Gate Park.

John had wanted to splurge. He'd made her dress up and ordered champagne.

Over appetizers, he gave her a pair of diamond studs.

Though they'd seemed huge, he'd assured her they weren't. They were each "only" a quarter carat, and surely she could wear them at work.

Like she would show up at the scene of a double murder in diamond studs. Instead of feeling grateful, she'd been furious. She hardly ever wore earrings. Occasionally, she put in the small pearl studs that had been her mother's. Only those.

To make matters worse, throughout their anniversary dinner, a constant trickle of people from Jim's political life interrupted them. The mayor's assistant was there with his girlfriend, a buxom blonde in her early twenties, as well as several "key supporters," as John had called them.

He spent as much time away from the table as he did at it.

He had eventually invited a wealthy older couple— the president of some big bank and his wife—to join them for dessert. When they were finally left alone, John complained he'd developed a headache and wanted to go home.

In the car, he'd insisted she put the earrings on.

Hailey had, thinking she would return them, that

they weren't anything Hailey wanted to own or wear. He glowed with pride, looking like a man she didn't know at all. Then, he said something she would never forget or forgive. "You're going to make a wonderful senator's wife someday."

Every decision about their future was made together. Whether Montessori preschool was worth the extra expense. How far apart the kids should be. How they would handle the after-school care. Which refrigerator to purchase when the old one died. Whether they should switch cell phone carriers. They sat at the round kitchen table and made lists of pros and cons, discussed and debated for days. It took nearly three weeks to decide on a preschool for Camilla.

Now he had chosen their future—his as a senator and hers as a political wife—without so much as a single joint discussion.

Within days, he was talking about his plans for running for office after he helped with his father's next election. In those conversations, he carefully skirted the conclusion he'd reached, that Hailey would need to quit the force. She saw it clearly—so translucent was the veil that masked his political ambition.

Two months later, three days after he'd said they needed to think about "how to wind down her career," Hailey had kissed Bruce Daniels.

A month after that, they'd started sleeping together.

But John was dead now.

The failures in their marriage didn't make a difference to him, wherever he was. Yet Hailey couldn't seem to break free of them.

CHAPTER 7

FIFTEEN MINUTES AFTER the girls' bedtime, Hailey's cell phone started to ring. It rang at eight-fifteen, then ten minutes later, then ten minutes after that. When Hailey finally answered, Bruce asked where she was, meaning *why aren't you on your way to me?* Finally, Hailey conceded that she would go over to his place. She needed to try to force herself to move on.

When Hailey came down in her jacket, Liz was downstairs in the living room, sipping tea and reading a novel. "The girls are asleep, and I thought I'd go out for an hour or so. Meet a friend for coffee."

Liz stood, smiling, and stepped around the chair to clasp Hailey's arm, as close as they ever got to an embrace. "I'm so glad, dear. I was wondering when you'd start dating again."

Hailey stepped backward, catching her heel on the area rug. "Oh, it's nothing like that."

Liz smiled softly, disappointed. "Oh. I understand. Have a good night, then."

Heat flushed her cheeks as Hailey looked away and searched for something to say. Hailey didn't want Liz to think she was lying, so she turned and nodded sadly, adopting what she hoped was an innocent expression. "Thank you, Liz. For understanding." And without meeting her gaze, Hailey left.

Liz grew up outside Washington DC. John had always said that his mother's family raised politicians. Both of Liz's brothers and her father were attorneys who had worked in the political arena, and her uncle was a lobbyist. John had also let on that Liz's family was very wealthy. He once commented that their house had been a gift from his grandparents, and for that reason, the deed was in Liz's name.

Liz had been quite ill for several years when she was a teenager. Her mother had been very concerned that Liz might never marry. Jim had arrived as a savior—not just for Liz, but for her mother as well.

It made sense that Liz put a lot of emphasis on Hailey not being alone.

When she arrived across town, Bruce came to meet her at the car, something they had starting doing after Hailey had been attacked in his lobby. For two weeks, she'd hidden the bruises from John, showered when he was out, wore long-sleeved pajamas and pants … John never noticed. That was how disconnected they were.

All that was history now.

The building still made her a little sick to her stomach. She never entered alone. She called from the car and Bruce met her at the door.

Inside, they sat in the living room of his apartment, a room Hailey hardly remembered seeing until after John's death. Before that, they barely made their way through the door before stumbling into the bedroom. But here, among the sleek, minimalist furniture, Hailey felt as though Bruce was someone she was meeting for the first time. "My ex picked it out," he'd told her once when she asked about the décor, though Hailey knew nothing about the ex, either.

Bruce handed her a glass of wine. "Malbec," he said, "From Argentina." He sat beside her, still in his shirt and suit slacks, still in his shoes, while Hailey slipped hers off, pulling her feet onto the couch. He rubbed her foot and nodded to the wine. "Like?"

"It's nice."

"Never touches oak. All stainless. Has kind of a clean taste, doesn't it?"

Hailey smiled. "It does."

"What's so funny?"

"Clean wine. I don't know." She thought again of the cork they'd found in Fredricks's coffin, and the laughter went stale in her throat.

Bruce moved toward her on the couch, draping her legs across his as he settled into the cushions. "No leads on the senator's shooting, I hear."

"None."

Bruce took a sip of wine, his expression thoughtful. "I heard Scanlan has got the CAP guys working with O'Shea on it."

CAP was Crimes Against Persons. The department handled assault, battery, robbery—any crime against a person aside from those that involved sex or death.

"They're trying to link your father-in-law's shooting to John's murder. All of it's on the hush-hush."

Hailey sat up and glanced at the wine as though it was the cause of her shortness of breath. "Really?"

Bruce pulled her feet back into his lap. "That's good, isn't it? Another lead."

First Hal, now Bruce. Neither would leave the subject of John alone.

She set the glass down.

"You don't want to talk about it," Bruce said.

Hailey lifted the glass and took a sip. "I don't."

He narrowed his gaze the way he did when he was working out a motive. "It makes you nervous, the idea that someone broke in again. Why do you stay there?"

This again. "I stay for the girls. Because Jim and Liz are their grandparents." How could she move? Who would help her raise Camilla and Ali? But Bruce didn't understand. He didn't have kids. But she wasn't just there for Camilla and Ali. She stayed for herself too. In her in-laws' home, she got to avoid thinking about where her life was headed.

First and foremost, she avoided dealing with her relationship with Bruce.

She drank from the glass, as much for the moment of reprieve from the conversation as for the warmth of the drink.

He was still watching her, waiting, and what she felt wasn't empathy or compassion, but simply frustration. She set the glass down, a little harder than necessary, and the wine sloshed over the edge, splattering the shiny tabletop.

Hailey thought of the rug, and saw that the drops hadn't reached that far. She stood to get a towel, but he caught her hand.

"I don't care about it." He pulled her back as she averted her gaze. "What's going on, Hailey?"

"Nothing. I'm tired. The case."

He tugged her hand, shook his head. "Not that stuff." He leaned forward and gently tapped her head. "In there. What am I missing?"

"You're not missing anything, Bruce, but Christ, the girls, the job. It's a lot. I'm living with my in-laws, my dead husband's parents. It's not easy to tell them I'm sleeping with another man."

"But you're not. We haven't been together in weeks."

"You know what I mean."

"Actually I don't, Hailey. I don't have any idea what you mean. I'm not sure you do, either," he said, the fierceness of his gaze relentless. "There's something else," he pressed. "What is it?"

She shrank back on the couch. "What do you mean?"

"Something changed after he died. Is it guilt? About us? Because he's dead?"

The wine had crept into her head and softened the edges of her thoughts. She reached for the glass again and took another sip. "There's guilt, sure."

Bruce edged forward as though narrowing in on a witness. "Because you loved me before he was dead?"

Tears filled her eyes. "Yes."

Bruce pulled her to him, continuing as though speaking from the inside of her own mind. "If you'd known he was about to die, you would've tried harder. You would've confronted him."

"Yes. Yes." Would it have helped? Could she have done anything to save them? If he'd insisted on a political career, could she have been the wife he needed? She had to believe they would have found a way.

He hadn't even seen the bruises. Didn't even notice that his wife had been assaulted. Or that she was with someone else. And he hadn't cared one bit about her plans for the future—for *her* future. It was all about him.

How would that ever have changed?

"Death makes us rethink everything," Bruce said. Then he gently narrowed in on the heart of it. "But you don't have a choice about it now, Hailey. You supported John the best you could, in a way he didn't support you." He tilted her chin toward his, wiped her tears with rough, flat fingertips. "He didn't support you."

"He just got caught up in the idea of a candidacy," she said.

Everything Bruce said was true. Still, she couldn't hear it—not from him. She didn't want to hear her lover criticize her dead husband.

"Okay, and maybe you could've made it better. You probably could have. You're amazing, and if he'd known how you felt, he'd have been an idiot not to fight for you. And John wasn't an idiot."

John had certainly acted like an idiot. She had to stop trying to rewrite the past. But every time she thought of the way their marriage had fallen apart, how distant he was, how cold … She remembered the night he died.

"I can wait," Bruce told her. A few moments later, he spoke again. "I've been looking at places in the paper."

"Really? You're moving?" Hailey asked, thankful for a change of subject.

He pulled her feet into his lap once more and began

rubbing them as though he could rewind the evening to where they'd been ten minutes ago, before either of them had brought up the subject of John. "Thinking about it. Looking for something bigger."

With one finger hanging in the air above the rug, Hailey traced a black triangle in its pattern. "Bigger?"

"I've got some feelers out at the Department of Justice."

"Wait. Now you're leaving the department?"

"We can't be together if I stay," he said.

Together. Did she want to be together? Bruce had never even met Cami and Ali. They were too young. Their dad had only been dead a year. Hailey stood and crossed the room to the window, gazing through it as though she could step out into the ether and drop down the three stories to the sidewalk, like Batman.

"Hailey …"

She didn't respond, watching the back of a sedan driving by Washington Park, the left taillight dark, wondering if the cops in the city had time to stop people for brake lights anymore. Couldn't imagine they did.

Behind her, Bruce remained on the couch as though he, too, was afraid she might be headed out the window.

He knew her as well as anyone, and still he tiptoed around her a year later, as though she'd become a fragile crystal vase, balanced on a table with only three legs.

Like Hal, Bruce let her get away without answering for the changes in their relationship. The less they asked, the less she felt an obligation to tell them anything.

"Okay. It's still too soon," Bruce conceded, and Hailey wondered when she had stopped thinking of him as Buck, the way she had when they were first lovers. When had he dropped from the pedestal she had put him on?

After a moment, he said, "I'd just like to be able to take you out, to go to a restaurant."

She turned from the window. "We can do that without you changing careers or moving."

"Maybe I'm ready for a change."

"Maybe you are." She returned to the couch, to her wine. "But it has to be for you. Not because of us."

"Agreed." Bruce reached for her hand, and she hesitated before giving it to him. Then she let him pull her back to the warm leather and press himself on top of her. She closed her eyes as his mouth opened against hers, his tongue, both familiar and tentative, gently exploring until she met it with her own.

"Buck," Hailey whispered, as though testing out an old emotion.

His lips left her mouth. Then he kissed her nose and sat up to look at his watch. "We should get you home. Are you okay to drive?"

It felt like being shooed out, by a teacher or a parent, and Bruce did this sometimes. Took on this selfless, caretaking role, leaving her wishing she'd stayed.

If John hadn't come up in conversation, she might have simply taken his hand, led him to the bedroom, and sought out the simple connection they'd had when this was an affair, rather than a relationship.

Buck was fantasy, the unattainable, painted in a light that was brighter than reality. But now he was transformed to reality, to Bruce, and in the white, hot spotlight stood John.

Dead John.

Bruce was right. Maybe things could've been better for her and John if they'd tried.

But he was right, too, that it was no longer a choice.

What he couldn't fathom—what Hailey couldn't explain—was that in the last minutes of John's life, she forgave him for every bad thing that had happened in the years before. Every harsh word, every cruel judgment and every selfish demand. Eleven months after his death, the memory of John that played was rarely any other than those last words he'd spoken, "Take care of the girls. Make sure they're okay."

The single memory made John incandescent.

No one else created even a glimmer of that light.

CHAPTER 8

HAL COULD HAVE used a workout, but he couldn't find the energy. Instead, he had gone straight home from the station. He'd pulled files on Dwayne Carson, who hadn't said a word after he lawyered up, and Jeremy Hayden, the gunrunner who was found dead in the upstairs closet during the sting operation. The two had similar rap sheets, but it was impossible to say if they ran in the same circles.

What was stranger yet was that neither one had weapons charges in the past. They'd been arrested for burglary, breaking and entering, a few assault charges, and a drunk and disorderly.

Nothing suggested they were involved in organized crime.

Hal brought the files home to look at again. He was too beat to stay at the station. He wanted a beer and his comfortable chair.

Inside his apartment, Wiley greeted Hal by wrapping herself around his leg and mewing for dinner. He lifted the calico under one arm and carried her inside, bolting the door behind him and walking through the dark living room into the kitchen. The red light on the home phone was blinking, alerting him to a voicemail.

It would be his ex-wife. Probably calling twice, if not three times. Sheila never called just once. Maybe his mother had called too. Once in a while one of his sisters checked in with him, but they never called his home line. Only his mother and Sheila did that.

Plus, Sheila had already called his cell phone a half dozen times today.

He set the cat on the counter and pressed the play button. Inside the refrigerator was half a container of Tunalicious cat food. The home phone tucked under his ear, he spooned the food into Wiley's bowl and waited for the message to start.

The first thing he heard was Sheila's standard hesitation, as though she was shocked that she had been connected to his number. As though her phone had rung too and some force was trying to pull them together.

"Hey, Hal, sweetie. It's me. Call me when you get in. I thought we could grab a drink or something. Old times, you know?" She waited again, maybe for him to pick up the phone, then said, "Okay. I'll talk to you soon," and hung up.

She never left her name.

Not that she needed to.

A man didn't forget the woman who charged up $40,000 in credit card debt in his name—after they had separated. It still rubbed him wrong, that she didn't say who she was. Maybe she assumed she was the only available woman who ever called him.

Maybe what bothered him was that she *was* the only

woman who called him, unless he counted his mother or sisters, or Hailey.

A computerized voice told him the time of the message was five-seventeen. The next one came at five forty-seven. Her voice was looser this time, the background noise louder. She was calling from a bar somewhere. At the end, someone called her name, a man, and she stopped midsentence and told him he knew how to reach her.

"That's it," she said, slurring her words. "I'm going to have to come over there."

"Shit," he said, wondering where she'd been calling from, how long he had to get out of his place before she showed up. According to the clock on the microwave, she'd left the final message twelve minutes ago. The last time Sheila came over, he'd refused to let her in and she'd spent the night in the hallway.

He set the cat food on the counter, filled the other dish with fresh water, and dialed his neighbor, Ken.

"Yeah."

"Ken, it's Hal. Any sign of Sheila out front?"

"Hang on."

Hal waited while Ken looked out. His neighbor's apartment was on the same floor as Hal's but faced the narrow alleyway of Natoma Street. Hal's apartment was on the west side, where only six feet of empty space lay between his building and a nicer-looking brick one next door. The alley was just wide enough for the garbage cans on the street below.

When it rained, his sill caught enough water to fill a Dixie cup. When it was hot, the alleyway grew stale, and as the air quivered behind the window glass, waves of garbage and tar smells rose from below. When it was cold, he hardly noticed it. Wind was the one thing that didn't fit between the buildings. Tonight, it looked like rain, but sometimes Mr. Tatsumi above him overwatered his plant, and what Hal mistook for rain was actually fern runoff.

"She still drive the white blazer?" Ken asked.

Hal rubbed his face. "Far as I know."

"I don't see her down there yet, man. You want to come hide out here? I got some beer."

"Your place be the first one she'll come to when I don't answer."

"Probably true, man. You best get out of the building."

"I intend to." Hal hung up, grabbed his coat and keys, and cracked the apartment door, listening to the hallway for sounds of Sheila.

Most likely she'd be drunk by now, and she wasn't quiet when sober. The only sounds coming from the hallway were from the upstairs neighbor's television. This was the time when his show came on, the one he liked to watch without his hearing aids. Down the hall, Frank and Angie Rossetti were fighting again.

Hal left the apartment and closed the door, taking the back stairs to the street, half running to his car. He took off down 20th Street, away from Dolores and Guerrero, the direction Sheila would come from, if she did actually come. But as soon as he turned right on Church, he found himself heading back toward the station. Better a night digging through clues than one spent listening to a drunk Sheila banging on his door.

He called in and asked to be connected to

Holding. When the desk answered, he inquired about Dwayne Carson.

"They've got him back in interview. Neill, I think."

"Can you patch me through?"

"Sure. Don't know if anyone'll answer, but here goes."

The phone rang four times. Hal was ready to hang up when someone answered. "Inspector Neill."

"Mike, it's Hal Harris from Homicide. I'm calling about Carson."

"Yeah. We're about to cut him loose. His attorney never showed, but the DA's office doesn't think we have enough to make a case."

The only lead they had, and it was a dead end. Hal wasn't ready to give up. "You know where he's headed?"

"No idea. Lives with his mother and four siblings in a one-bedroom apartment in Hunters Point. Father's AWOL."

Hal hated the statistics about the percentage of black men who weren't involved with raising their children. "Lot of 'em are."

"Right. Mom works two jobs. You know how it goes."

Hal thought about the business card Carson had for Martin Abbott. "The high-priced attorney bailed on him?"

"According to the jail, Carson never talked with him, but who knows? Maybe Abbott got a message to Carson another way."

Hal rubbed his head. "I was sure Roger would find something."

"None of the prints on the weapons in the trunk matched Carson's," Neill said.

"Defense would argue Carson was just in the wrong place at the wrong time," Hal said.

"DA's office suggested we push him to give us something and cut him loose."

"Did it work?" Hal asked.

"He did give us another name, the guy he said picks up the guns."

Hal turned down 14th toward Harrison. "Who's that?"

"Name's Willie Redd. He's the one who held Matthews at gunpoint."

"I remember," Hal said, his chest tightening again at the memory.

"Yeah. I'll bet." Neill paused a beat. "Since Redd can't talk from the grave, we don't have much left."

"It seem weird that Carson knew Martin Abbott? You ever heard of Abbott taking on a case like this? Doing pro bono or something?"

"Pro bono? I don't think you can even have dinner with Abbott without paying his hourly."

That matched what Hal had heard too. Why would Abbott suddenly take interest in a kid like Carson? "So it seems weird, right?"

Neill paused, sighing. "Yeah, it does."

There was no way Hal was going back to his apartment until a couple of hours had passed.

Six months ago, he'd have gone to Hanlon's to hang with his old buddies from patrol, maybe Beyer or one of the older stiffs in Homicide. Those guys were there most nights, and it wasn't so bad to show up from time to time, hang out, and listen to the old stories they loved to tell again and again.

But twice in the past month, Sheila had shown up there.

Once, she'd left with a rookie patrol officer, a kid Hal didn't know. They'd gotten out the door and into her car, or so he heard, when a couple of older guys, friends of Hal's, had broken it up and told the kid off.

The kid actually came back into the bar to apologize to Hal.

"No skin off my back," Hal told him, but he was lying. Sheila carved little bits off him every time he saw her. And just because she'd been run off once, didn't mean she wouldn't be back.

Out the window, Hal passed a line of patchwork tents set up under the freeway overpass. A dozen of them. Maybe he'd go to the station anyway. Maybe he'd learn something to help them. Hell, they needed a break.

"You still there?" Neill asked.

"Yeah. Actually, I'm close to the station," Hal said. "Maybe it's worth following the kid when he's out, see where he goes."

"Tonight?" Neill asked.

Maybe it was desperation or maybe it was something about Carson. These kids weren't that different than he was at that age. He just got lucky, ending up on the right side of things. Unlike these kids, his father had been there, right up until his death. "What the hell. I'm in the area. You processing him now?"

"Yeah. He should be out in about twenty minutes, half hour. Give me your number and I'll call you when he's on his way out."

Hal sat on the darkened street across from the main

entrance to the department for ten minutes before his phone rang.

"Harris," he answered.

"Hi," Sheila said. "I thought you were avoiding me," she continued, her voice soft and slurred in a way he remembered finding sexy once.

He cursed silently. He hadn't looked at the damn screen. "Uh, I'm working, Sheila."

"Okay. I just wanted to call and see how you are. I left you a message on your home number too."

Three.

"I've got to go, Sheila." Before she could start up again, he said, "I'll catch you later," and hung up.

When his phone rang again, he checked the number before answering.

"It's Neill. Carson's on his way out."

"Thanks."

"Call me back if you learn anything helpful."

A few minutes later, Dwayne Carson appeared.

He pushed the front door open halfway and stopped. He glanced back and stepped out fully as a young prostitute pushed by him, talking over her shoulder and swinging a pink, sequined handbag as she tottered down the stairs in high, strappy red heels.

Carson remained against the concrete façade of the building before descending the stairs and standing beneath the marble plaque where the department's credo was inscribed.

"To the faithful and impartial enforcement of the laws with equal and exact justice to all."

Carson scanned the street, looking for his ride,

maybe. He appeared to be a different person now, much less confident in front of the building than he had been inside it. Something about the way he surveyed his surroundings—the sidewalk, the buildings, the highway overpass a few blocks down—was tentative and wary.

When Carson finally started toward the street, he stepped gingerly, as though expecting a landmine, then went only a few yards before dropping to one knee to tie his shoe. He did this with his head up, still searching.

He was afraid.

What the hell did Carson think was going to happen in front of the police department?

Carson started walking east, moving quickly. Head down, arms crossed, he hugged the inside of the sidewalk, confusing a group of cops walking in the opposite direction, who expected him to pass on the right.

As Carson walked, he kept glancing over his shoulder.

Half a block down, he ran straight into a man in a suit, someone from the DA's office, Hal thought. Carson didn't pause, ducking around the guy and running a few steps before slowing again. His stride was rigid, his arms fixed across his chest. He looked like a man struggling with the urge to sprint.

Despite Carson's behavior, Hal couldn't locate any sign of danger. With Carson now almost a block ahead of him, Hal put the car in gear and started forward. A car backfired on the freeway, and Carson jumped as though bullets had been fired.

Hal palmed his phone. He could call for backup, but what the hell would he say? He had an antsy gunrunner?

He pulled to the curb again when a black sedan with no rear plate steamed by, almost clipping his side mirror.

It looked like a gang car.

Hal's gut told him something was up.

He palmed the car's radio. "This is five-Henry-one-seven requesting backup on Harrison Street, in front of the department." He tried to remember the name of the street one down but couldn't. "Possible one-eight-seven in progress."

As dispatch confirmed the request, Hal hit the accelerator. The sedan was already thirty yards ahead.

The driver honked the horn and Carson spun and ducked. Hal was too far back to do anything, could only watch as a hand reached from the driver's side …

Carson's expression turned from fear to relief.

Running, Carson crossed the street and circled to open the passenger door.

"Shit," Hal said, feeling like an asshole.

He lifted the radio to cancel his call.

The gunfire started.

Hal ducked instinctively and then sat up to search for the source of the gunfire. He drove toward the shots, trying to get a look at Carson.

An oncoming car blocked his view. By the time it passed, cops all along the street were moving to get pedestrians down to the ground.

The black sedan jolted to a halt.

Hal swerved across four lanes of traffic to park behind it. The second shot hit the sedan's driver side window, which burst in a spray of glass. The next struck high on the windshield of Hal's car. Sharp screams filled the street as Hal cracked his door and dropped to the blacktop.

Cameron Cruz, a department sharpshooter, pulled two young women to the sidewalk, drawing her weapon.

In the line of fire, Hal was forced to remain where he could use the car as a shield. Moving awkwardly, he dragged himself on his elbows until he was behind his car, then rose slowly to survey the scene.

Another round of bullets fired, exploding glass and chipping the brick off the building above his head. A flash of movement from the right drew his gaze. The shooter. Crouched in the narrow alley, he wore a ski mask and black clothes.

Hal ducked as more shots were fired. The sound of a revving engine pulled him to his feet. A cop in uniform jumped in his line of fire, and Hal pointed his weapon to the sky just before he took the shot.

"Goddamn it!" he shouted.

The cop turned back, mouth agape.

The shooter took a last shot and jumped into a gray Honda Civic.

Rounding the corner, Cameron Cruz sprinted down the alley. She stopped, took a stance, and shot twice. Her bullets struck the Civic's rear left tire and the back window. The car swerved, straightened, and then took off around the corner.

As the cop he'd almost shot called in the Civic, Hal ran toward the parked sedan that had picked up Dwayne Carson. He yanked open the door, and a wounded Dwayne Carson rolled into Hal's arms.

"Where did the guns come from, Carson? Where did you get them?"

Carson's eyes rolled back into his head. His shirt was dark, the cotton warm and slick with blood.

"Come on," Hal shouted, shaking him. "Tell me who did this to you."

Carson blinked. He licked his lips, spoke in a whisper. "Regal."

"Regal? What the hell is Regal?"

Carson's lips fell open and his body went limp.

He was dead.

CHAPTER 9

HAILEY DOUBLE-PARKED HER car behind the police barricade in front of the department. Dwayne Carson was dead.

Cameron Cruz stood on the street, talking to Roger Sampers. Shelby Tate was examining Dwayne Carson's body. It was going to be another long night for the crime scene team. Gathering evidence at an outside scene was a slow process.

"I figured you'd be in bed by now," Hal said, surprised to see her.

Her cheeks grew hot. "I ran out for a bit after the girls went down," she said without meeting his gaze. Did she look like she'd just left Bruce's? She ran her fingers over her hair, told herself not to fidget. "What are you doing here?"

"Sheila left a bunch of messages at the house, so I came back to the station."

"What's she done now?"

"I don't know. I didn't see her."

Hailey was relieved. Sheila was bad news. And somehow, she still had a strong grip on Hal.

"I left so I wouldn't have to," Hal said.

"Sorry."

"She is who she is."

Relationships were complicated. Hailey knew that better than most. She had trouble imagining how Hal had ended up married to someone so troubled. Whenever Sheila inserted herself back into his life, Hailey worried for him.

She nodded to the scene. "What happened?"

Hal rubbed his head. "I watched the whole thing. Dwayne Carson gets released. He looks nervous, edgy. Makes it to the end of the block when his ride shows up. Dude's getting into the car when a Honda Civic comes down the alley just east of the department parking lot. Guy in a mask unloads a shitload of brass." He rubbed his head. "Carson died right in my arms. I pushed him to tell me who did this to him."

"And?"

"Regal."

"Regal?" she repeated. "What do you mean?"

"That's what he said."

"Isn't that like a chain of movie theaters?"

"Right," Hal said, his tone clipped. "And a guitar store and the second name of a scotch whiskey. First name is Chivas."

"Okay," Hailey said. "How about the driver? Maybe we can talk to him."

"No." Hal's voice dropped. "He didn't make it either."

Two more victims.

"Shoulda stayed home and waited for Sheila," he muttered.

He didn't mean that, did he? He couldn't get back together with Sheila. Hailey wanted to ask if he was okay but sensed he didn't want to talk about it. He needed time to process. She focused back on Carson. "It was like he knew someone was coming for him. Did he seem worried when you interviewed him?"

"Not at all. That's why I think it had to do with Abbott."

"Martin Abbott had him shot?"

"Who knows," Hal said. "Someone gave the kid Abbott's business card. So maybe they've got some sort of system set up. Carson calls Abbott, thinking he's calling an attorney who is paid to help him …"

"And they send someone out to kill him? Christ," she muttered. "That means they have to have someone in Abbott's office."

"Right."

"Who caught the murders?"

"Kong and O'Shea. They're en route." Hal studied her. "Were you out on a date?"

Hailey shook her head. "God, no."

Hal's stare felt intense. Like he didn't believe her. It felt like that more often now.

"I could use a drink," Hal said.

Hailey didn't want to go out with him tonight. He was wound up, in the kind of mood to push. "You think she'll still be at the house?"

"Nah. She'll be gone by now."

"I'll see you bright and early, okay?"

She turned and walked away before he could mention

drinks again. On the street, Shelby Tate stood with Linda James and Cameron Cruz.

"Heard you had an exciting night," Hailey said, stopping at the group.

"I'll say," Cameron agreed.

Shelby Tate peeled off her gloves and stretched her arms. "I need a beer."

"I could use a drink," Cameron agreed.

"Count me in," Linda James said. "Hailey?"

The girls were asleep, so she wasn't in a rush to get home. Hailey glanced at Hal, who was now talking with O'Shea and Kong.

As Hailey turned back to Cameron, she could feel the electricity of the scene coming off her friend. She'd once heard someone say that live gunfire felt a lot like being on stage, and cops and performers felt similar emotions when they were leaving the scene, or stage.

They were right.

Which meant the Rookie Club needed a drink.

"Why not?"

"Tommy's?" Linda asked.

"Where else?" Cameron said.

Hailey gave Cameron a hug. "I heard about Diego." Cameron's boyfriend had been killed in the line of duty a couple months back. "It gets easier."

Was that true? Some days it was easier.

Cameron wiped her eyes. "Thanks."

The two women had known each other as long as Cruz had been in the department, and they were both members of the Rookie Club.

"We've missed you."

Hailey used to make it every few months. She hadn't attended a Rookie Club dinner since John's death. "I know. I'll get back, I promise."

"You can start tonight," Cameron said. "See you guys there."

As Hailey drove through the city, she realized she was looking forward to a drink with these women. Maybe it was the energy of the scene sinking in or just a break from conversations with Bruce and Hal. These women weren't going to ask her if they had any leads on John's death or if Jim was involved in this gunrunning operation.

Despite a full house, the Rookie Club women had managed to secure a table at the back of Tommy's when Hailey arrived. They waved her over as a waiter was taking drink orders. "Corona for me," Hailey said as she took a seat next to Shelby and across from Linda James and Cameron.

Next to Cameron was Ryaan Berry.

Linda introduced them. "Cameron's giving us the blow-by-blow."

"I took a second shot as he ducked back into his car," Cameron said. "Hit the rear tire. Watched it blow, but he took off. Not sure how far he got on that wheel."

Linda glanced at her phone. "He got far enough. We surrounded the area and set up roadblocks. So far, nothing."

"He shot five bullets and downed two victims. That's some good shooting," Ryaan commented.

"Both victims were shot in the torso," Shelby added. "I'll know more after the autopsy tomorrow, but I'd guess the driver's wound was two inches from his heart."

Hailey remembered what it was like to be in this group of women. All these sharp minds, all this expertise. From the outside, they could have been a group of stay-at-home moms, but they were some of the best law enforcement in the city.

"And that guy was standing at fifty yards," Camron said, shivering. "I couldn't shoot any better than that."

The waiter returned with their drinks and a huge order of nachos. "I'm ravenous," Cameron said, passing out the small plates.

"I'm starving too," Jess agreed as they all dug in.

"Any leads on who would want him dead?" Shelby asked.

"Someone who didn't want him to talk," Ryaan said.

The table was quiet a moment. If they had been able to hold Carson, maybe on the stolen weapon, he might be alive. Maybe that would have given them the time to get more answers. Hailey took a long draw on her beer, grimacing at the bite of the carbonation. There was no use second-guessing the process. It was what it was.

"Do you know who's at the top of the food chain? Who's in charge?" Jess asked.

Ryaan shook her head. "So far, we've identified a bunch of the guys on the street, but we aren't having any luck tracing the guys who are running things."

Hailey thought about Carson's last word. "Does Regal mean anything to you, Ryaan?"

"Regal?" she repeated.

"Hal said that was Carson's last word," Hailey explained. "As he was dying, Hal asked him who had done this to him. He said, 'Regal.' Or that's what Hal thought Carson said."

Ryaan shook her head slowly.

"Maybe a street name for someone?" Cameron suggested.

"Maybe. I've never heard of Regal," Linda commented.

"Regal Theaters is what comes to mind for me," Shelby said, smiling.

"There's a Regal Insurance Group," Ryaan said slowly. "They have kind of a niche place in the market."

"What do they insure?" Hailey asked.

"They insure against weapons loss."

Weapons loss. "The type of company that would insure someone like Hank Dennig's company?"

"Yes," Ryaan agreed. "Dennig Distribution would be exactly the kind of client Regal would insure."

"I've got to call Hal." Hailey put a twenty on the table and excused herself.

She was dialing before she hit the street.

CHAPTER 10

HAL DIDN'T ANSWER his phone, so Hailey left a message about Regal. Maybe he'd decided to go out after all. Hailey was surprised when he didn't call back. The whole drive home, she kept her phone in her lap, waiting for it to ring. It was after ten o'clock. Maybe he'd gone to sleep?

By the time she reached the house, the energy she'd felt from the lead was gone, and she was exhausted. She climbed the stairs to the house, let herself in, and stepped out of her shoes.

A light flickered from the living room fire and Hailey stepped into the dark room.

Jim sat in the big chair, which he'd pulled almost to the brick hearth.

"Jim?"

The bandage on his ear and the deep circles under his eyes made him look older.

"Are you okay?" Hailey asked.

He rubbed the bridge of his nose absently, his gaze set on the fire. "Can you come in for a moment, Hailey?"

She set her purse and jacket on top of her shoes and sat in the chair across from him, pulling her feet under her.

Though the room was warm from the fire, the same deep chill she had felt since John's death slid under her skin. "What is it, Jim?"

"I should have shared this with you sooner." He handed her a number ten envelope. "It was wrong to keep it from you."

Hailey lifted the flap, unsealed, and drew out a white page.

When she unfolded it, she saw it was a photocopy of a letter, the bottom signed Nick. "Fredricks?"

"We knew each other some time ago."

The top was dated November 15, 2003, about five months before Nicholas's death. Trembling, Hailey read it through twice before pausing to consider what it meant.

Only nine sentences long, the letter was vague. After reading it a few more times, she decided the threat in the letter was intentionally cryptic.

In the first three lines, he praised Jim, commented on the specifics of his voting record and on his handle of the issues facing those "not enjoying the same economic prosperity" as they did.

Midway through, though, the tone changed.

I am concerned how recent events might change the direction of your platform. I would so mourn the loss of you as an ally, Jim, particularly, of course, in light of our shared interests.

Fredricks made no specific reference to what the recent events were, or what he meant by shared interests.

It was the last three lines that made the skin on her neck and shoulders tighten with chills. There, Fredricks had added a quote. One Hailey had recently learned was Jung …

Knowing your own darkness is the best method for dealing with the darkness of other people.

Then Fredricks wrote: *I know your darkness, Senator.*

The letter the police had found lying next to Jim, after he'd been shot, had ended with the same last line.

When Hailey was done, Jim reached for the page. She hesitated, then handed it over.

"Who shot you, Jim?"

"I don't know," he said. "I honestly don't."

In the last year, she'd gotten to know Jim well. She'd watched him interact with Liz and Dee and had noticed that he glanced away at the end of an answer that wasn't entirely truthful. *I'm not worried about anything, Liz*, he would say, but his eyes focused downward.

His furrowed brow, the pull of his mouth. Gone was his smooth politician expression. He wasn't lying now.

"Do you know how Fredricks died?" she asked.

Jim's gaze flashed to hers. "He was shot."

"It happened just blocks from here. What I meant was—did you ever have a theory about why he was shot? You knew him."

Jim stared at the fire, the threads of yellow and red reflecting in his eyes, casting his skin orange. "I thought about it a lot—I still do. Nick had some trouble in his earlier years. He immigrated to the States from Germany in high school. His family moved to Brooklyn, and after school, he went to work for the NYPD."

She knew this already. "Do you know what he did for the department?"

"He worked in media relations, writing mostly. After that, he moved to Washington to get involved in policy—specifically, gun policy."

"Do you know why he left the department?" she asked.

"I don't think it suited him, working for the police."

"Meaning?" Hailey prompted.

"He was outspoken about his beliefs," Jim said. "DC suited him better, although, even there, he was outspoken at first."

"You think he might have been killed because someone didn't like his politics?"

Jim let out a short laugh. "Most of Washington would be dead if people killed over politics."

It was true.

"The shooting never made sense to me. He'd been a pacifist for a number of years, and he was a well-respected thinker. The police assumed it was random violence. His wallet was stolen, and his watch."

"But in this neighborhood?" Hailey asked. "It's hard to imagine a holdup here."

"It is very disturbing," Jim agreed.

"What does he mean about 'your darkness'?"

Jim shrank then, still staring at the dying flames in the hearth. "This is messy, Hailey."

She felt the chill dig deeper under her skin. "What do you mean?"

"I mean, it's messy." He stood. "I'm going to need a drink. You want one?"

"Please." Normally, she would have said no, but it had been a long day. Jim returned with two crystal glasses, half filled with dark, amber liquid and perfect squares of ice. He set one in front of her.

Jim and John used to sit in this room, drinking from these two glasses. She couldn't bring herself to pick up her drink.

"Dee and I were adopted," he began.

"I knew that. By your aunt and uncle."

"My mother's sister and her husband," he said. "Dad had been in the war, and we were all living in a Quonset hut community, down in L.A. The war really messed Dad up, wrecked him, really. Dee and I were just kids." He closed his eyes, cupped the drink between his hands, resting them on his belt.

"I was seven. Dee was five. Dad brought back a Luger, something he'd pulled off some dead Nazi, I guess. He never really told the story, but he loved that gun. Worshipped it."

Hailey didn't touch her glass.

"When he got really drunk and passed out," Jim continued, "I used to take it off him, carry it around, and pretend to shoot Nazis."

Hailey shivered.

"It was never loaded," Jim went on. "He'd only gotten three bullets, and he always hid them separately. He thought they were worth something. The jackets were covered in green enamel, the way German bullets were during World War II. He called them his emeralds.

"One night, when he was really drunk, I took the gun out to play with it in the dark." He paused. "A little girl … Dottie."

Hailey feared where the story was going. John should

be next to her. Did he know this? She took a drink from the glass, cringing at the clinking sound of the ice.

"A black girl," Jim went on. "Those hut communities were mixed then. She appeared beside me. Scared me, so I dropped the gun. She got to it first, took off running with it.

"Her older brother was a bully, a kid as big as a truck, skin so dark you could hardly see his eyes. And mean. Just angry and mean. Their dad hadn't come back at all, and rumor was he'd been released from the army but just hadn't come to get the kids or their mother, who was a fragile little lady, not much bigger than me and Dottie."

Something creaked in the hall. Jim frowned and rose, crept from the room, and returned a minute later.

"Does Liz know this story?" Hailey asked.

He shook his head. "No one does."

So John didn't know. Would it have changed how he saw his father? Would it change the way *she* saw him?

"Dee?"

"Well, yes. Dee knows because she was there and my parents. And there is one other person who knew."

Hailey waited, but he shook his head as though the answer would have to wait.

She sensed it already, how the story would end. She wished she were under her covers, asleep.

How many more secrets could she keep?

"So Dottie took off with Dad's gun. She was wearing a pair of khaki pants rolled above her ankles, pants that had been her brother's. Rolled up like that hid the places where he'd torn through the knees. The only things I could see in the dark were her bobby socks, a dirty white color, the little lace ratty along the top."

Jim squinted as he spoke, his eyes partially shuttered, as though he was describing a picture he had in his head. One he'd had for more than sixty years.

"She stopped once or twice, pointed the gun at me, yelled 'Bang. Bang.' Like some sort of joke…

"I couldn't keep up with her. The only thing that kept me running was the thought of what would happen if her brother got hold of that gun, or if my father woke up the next day and it wasn't there.

"The place was so dusty, it was like running through a swarm of flies. We reached the lot where the older kids used to play with this one ball that the whole place shared. It was empty.

"I was so thankful that her brother wasn't there, but she didn't stop. Dottie kept running, laughing, and calling back to me that I was a sissy boy because I couldn't catch her."

Jim took a long drink. "Finally, she slowed down enough for me to lunge at her, knock her down. I held her down. I was so angry, and she just kept going on. 'You just mad because you can't run as fast as a girl,' she said." His lips narrowed. "It was true too, but I wanted her to take it back."

He paused and raised his glass. The crystal caught the fire's light, like faceted stones of red and orange in his fist. "I pointed the gun at her—to scare her."

Hailey drained her glass, preparing for what Jim would tell her. Seven years old. Camilla's age.

He cupped a hand above his eyes as though shielding his face from a bright light. Hiding his emotion. Jim rarely showed emotion. Visions of the night John died—the shot, Jim's scream, Ali in his arms.

Hailey felt herself trembling, something inside her knocking and shaking. She wanted to leave, to run, but instead, she gripped the arms of the chair, holding still.

Jim patted his face as though splashing water on his skin. His eyes were red, the skin beneath them flushed. "Dottie and I struggled for a couple minutes, me on top of her, trying to get her to tell me I wasn't a wimp." He sighed. "The things that mean so much when you're a kid." He stopped, staring back at the fire, his face burning with adolescent shame.

"What happened, Jim?"

"A few minutes later, she pushed me off and got up, turned away. She was just stronger than me. Not much bigger, but stronger. She called my dad a no-good drunk." His face trembled and he cupped a hand over his mouth. "God, he was a no-good drunk, but hearing her say that made me shake with fury. Part of it was that she was a girl."

Hailey could imagine the fear he'd had of his father, the punishment that would come from losing it. The drinkers were the worst. Of all the killers she'd dealt with, the alcoholics were the meanest.

"But I think the bigger part of it was that she was black. It's a terrible thing, that kind of hate." He straightened his back as though preparing to receive the verdict in his case. "I pointed that gun at her and I pulled the trigger."

Hailey collapsed back into the chair. "Oh, God."

"I don't remember looking down at it, figuring out where the trigger was or anything. And I'd never shot a gun before." He met her gaze. "I've never shot one since either. I've got no idea how I did it, but I wanted her to be sorry, and I pointed it at her. It exploded, knocked me flat on my backside. I hit my head on a rock. When I got up, stunned, I tried to find her in the dark. For a second, I thought she'd run off, but then I saw her socks. Those white socks. When I saw the blood, I pissed my pants and ran like hell."

"She died?"

"She died," he said as though the words caused him physical pain.

Hailey leaned forward and set the glass down. Jim tipped his own to his lips until the amber disappeared. Then he set his down too. He was crying.

John's death. That was the only other time she'd seen Jim cry. "No one heard the shot?"

"That field was out from the huts, close to the tracks. Trains passed by at all hours and if anyone heard the shot, I always figured they thought it was a train or a car on the freeway a few blocks down."

"What did you do?" Hailey asked.

"That night? I ran home with the gun and got my mom. She was the one who could handle that sort of thing, though Dad happened to have sort of sobered up that night too. Relatively, anyway. Mom told Dee to stay in the hut, but she followed us. Dad decided to tell the police that he'd done it, been playing around with the gun just like I was, and it went off accidentally. Mom begged him to tell the police the truth, but he'd made up his mind."

His father had sacrificed himself for his son. Of course he had. That was what parents did. It was what John would have done too. Anything for their kids.

"God, that night is still so clear. Mom and Dee crying, Dad trying to sober up, and me standing there in wet pants, thinking I loved my dad more then than I ever had before."

They sat for a few moments in silence. Hailey thought about the boy who'd been shot at the police station—Dwayne Carson. Seventeen.

How many young victims had she seen in her time in the department?

Too many. Way too many.

"That's why that night—when John …" Jim whispered.

She didn't want to talk about the night John was killed. "Who else knew?"

Jim looked up. "Who knew what?"

"Who was the other person who knew about Dottie? Aside from Dee."

His shoulders dropped, folding in until they nearly touched.

"If you never told anyone, who did?" Hailey remembered what he'd said, that Dee had felt guilty. "Dee. Who did she tell?"

He shook his head. "She'd never tell anyone." His expression faltered, a frown tugged at his lips. "Never again."

"But she told someone once."

He nodded.

"I need to know who it was, Jim, who she told."

His Adam's apple bobbed against the thin skin of his neck like a knife carving a path. "Nicholas Fredricks."

"Damn," she whispered.

CHAPTER 11

HAILEY CAME OUT of the den and ran straight into Dee. Hailey jumped backward.

"I didn't mean to scare you." Dee peered into the den. "I just got back from dinner with Tom, and I was checking on Jim."

Jim's voice drifted through the doorway. "I'm big enough to take care of myself," Jim snapped.

Dee didn't seem fazed, but left him alone. This was the third or fourth night in a week that she had been out with Tom Rittenberg. She seemed different too. Less stressed, happier. Things with Tom must have been getting serious.

Hailey followed her toward the kitchen. How long had she been there? "Did you hear our conversation?"

Dee sat at the kitchen table. "I know he was talking about Dottie." She fingered her locket. "And Nick."

"Nick."

Dee knew him too. More than knew him. Hailey studied the locket, the way she worried it. Hailey didn't think she'd ever seen Dee without it.

Dee caught Hailey staring at the necklace. "The locket was a gift from him."

Dee and Nick had been together. "You met through Jim?"

"No. We met through some mutual acquaintances in DC. He came back here for me. He'd gotten a teaching position at Cornell, and I'd planned to go with him in the fall. We'd started talking about getting married."

"And then he was killed."

"Yes."

A twelve-year-old murder. John's aunt was in love with a man who had been killed. How had she never heard about it? John had never so much as mentioned that Dee had been with someone. She could see Jim keeping it quiet, but why hadn't John told her? Did he not know? And Liz?

"I'm so sorry, Dee. I didn't know."

"It was a long time ago."

Twelve years didn't seem that long. Ali would still be in high school. Camilla would be in college. They would still be missing their father. "I don't think I'll ever get over John's death."

Dee looked up. "No. I don't imagine you will."

The words struck hard. Of course she wouldn't get over John. But she'd expected Dee to say something different, something like, "It gets easier."

But maybe it didn't.

The cop in Hailey took over. "Can you think of anyone who would have wanted to hurt him?" Hailey asked.

"If I knew who might have killed him, I wouldn't have kept it to myself."

"Of course not." It was a stupid question. Dee would want to find his killer as much as anyone.

"But Nick did have a way of getting people worked up," Dee admitted. "He and Jim used to get into it all the time."

"I can see that," Hailey said. "What was Nick's perspective?"

"His background made him see things differently. He'd come from Germany where his family was very poor. America was this wonderful place where life would be different, where they could finally have enough. And it *was* that way for his parents. They had enough to provide for their kids, to feed everyone. For them, that was a lot. It was enough."

"And for Nick?"

She smiled softly.

"He wanted this country to live up to that ideal he had in his mind. He wanted to see it the way his parents did. After high school, he worked in the police department. Three of his cousins were already on the force. He wasn't interested in being an officer, so he took a job with administration. He worked with their press office until someone realized how well he wrote. After that, he wrote all sorts of things for the department—speeches mostly, but press pieces and articles for the *Times* and the *Post* about the complexities of holding people to the law, but not limiting their freedom."

"Sounds like someone we should be listening to now."

"They still teach his articles in a few criminal law programs."

"He left the department abruptly, right? What happened?"

"The police took a call about a child hanging around the grounds of an inner city high school. It was late at night, and there was no one else around. The caller said the child might have a weapon. The officer came to the scene—this is before the days of cameras and cell phones recording everything. The kid was shot. The officer swore he had a gun, but there wasn't a gun on the scene, and no one else could corroborate his story."

Hailey could already hear the end of the story. The police wanted to cover it up. "Nick was supposed to write about it."

Dee nodded. "A speech for the police chief, actually."

"And they wanted him to lie."

"More like misdirect," Dee said. "It was to prevent a riot, they told him."

"He refused," Hailey guessed.

Dee's fingers trembled as she touched the locket again. "He refused." She wiped her eyes. "It's ancient history now," she said. "Tom says I need to focus on the future and try to put it behind me." She retrieved a prescription bottle from her purse and shook out two small yellow pills. "It's harder than it should be."

Hailey wondered what the medication was.

Dee took the pills with the water sitting on the table in front of her.

Maybe it was something to help her sleep.

Hailey wanted to find a way to reach out to her, but Dee gathered her things and walked from the kitchen as though they'd been discussing the weather. "Good night," she called as she headed down to her basement apartment.

"Good night, Dee."

*

Hailey spent much of the night awake, staring at the ceiling. She couldn't shake the story of Dottie's death, and she didn't know what to do with it.

She was desperate to talk to Hal.

But how could she? Doing that would betray Jim, betray John.

Her relationship with Hal used to be so simple, so honest. She had trusted him with everything.

Until the affair with Bruce had started.

She didn't know how to tell him. They didn't share those kinds of things, never had. Even through Hal's divorce, they hardly spoke of relationships outside of work. What Hailey knew about his ex-wife, Sheila, had come from other sources.

She'd wanted to support him, to be helpful—but she didn't know how. In the end, they'd never had a real conversation about Sheila.

So how could Hailey possibly tell him about an affair?

And why would she?

John's death made things that much more complicated. Now she held Jim's secrets as well.

The letter Jim received when the shot was fired in the front hall—the letter in the white FedEx envelope with the anti-NRA button pinned to the clear plastic—that linked him to Nicholas Fredricks.

That linked Jim to the other deaths.

Which linked Jim to their investigation.

Which meant she had to tell Hal. Immediately.

Would Hal believe Jim's story?

Hailey believed Jim because she had to. Since John's death, Jim was the only person she could speak with openly.

Getting Hal to trust Jim would be more difficult. Their job brought a natural distrust of people with money and power. It wasn't simply a matter of jealousy. It was that people with money and power used it to try to control the police. And they did things like pick which investigator they wanted on a certain crime—the way Jim had called in a favor so Hailey would land on the Dennigs murder.

She also knew that John's death added to Hal's distrust of Jim. An unsolved murder was not something people took lightly—especially people like Hal. Whatever Jim did—whether he called the inspectors daily or let the police handle the investigation without interfering—it all looked suspicious to Hal.

Just as it would have looked to her if she were in his shoes.

It didn't help that she'd bailed on having a drink with him to go out with the Rookie Club.

Those were her first thoughts when she woke, feeling both groggy and panicked.

Her cell phone battery was dead. She'd forgotten to plug it in the night before. The alarm hadn't gone off. Jim was already gone when she came downstairs, so she'd missed her chance to talk to him.

Nicholas Fredricks had known about Jim's childhood shooting incident, and he'd used it to manipulate Jim into changing his politics. Which meant he'd probably used the same tactic on others. The case file on Fredricks's murder suggested Fredricks was known for playing fair, but what he'd done to Jim wasn't fair.

Maybe Fredricks had squeezed someone too tight. But Fredricks had been dead twelve years. Any information about who he'd worked for was long gone by now.

The note Jim had received when he was shot made reference to the old correspondence with Fredricks as well as "an old special," the gun that was used to shoot Jim.

The logical conclusion was that Nicholas Fredricks had told someone else about Jim's past.

That person was their best suspect in all of these deaths.

Now, she had to figure out who that was.

Hailey arrived at the station and was heading up to her desk when Hal caught her in the stairwell. "You get my message?"

"You get mine? About Regal?"

"Not now," he said. "Did you get the message I left this morning?"

She shook her phone. "No juice. One of the girls must have taken my car charger."

"You read the paper this morning?"

She'd gone to bed late, woken up late. "No," she said, dread slowing her down. "Why?"

"Come on." He started down the stairs.

"What's going on?"

Somewhere above, a door clanged open.

"I'll take care of it, Captain," came O'Shea's voice.

"Now," Marshall said with a grunt. His voice echoed in the hallway.

Hailey didn't miss the anger in his voice.

Hal pressed his finger to his lips, pulled her along.

"What's going on?"

Hal shook his head, continued down the stairs, past the door to the main level, and down toward the basement. He tugged on the door, which was locked, and instead pulled her into the small hidden alcove under the stairs. They waited until the voices silenced.

"Press conference out front in ten minutes."

Hailey leaned against the cold wall. Jim would have woken her if he knew something. He wouldn't have wanted her to be blindsided. "Press conference? For what?"

"Fredricks, for one. And they caught Carson's shooter."

None of that warranted hiding under the stairs. "How'd they get Carson's killer so fast?"

"Guy called to confess."

"Okay. It's weird, but you didn't pull me down here for that. What's really going on?"

"Someone leaked the shooting—the senator's shooting."

Jim.

How had Jim missed it? Why hadn't he contacted her?

He'd had more to drink last night, but someone would have warned him—someone at the office, or Dee. "Do you have your phone?"

"He already knows. He called me a half hour ago when he couldn't reach you."

The air caught in her throat. "What did he say?"

Hal hesitated, scanning her face, the unanswered questions in his eyes. "He asked that you call him after the conference."

Jim's shooting would have the press digging up the past. Of course they would want to link this shooting to John's death. She imagined the headlines. Father shot one year after son. The killer missed this time. "How'd it get out?"

"It's a good question. Marshall's going nuts looking for you. He wants you there."

She was about to be the centerpiece of a damn press conference. Why hadn't she charged her phone? She'd stayed up too late. Drank with the Rookie Club, then with Jim. What if they made her speak?

"We'd better go," he added.

She grabbed his arm, stopping him. "There's something I need to tell you."

He turned back, his expression grateful. Too grateful. She had let him down. How many times had she given him only part of the truth? And now she was going to do it again.

She looked away. "I have a lead that you're not going to like."

"Okay."

Hailey forced herself to meet Hal's gaze. "Jim got a letter—a while back—from a guy who didn't support his politics…"

Hal raised his brow.

"I just found out about this letter last night," she said.

"What's this letter got to do with us?"

"The guy quoted Jung."

"Jung," he repeated.

"Right."

"So he got a letter from the same guy who sent the note with the warning shot?"

She shook her head, measuring it out. "No. This letter came thirteen years ago."

Hal blew out his breath.

"From Nicholas Fredricks," she said.

"Shit."

A door slammed above them, and Marshall came into the stairwell, cursing. Hal turned and climbed the stairs, three at a time.

"Marshall," he shouted as she followed. "She's here. I got her."

"Thank fucking God," Marshall hollered down the stairwell.

"Hi, Captain," Hailey called up.

"Where the hell have you been, Wyatt?" he barked. He was breathing heavily and already tugging at his tie. "Forget it," he went on. "Let's just get out there before the press starts reporting more bullshit about the police not being cooperative."

Hal held open the door as they entered the lobby. On the front steps of the hall, a mob of cameras and reporters shouldered one another to close the extra millimeters of space between them.

Homicide Inspectors O'Shea and Kong stood on the far side of the microphone, along with Ryaan Berry of Triggerlock. O'Shea nodded to her. There would be new pressure around John's murder investigation. More questions, more theories, more dead ends. How long would she have to go through this?

Marshall scratched at the skin beneath his collar and

craned his neck as though to relieve the pressure. "Okay," he said, raising his palms to the crowd.

"Ladies and gentlemen." Marshall fingered his neck where a trail of red on the skin looked like the path of tiny fire ants. "The body of Nicholas Fredricks was disinterred yesterday by Inspectors Wyatt and Harris as part of an ongoing investigation that I am not, at this time, at liberty to discuss."

The crowd began to lob questions.

A shooting on the block of the police department was big news. Why hadn't Hailey thought to check the paper? Or her phone?

Because she had been distracted by Jim's story, by the confrontation with Dee, by the discovery about Regal Insurance… She was distracted.

"In the matter of the shooting that occurred yesterday at twenty-one hundred hours down the street from where we're standing—" The cameramen swung to film the street, though any evidence of the crime was gone. "We received a phone call early this morning from a suspect who has claimed responsibility for the two murders. At this time, the suspect is in custody."

"Is this shooter responsible for the other deaths?" asked the ABC correspondent, a thin blonde whose lips were lined in the exact rose hue of her sweater. She glanced down at her notepad. "Hank and Abby Dennig of Pacific Heights and Colby Wesson of Placerville?"

Hailey froze. Did the press know about the buttons found at each of the scenes? They had managed to keep that out of the press until now. She wanted to look at Hal but didn't dare.

Face forward, keep a blank expression.
Don't give anything away.

As soon as the reporter's voice faded, an onslaught of other questions flew through the air.

Marshall waved both hands, palms down, into the crowd as though to flatten their voices with the heels of his hands. "Please." He pointed to another reporter, halfway back in the crowd.

"*Guardian* here. What about the shooting of Senator James Wyatt a few nights ago? Do you have a suspect?" he called out.

There it was. Jim's shooting. She hoped to hell that wasn't leaked by someone in her own department. What if she was wrong, and this did have to do with Jim? She'd never heard the story of Dottie before last night. Liz didn't even know about it.

What else might Jim be hiding?

"Do you believe the senator's shooting is related to these others?" ABC asked. "And is there a possibility that the shooter in custody is responsible for these other deaths?"

"At this time, we have not confirmed any connections," Marshall said evenly, smoothing his tie. "But we have not ruled them out, either. Inspectors on both cases are working in close cooperation … as we always do," he added, motioning to Hal and Hailey on one side of him, Kong and O'Shea on the other.

"One more question," Marshall said, steering his gaze away from the *Guardian* and ABC.

"Isn't Inspector Wyatt the daughter of Senator

Wyatt?" the *Guardian* yelled out. "How does that impact your case?"

"Do you feel personally threatened, Inspector Wyatt?" added ABC.

Marshall frowned and glanced over to Hailey, nodded her to the mic. "I am Senator Wyatt's daughter. Daughter-in-law, actually. For that reason, I am not on the team investigating the shooting incident at his home."

"She'd probably love to see him in cuffs," joked a reporter Hailey didn't recognize. CBS, maybe.

"And no, I don't feel threatened," Hailey responded, focusing on the line around ABC's full lips. "I have total faith in the department's ability to find whoever is responsible for shooting Senator Wyatt, and I have faith that my partner, Inspector Harris, and I will find the killer who took three lives last year."

"Wasn't your husband also shot by an intruder in Senator Wyatt's home last February?" the *Guardian* reporter called back. "That case was never solved. Do you still have faith that the department will find *his* killer?"

Hailey held his gaze, though her legs were unstable beneath her. For months after John's death, reporters and newspapers had pressured her to do an interview. What a story it was. Homicide inspector's husband murdered in his parents' home. Case unsolved. It had everything the press loved—tragedy, human interest, intrigue, death, and an opportunity to point to the police's failure.

Hell, it could be a movie.

Even now, over a year later, the press still called O'Shea to ask about any new developments. Every time, he made sure she knew, brought her up to date on what angles he and Kong were working.

How she prayed it didn't start all over again.

"Are you considering the possibility that his death is also related?" the *Guardian* reporter shouted.

Marshall put his hand up and stepped forward again. Hal motioned her back toward the building.

"That's all we have time for now," Marshall said.

Hal led her to the elevator. She usually took the stairs—the old elevators rattled and Hal always seemed uneasy in small spaces.

She had no energy for walking.

Marshall slid in beside them, as did O'Shea and Kong. Hailey stood pressed to the cold steel back wall of the box.

"Damn piranhas," O'Shea said. "Always digging up the dead. Over and over, I tell you," he went on, with the hint of Irish brogue that appeared when he was performing, as he was now.

She and O'Shea were never close. Maybe that was why Marshall assigned him to John's shooting. Since then, she avoided him as much as possible. The good news was that he tended to avoid her too.

"You'll brief her on the shooter suspect," Marshall said to Hal, ignoring O'Shea. Hal nodded, and Marshall clapped once as the doors opened on their floor. "Good. Let's get to work then."

As he stepped off the elevator, Hal pressed his palm to the bare skin of his scalp. She tried to read his expression. Was he thinking about the letter Jim had gotten from Nicholas Fredricks with the same wording as the letter that had accompanied a bullet thirteen years later?

Because she was.

That and a dozen things Hal didn't even know about—Dottie's shooting and the fact that Dee was dating Tom Rittenberg, but she'd been in love with Nick Fredricks.

How Hailey wanted to tell Hal all of it, lay everything out so he could help her work through it.

But how could she? How could she tell him all of the ways in which her family might be involved and still ask him *not* to jump to that conclusion? Not to insist that it all related to Jim.

Because it didn't. It couldn't.

She and Hal needed to talk about the letter Jim had gotten and form a plan. "We're on this shooter guy?"

Hal nodded. "You mean the guy who killed Dwayne Carson? Guy named Robbins. He's over at General with a gunshot wound to the head."

Gunshot. "Wait. What gunshot wound? I thought none of us got a good shot off on him."

"No one did," Hal confirmed. "At least not in the alley."

"So who shot him?"

"Guess Robbins had a disagreement with one of his boys—a kid named Kenny Fiston—after he offed Carson. They shot it out in his apartment up in Hunters Point, around ten o'clock last night, around an hour after Carson died. Fiston's dead and Robbins took a bullet to the brain. Lucky for him, it was a little bullet."

"It doesn't usually take a big one."

"Yeah, well, he's also lucky, 'cause it caught his skull

at just the right angle. Circled inside the skin, but never penetrated the cranium." Hal raised his brows. "That's some luck, eh?"

"You're saying Robbins took a close-range shot to the head and is alive to talk about it?"

"That's what I'm saying. Kid's fine. Little flesh wound is all. Well, some good bleeding 'cause it was his head, but no permanent damage."

She frowned. "Who called the ambulance?"

"Neighbor."

"It's unbelievable," she said.

"I know. Doctor over at General said he'd never seen anything like it."

"And now he wants to confess to murdering Carson?"

Hal shook his head. "Yeah, like maybe Robbins found Jesus last night, wants to do his penance, and get started on a new life."

"Maybe he realized how quickly friends can turn on you and decided he'd be better off inside," Hailey said. "What do you know about the friend?"

Hal leaned back on his heels and recited from memory. "Name's Kenny Fiston. Friends called him Fish. Three priors for firearms: illegal possession and intent to sell. Served ten months for one, eighteen for another. The last charges were dropped in exchange for information."

Hailey tried to fit Kenny with Dwayne Carson. They had similar backgrounds, were close to the same age. Ryaan had said that Triggerlock had only identified the low-level guys. Hunters Point was the projects. If they'd shot it out there, Fish wasn't running the guns—he was another street kid being used. "Who was his attorney?"

Hal raised a brow. "You mean like Martin Abbott?" He shook his head. "No such luck. And according to Neill, none of 'em have ever had representation. Ballistics is running the gun found on Robbins—the kid with the bullet in his head—to see if it's a match to the weapon used to kill Carson." He nodded toward the department. "You need anything in there, or should we head over to General?"

Hailey wanted to touch base with Jim on the press conference and to assure him that she wasn't going to share their conversation from the night before. But there was no privacy inside the department. "Let's go."

"You can tell me about the letter on the ride over."

Before she could respond, Cameron Cruz appeared around the corner, almost running. "They told me you guys were here."

"And here we are," Hal said.

"What's going on?" Hailey asked.

"I heard you guys were heading over to talk to Robbins, the guy who confessed."

Hal nodded. "That's right."

"Mind if I come along?" she asked, wringing her hands. "By the way, that was fun last night."

"Last night?" Hal repeated.

"A bunch of us went out," Cameron said.

"It was just some of the women from the department," Hailey added awkwardly.

Hal glanced at her, but she avoided his gaze. She had bailed on him and gone out with the women instead. Because they were easier. They didn't probe. They didn't look at her… like that.

Hal stared at Cameron. "Why do you want to come to interrogate Robbins?"

"It was the closest I've ever been to a shooting."

"Kind of strange since you're a Specialist," Hal said. It might have been a joke, but his voice held an edge.

Cameron didn't seem to notice. "Right, but I'm usually up on a roof somewhere."

"So, why do you want to come?" Hal asked again.

"That shooter was a professional," Cameron said. "He wasn't anything like the kids we took down trying to sell those guns."

"What do you mean, professional?" Hal asked.

"His stance, his aim. He had a lot of practice. Probably a decade of it," she said. "From what I hear, Robbins, the suspect you have, doesn't fit."

"Robbins confessed," Hailey said. "Why would he do that if he wasn't guilty?"

Cameron shrugged. "I wouldn't know that. I just know that I watched the guy who killed Dwayne Carson. I don't want him on the street. I'd like to offer some help if I can."

"Sure. I'd love an honest opinion," Hal said and his gaze pinned Hailey. His anger seemed to burn her skin as he added, "For a change."

CHAPTER 12

HAILEY GOT INTO the backseat. Hal drove. He knew it was an asshole thing to say. He was pissed. He had a right to be pissed.

While Cameron talked through her version of last night's shooting, Hal strained to listen to the phone conversation Hailey was having with Jim in the backseat. "Hal and I are on our way to see a suspect," was the one thing he'd heard clearly. The answers from the backseat shrank to one word. *Yes. No. No. Yes.*

"I know," she whispered and Hal felt a chill ripple across his scalp.

The gentle tone of her voice, the reassurances—as though John were on the other end of the phone. What hold did Jim have on her? Why did she trust him? She could barely stand her father-in-law when John was alive, but now they were thick as thieves.

And at the same time, she had stopped confiding in Hal.

Her partner.

When he caught her eye in the rearview mirror, she turned away as though she hadn't seen him.

There was something in her refusal to meet his gaze.

Sheila had done the same thing—like a refusal to let him in.

As they walked into the hospital, Hailey pushed the thick curls from her forehead and held her chin up as though preparing for the fight.

The old Hailey again.

When they arrived, Mike Neill, an inspector in Triggerlock, sat just outside the arches of the metal detector at the entrance to the hospital's jail ward.

When they were through security, Mike pulled a stack of folded pages from his back pocket. "Here are some images of the scene. Also, they matched the gun found on James Robbins to the bullets that killed Dwayne Carson and Griffin Sigler, the driver of the car."

Hailey stepped forward. "Hal said Robbins was shot in the head?"

Mike nodded. "You're skeptical too?"

"A little."

"Join the club. I've been with the medical examiner all morning. The shooting scenario at the apartment doesn't work the way Robbins is telling it."

"He's lying about him and Fiston shooting each other?" Cameron asked.

"Absolutely," Mike said. "The way he tells it, he gets home from shooting Dwayne Carson, and Fiston comes to his place. According to Robbins, the two kids are seated on couches. But according to the ME and the surgeon at General Hospital, each gunshot wound was delivered at a downward angle. That means both of them were shot by someone standing above them. That's not possible if they shot each other."

"Is it possible that one or maybe both were shot while standing and then sat down?" Hailey asked.

Mike shook his head. "Blood spatter shows both boys were shot while sitting on the couch."

"Opposite couches," Hal confirmed.

"Right."

"How far apart are these couches?"

Mike studied the pages until he found what he was looking for. "Five feet, seven inches between the two boys, but the couches don't sit face-to-face. They're set up like an L, at ninety degrees, more or less."

"The angle sounds wrong," Cameron said, speaking for the first time since they'd left the car. She pointed to a photograph of Kenny Fiston. "If they shot each other, the entry wounds should have been more or less parallel."

"You're right." He turned back to Mike. "Did CSU test the trajectories to confirm if the shots were fired from those positions?"

Mike shook his head. "They took photographs and did the measurements, but they're four weeks out to run those kinds of scenarios. Too much other stuff to work on and trajectory work is time-consuming."

"They test for gunshot residue?" Hal asked.

"Yep. GSR positive on both of them."

"What about other bullets?"

"They found two others," Mike said, flipping through the report. "One slug in the wall and one in a baseboard."

"One from each gun?" Hal ventured.

"Good guess."

"Sounds like a setup," Hailey said.

"What do we know about this kid Robbins?" Cameron asked.

"No record. No truancy issues. Parents are both gone, but he works at a dry cleaner on Cesar Chavez and helps raise his kid sister."

"And he confessed to shooting both Dwayne Carson and Kenny Fiston—who was his friend—inside his own apartment?" Cameron asked.

"That sums it up," Mike said.

"Doesn't sound right," Hailey said.

"He's in room 6110," Mike said. "I've got to get back to the station for a briefing. I'm meeting Kong and O'Shea here to interview him in a couple of hours, but call if you learn something."

"Will do," Hal agreed. Kong and O'Shea had been assigned Carson's murder case. Hal was here because this thing related to the earlier murders. He felt it in his gut.

He had a bad feeling, that tightness in his chest, the light-headedness that reminded him of the back of that patrol car after his father's death. Even with effort, he couldn't quite shake it as they made their way to room 6110.

Two officers guarded the door. Inside the room, the overhead lights were shut off. The outside light created striped shadows between the thin slats of vinyl shades.

A low, intermittent beep was the only noise in the room as the patient turned his head slowly from the far wall.

James Robbins wore a hospital gown in prison orange.

Though he had dark skin, the kid's angular nose suggested mixed ancestry.

Maybe the shooting was a gang thing. Maybe it had nothing at all to do with their case. Maybe the timing of Carson's murder—just after he'd been released on charges related to the guns stolen from the Dennigs—was coincidence. For all they knew, this kid Robbins might have been tracking Carson for weeks.

But if Carson's death was gang-related, why did the victim look so scared coming out of the station? At the Triggerlock sting, he didn't look scared. If he knew he was a wanted man, he should have been afraid then too.

No. Something had changed after Carson pulled Martin Abbott's business card from his pocket.

Lying in the hospital bed, Robbins watched them with narrowed eyes, a little dull. He tried to lift an arm, but the white Velcro restraints on his wrists held him to the bed. Instead, he turned his head to wipe his face on the shoulder of his gown. Thick white gauze circled his head like a sweatband. Above and below the bandage, he wore his hair in an Afro. It was a little long but clean and evenly cut.

Bruises had formed under both eyes. They were deep violet half-moons above angular cheekbones. The whites of his eyes were yellow, his pupils tiny.

Without speaking, Hal set the recorder on the rolling table by his bed. That close, Hal smelled the kid's sweat, pungent and acidic. He smelled scared. "You want, I can loosen those." Hal pointed to the restraints.

The kid licked his lips, nodded. "Yeah." Cleared his throat and added, "Please."

Hal ripped them open, and immediately, the kid rubbed his wrists.

Hal glanced at the thin, delicate arms, not much bigger than Sheila's, as he stretched his arms straight and bent them again, as though his elbows ached. The inside curve of his arm was free of track marks, his face clean of scars. Not even a nick from shaving.

"Better?"

The kid nodded. "Thanks." He turned to the cup of water on the table. "You mind?"

"Go ahead." Hal waited while he drank the water and wiped his mouth with the back of his hand. Then the kid refilled his glass from a small pink plastic pitcher and drank that down too. When he was done, he placed his cup back on the table, crossed his hands, and stared at the white beds of his fingernails.

Hal looked too. Clipped, cut. No dirt. A well-groomed kid.

There were well-groomed killers, he told himself.

Sure.

The kid nodded that he was ready, and Hal made a show of pressing the red record button before stepping to the end of the bed. Hailey moved in beside him, while Cameron remained at the door.

Hailey caught Hal's eye, but Hal ignored her. He was in charge of this one.

"You know why we're here?"

The kid seemed to have some trouble swallowing but nodded. He glanced at the recorder. "Yes," he said, his voice raspy.

"Please state your full name."

"James Charles Robbins."

"Date of birth?"

"December 10, 2000."

"Age?"

"Sixteen."

"Mr. Robbins, do you understand that this conversation is being recorded?"

He rubbed the bandage on his head gingerly. "I do."

"You also agree that you are not being forced to talk to us."

"Yes, sir. I understand."

"And you understand that it is your choice to not have an attorney present?"

"I don't want an attorney." He paused. "Thank you."

Robbins was an easy interview, helpful and polite, made eye contact, spoke with proper grammar—the kind of kid a dad would be proud of. Not the kind of kid Hal usually interviewed for murder. He came across more like an awkward high school debate student than a killer. But he was scared. Just like Carson had been.

Who had scared these guys? And why?

Hal walked him through the details of the day before, beginning with when he woke. Only when the interview reached the point when Dwayne Carson and Griffin Sigler were killed did his demeanor change. His posture stiffened, his voice cracked, and he stopped making eye contact. "We went down there—me and Fish."

"Fish?" Hal asked. "That's Kenny Fiston?" Robbins nodded.

"So you and Kenny went down to the police station?"

"Yeah," Robbins said. "Fish drove and I shot them. Then, I shot Fish."

James Robbins was a bad liar. Bad liars didn't make it in the world of crooks and gangs. Lying was more essential than being able to shoot or fight.

In that world, lying was on par with breathing.

Hailey stepped away.

Cameron shook her head.

Hal studied Robbins, waiting for something to give. But the kid kept his mouth closed.

"You said you shot them. Did you know who they were, these guys?" Hal asked.

Robbins shrugged. "Some guys." When Hal pressed, he added, "They owed Fish some money."

"And who shot Fish?" Hal asked him.

His Adam's apple bobbed like a buoy he was trying to hold under water. "I did."

"So you shot two men in the alley beside the police station then you went home and shot Fish?"

Robbins blinked and nodded.

"Out loud, please," Hal said, losing patience.

Something in the kid looked dead then, his eyes heavy, almost closed, as he turned his mouth down to face the recorder. "I shot Fish."

Hal had been handed confessions before—once when a guy split his wife's head open with a tire iron, once when a babysitter had accidentally smothered a child, but almost always there were strong emotions at work—bottled up aggression or boiling anger or profound sorrow, regret—hell, something. This kid showed nothing. "You want to tell us why you shot your friend?"

His shoulders dropped and his chin fell. "He stole something from me," he said flatly.

"What did he steal?" Hailey asked.

"It don't matter."

Hal noticed it was the first time his grammar had slipped. "A woman? Money?"

The kid nodded like he was being offered free samples. "Yeah."

Hal pressed his palms into the bar at the foot of the bed, leaned in. "Well, which was it, James?"

"Maybe it was both." Before Hal could ask another question, Robbins said, "I'm done talking now."

Hal waited another minute, one last holdout, but Robbins remained silent. Hailey tucked the digital recorder into her purse and left the room. Hal stayed back until all the women were gone. "You sure you done talking?"

The kid looked away.

Hal left. Outside the door, the guard stopped him. "He cuffed?"

Hal shook his head. "That kid don't need to be cuffed."

Guard shrugged. "Policy, man. You know how it is."

Halfway down the hall, he met up with Hailey and Cameron, who stood talking. Cameron turned to him. "Did you watch his hands?"

Hal tried to picture the kid's hands. Clean hands.

"No," Hailey said. "Why?"

"He's left-handed."

The kid had scratched his head with his left hand, but he'd been scratching that side.

"Which hand had gunshot residue?" Hailey asked.

Hal flipped open the ballistics report Mike had left and skimmed through several pages while Hailey paced the linoleum. Finally, he found it. "Shit."

"Right hand?" Cameron guessed.

Hal nodded, his gaze on Hailey, who had halted. "Right hand."

"That's not all," Cameron said. "The shooter I watched was left-eye dominant."

Hal was impressed. He hadn't noticed either of those things. He'd been distracted with Hailey and her secrets. If he couldn't trust his partner, how the hell could he stay on task?

Focus. "How do you know someone is left-eye dominant?" Hal asked.

She tilted her head to demonstrate. "You can tell from the way he pitched his head when he fired." She looked back at Robbins's room. "This guy's not the shooter. I'd testify to it in court."

"Now remember," Hal said. "You only saw him for a few minutes on the street. It was a stressful situation. You said it yourself—you've never been that close to a shooting before."

"It's true," Hailey said. "Are you sure you're right?"

"It's my job to watch people with guns," Cameron said, "although I'm usually farther away. That shooter last night—he used an Israeli shooting stance. That's something taught in training schools." She squatted down, held her hands up, left cupping the right. "It makes the shooter a smaller target, provides good balance for better aim." She rose to her feet and hitched her thumb toward the door, the frenetic energy she'd had at the department back again. "That kid in there didn't learn to shoot at any school, if he's ever fired a gun. If he knows how, he learned it on the street, and I'd bet my next paycheck that he wouldn't use an Israeli shooting stance."

"Okay," Hal said. "Now, we just have to prove it."

"Ask him to show you how he shot the gun," Hailey said, shrugging. "Have him demonstrate."

Hal didn't want the wrong guy, and if Cameron was right about any of it—gunshot residue, eye dominance, shooting stance—then Robbins was the wrong guy. He'd known Robbins wasn't their shooter as soon as he laid eyes on the kid. Cameron's observations only made him all that more certain.

"I'm telling you," Cameron said again. "That guy didn't do it."

Hal nodded. "I remember the shooter squatting." Fear was motivating this kid, which meant there was someone out on the street Hal needed to find. "Let's do it."

When they walked back into the hospital room, Robbins glanced at Hailey before focusing on Hal. He edged himself up in the bed. Hal undid the binds and stepped back. Robbins rubbed his wrists again, wincing a little this time.

"They do those up too tight?"

Robbins glanced down, shrugged. "A little."

"I'll make sure they're looser next time."

"Thanks." He scanned the group. "You got more questions?"

"A few." Hal took his notepad from his shirt pocket and wrote, "Is there a bug in here?"

"We just wanted to confirm a couple things," Hal said as he passed the notebook to the kid.

Robbins frowned at the note. "What?"

Hal took the sheet back, wrote, "Microphone? Someone listening?"

Robbins shook his head. "I don't know what you're talking about." His gaze tracked around the room. No. The kid didn't suspect a bug, so he was lying for another reason.

Hal slid the notebook back in his pocket. "Are you okay to stand?"

Robbins shrugged. "Sure. Why?"

"We want you to show us something." Hal helped him out of the bed, and when Hal handed him a cell phone, Robbins took it with his left hand. "What? You want me to call somebody? I don't have nobody to call."

Hailey's turn. Good cop. "We want you to pretend it's a gun and show us how you shot those men."

Robbins tipped his head to the side. "Come on, lady. That's crazy."

"No, it's not," Hal snapped. He fought to control his temper. A young black kid with his shit together, and he was going to confess to a crime he didn't commit. These street kids didn't have a chance as it was. Why the hell would Robbins make it worse for himself?

Hal didn't care. He wasn't going to let Robbins go down for a murder he didn't commit.

If he wasn't the shooter.

He wasn't, was he?

The kid straightened. Giving in, he lifted the phone

toward Hailey and then shifted his aim to the wall. "Bang, bang."

The "gun" was still in his left hand.

Hal glanced at the spot on the wall where the bullets would've punctured the plaster. The kid had started to aim at Hailey but then turned his aim to the wall instead.

Pretend bullets from a pretend gun.

"Now do it for real," Hailey instructed. "Show us exactly how you stood when you shot those guys."

"It's a phone."

"Do it and we'll leave you alone," she promised.

He hesitated and tossed the phone on the bed.

"Man, you didn't shoot them any more than I did," Hal said, his voice a low whisper, thankful there would be no record of his words.

Robbins waved them off. "That's crazy. I'm giving you a full confession. What more do I need to do 'fore you arrest me?"

"Sit down," Hal commanded.

The kid's bravado sank as he did.

"Tell us about the car," Hailey said.

Robbins licked his lips, shrugged.

"Where'd you get it?"

"Fish dealt with that."

"You rode in the back?"

He looked up at Hal. Then his gaze skittered over the others. He knew they didn't believe him. "I don't remember."

"You don't remember?" Hal asked, voice booming.

Robbins shrank smaller. "We'd been smoking."

"Smoking?" Hal repeated.

"Yeah, smoking. We had some Pump, some amp, Dizzy D. You know, Crack," he added, his own voice splitting over the word.

"You remember how you got the guns?" Hal asked.

"Fish got 'em."

Hailey handed her notebook and a pen to Robbins. "Write out your full name and address."

He hesitated before taking the pad and pen then began to write. With his left hand.

From her place against the door, Cameron emitted a tiny moan.

"You happy now, lady?" he said and slumped against the headboard.

Hal sat on the edge of the bed. The anger he normally felt with lying punk kids had been replaced by something more like empathy. "I would be a hell of a lot happier if I knew how a left-handed guy fired two perfect shots with his right hand in front of a couple dozen witnesses."

Robbins's gaze slid back to Hal and then away again. He blinked, his lids resting closed just a moment too long. When they opened again, he stared at the far wall.

"I guess we asked all our questions." Hal let the kid have some more water and replaced the bindings himself, leaving enough space for two of his own fingers to slip in easily.

Then he led the procession out and told the guard that the prisoner was bound. No one spoke as they rode down the elevator, during which Hal held his breath, or in the short walk through the hospital doors and into the parking lot.

Finally, when they'd climbed in and Hal had started

the car, Cameron spoke from the backseat. "What are you going to do?"

It was a damn good question.

"Got to figure out a way to get him to tell us who really shot those guys," Hal said softly, hearing the defeat in his own voice.

How the hell would they do that?

CHAPTER 13

HAL AND HAILEY didn't have a chance to talk about the letter Jim had received from Nicholas Fredricks. They'd been busy with James Robbins, but Hailey felt the tension mounting again on the ride back to the station. Cameron sat in back and provided conversation, but the closer they got to the station, the worse Hailey felt.

When they entered the department, the letter to Jim from Nicholas Fredricks was sitting on her desk in a clear, plastic evidence bag.

She felt sick to see it. Why did Jim confide in her? No. It was the right thing to do. It would lead them to his shooter. But talking to Hal about Jim would not be easy.

Kong sat in the center of Hailey's desk, between the two tall stacks of case files, his legs dangling over the edge.

"There you are," he said as they came in.

"Get off my desk, Kong." Hailey dropped her purse into her bottom drawer, and carried her mug toward the coffee machine in the tiny copy room. Someone had left the pot on all morning. What was left in the bottom was thick and burned. Hailey dumped it into the trash and started a fresh pot.

Kong was a big jokester. He and O'Shea had large personalities. They were loud and outgoing, always hassling each other in jest. It worked for them. It didn't work for her. It never had, but it was much worse since John's death.

When she turned, Kong was leaning against the doorjamb, which made the room seem even smaller than it was.

"Any word on the officer who was shot in the sting?" she asked.

"Still in ICU," Kong said. "Doctors are optimistic, though."

Optimism. She could have used some of that right now.

Hal stood at her desk, reading the letter. When he looked up at her, there was anger in his expression. Hailey turned her back on both of them, watching coffee fill the stained glass pot in a slow, constant dribble.

Growing impatient, she switched her mug for the pot so the coffee brewed directly into her cup. The few drops of spilled coffee sizzled and hissed beneath it.

On the side of the mug, Ali, Camilla and John smiled in the matching plaid robes she'd given them four or five Christmases ago. John's hair was tossed, and tufts stuck up in back where he'd slept on it. Camilla's curls were a nest around her round cheeks, one of them bending into John's chin, while Ali's straight hair formed a halo of static electricity.

She'd found the mug when she'd packed up the house for sale. It had been a joke gift from John, the kind of gifts they used to exchange on Valentine's Day.

Before the campaign talk. Before John became like Jim.

She was sure John thought she'd never use it.

Maybe she wouldn't have if he hadn't changed so much … if he hadn't died.

Hailey blinked hard and removed the half-full mug from under the stream, replacing the glass pot.

Taking a moment to pull herself together, Hailey turned the image from her view, added two white sugar cubes, mixed it with a stir stick, and turned to face Kong, "King" as some called him.

"You hear about this letter?" Kong asked.

"Last night. Jim told me." She walked to her desk and looked down at it. "Where did it come from?"

Kong sat again on her desk, but before he could get comfortable, Hailey waved him away. "Move it, Kong. I'm not in the mood."

"Came today. From the senator's office, delivered directly to O'Shea."

"Well, the guy who wrote that letter is dead," Hal said.

Kong nodded. "I know." He turned to her. "But whoever shot your dad isn't."

"Father-in-law, King," Hal corrected. "He's not her dad."

The reference didn't bother her. These days, Jim was like a dad. "I'm sure that's why Jim sent it over. He thought it would be useful to compare against the letter he received last week. He's trying to help."

Hal pressed his lips together and said nothing.

"What do you think of Robbins?" Hailey asked.

"Kid didn't shoot his friend, I'll tell you that." Hal sat up. "I'm going up there, take a look at his house after work."

"I'll go with you."

He shook his head and stood. "You go home to the girls. I'll call you after."

Hailey lifted the stack of mail into her lap, thumbed through it, and tossed out a stack of catalogues offering bulletproof vests and holsters, then another with a listing of seminars for detectives, one in Hawaii, another in Florida. Something slid through her fingers and landed on the floor.

A number ten envelope. Hal lifted it from one corner. It was addressed "Harris and Wyatt." No postage.

Taking the scissors from the can on her desk, Hal cut it open and slid out the contents.

The top read *San Francisco Chronicle*, June 28, 2012. The headline read: "S&P 500, Tech Stocks … now Illegal Guns." The byline was someone named D. Blake, and the tag read "Chronicle Staff Writer." It was a short piece, maybe two square inches on the page.

> *An unnamed East Coast fund manager has been accused of diversifying client investments into the sale of illegal guns. Few details have been released by insiders, who are pushing for an investigation into the one-man hedge fund allegedly investing client funds in stolen weapons.*
>
> *According to sources, several referrals to the fund have come from heads of Fortune 500 companies and members of congress. The fund is also accused of using gang members to make street sales up and down the eastern shoreline. The SEC has made no announcement*

regarding their intent to investigate. Randall Lockhead, Deputy Assistant Director (East) for the Bureau of Alcohol, Tobacco, Firearms and Explosives, was also unavailable for comment.

At the bottom right corner, someone had scrawled, "No source, no story!"

"How long's that stack been there?" Hal asked.

Hailey tried to think if she'd looked at it yesterday. "Late last week maybe."

Hal pulled an evidence bag from the kit at her feet and dropped the letter in a clear Ziploc bag, still holding it by a corner.

"I'm going to make a copy, get it to the lab. You want to call the paper, see what you can find out about Mr. Blake?"

Hailey was glad to have a moment alone with her thoughts.

Members of Congress. Just the words made her antsy. Even if she believed Jim had nothing to do with these guns—which she did—there were just too many innuendos pushing the police in his direction.

She took her cell phone to the women's room. Alone, she dialed Jim's direct office line. Dee answered and said he was in a meeting.

"I'll call back," Hailey said, wishing Jim would learn how to text.

"Is it about John's case?" Dee asked.

"What?" Hailey said, fighting to sound normal. "No."

"We saw the interview this morning. I thought you looked strong. Jim did too. You handled yourself well."

"Thank you, Dee. Will you tell him I called?"

"Of course. Nothing I can help with?"

She thought about the article. "Have you ever heard of someone named Blake? D. Blake?"

"I don't think so. Is he one of Jim's colleagues?"

"No. He's a reporter."

"I can look through the press files I've got. I save everything related to Jim or the campaigns."

"That would be great," Hailey said.

"No problem. I've got something to finish up here. Then I'll get right on it."

"Thanks, Dee."

Back at her desk, Hailey called the *Chronicle* to follow up on Blake. She spoke to the publisher's assistant and faxed her a copy of the letter.

While she waited for the publisher to call her back, Hailey called down to the DA's office to get the status of the warrant she'd requested—the financial records for Nicholas Fredricks's funeral.

"We're taking it to the judge for a signature tomorrow," the ADA told her.

"Good. I'm also wondering if you can get your hands on a list of everyone who would have access to the phones at Martin Abbott's law firm—secretaries, paralegals, that kind of thing."

"You want us to subpoena Martin Abbott?"

She could have done without the pushback. She was trying to solve some murders. "I guess I could get Tom Rittenberg to call and request your help in solving his daughter's murder. I was sort of hoping I wouldn't have to. It's an employee list. Not a client list."

"I'll see what I can do."

Hailey thanked him and hung up. She added D. Blake to the list of outstanding items in the case. The others read:

Talk to Shakley.

The officer shot in the sting. Next to it, she wrote, *Still in ICU.*

Who paid for NF funeral?

She could follow up on that one tomorrow—if the warrant came through. She made a note there too.

Hear from NYPD about NF.

She added a question mark. She couldn't imagine they would call her back, but she'd keep it on the list.

Martin Abbott link.

That one would have to wait too.

Jeremy Hayden.

The dead gunrunner killed during the sting. She underlined his name.

None of the pieces even felt connected. Abbott and Fredricks and Hayden and now this guy, Blake. These people didn't know each other—there was no indication that their paths had ever crossed.

Why were they all part of this case?

She called over to the juvenile detention center and left a message requesting Jeremy Hayden's record. Added it to her notes.

She'd opened up a blank incident report to begin filling in the details of Fredricks's vandalized corpse when her desk phone rang.

"Wyatt," Hailey answered, expecting Jim.

"This is Carl Phillips. I'm the Deputy Publisher with the *Chronicle* returning your call regarding Donald Blake."

Hailey felt a jolt of energy. "Thanks for calling." D for Donald. Progress.

"I got the article submission you faxed, but I'm afraid I don't have a whole lot to offer you. Both the publisher and I are relatively new. I've been here about two years, Stan about a year and a half. This was before our time. I checked the graveyard, though, and I was able to confirm this article was never printed."

"And Donald Blake is no longer there?"

"No. Jeez, he's been gone two years now."

Reporters obviously came and went. She was surprised the director had called her. "That's no problem. Do you have a forwarding number for Mr. Blake?"

The line went quiet.

"Mr. Phillips?"

"I'm sorry, Inspector. Mr. Blake died. He's dead."

Hailey sank against her chair, the wheels screeching on the linoleum. Dead. Another death. "How did he die?"

"God, it was a terrible tragedy." He lowered his voice. "Really shook up the team."

"How did he die?" she asked again.

"He killed himself after his family died in a gang shooting. They were driving and got caught in the middle of a turf war."

A gang shooting.

How big would this thing get? Abby and Hank Dennig, Colby Wesson—they weren't just murdered.

It was like they were assassinated. But why?

Hal walked through the department doors. He caught her eye and stopped.

"Shot?" she repeated into the phone.

Hal raised his brow.

Hailey put the phone on her speaker. "Can you repeat that, Mr. Phillips? My partner Hal Harris has just joined me."

"Uh, sure." He spoke louder, the way people did when they were on speaker phone. "Yeah. Donald Blake was driving. He was injured, but the steering wheel probably saved his life. The others were caught in the crossfire and killed instantly. Don survived, but he took his own life a few months later."

Hailey watched Hal's reaction as the words struck him. He stood straight, arched backward. The knot of muscle in his jaw looked the size of a golf ball.

"Yeah, it's really tragic," Phillips went on. "Like I said, people here are still upset."

"When?"

"Would have been the summer of 2013."

"Do you know where he lived?" Hal asked.

"Uh." Phillips seemed to jump at the sound of Hal's deep baritone. "Not exactly. Oakland, I think. But in a safe neighborhood. From what I know."

"You've never seen that article submission before?" Hailey asked.

"No. It seems so weird that it came up after all this time. Where did you say you got it?"

"We received it here at the station," Hailey said.

"Do you know where the shooting happened?" Hal asked.

"Like I said to Inspector …"

"Wyatt," Hal said.

"Right. Like I told her, I wasn't here, but I know the deaths were ruled a gang shooting. He was with his family—taking his kids to the Oakland Zoo."

Hal wiped his face with a hand that could easily palm a basketball. "You have the story? About the shootings?"

"I'm sure we do somewhere. I could fax it, if you'd like."

Hailey thanked him for the help and hung up. The phone on Hal's desk rang and he crossed to answer, leaving Hailey with her thoughts. Did the list of victims begin as far back as Donald Blake's family? Were all these deaths related? Jim and Shakley were alive, but so far, they were the only ones.

No, James Robbins was alive, too, but with that bullet in his head, that could only be called a miracle.

Why was Jim still alive? There was no question that these guys could shoot and shoot to kill. Why miss Jim?

Hailey pushed the thoughts of her father-in-law aside as she called and left a message with Oakland PD's homicide department to get more details on the Blake deaths. Hanging up the phone, she took a breath as Hal returned to her desk.

"What now?" he asked.

As soon as the words were out, her phone rang. She lifted the receiver, hoping it wasn't Jim. She didn't want to have an awkward conversation.

"It's Lusheng, darling. I've got your file."

Hailey had to smile at the sing-songy voice of the man who kept the records at the juvenile detention center.

Lusheng was smaller than more than half the inmates and openly gay. Somehow, he'd managed to stay in the position for more than ten years. Hailey loved his spirit. "Lusheng. I just called down there ten minutes ago." She put the phone on speaker.

"You know flattery will get you everywhere," he cooed. Hal shook his head.

"I can fax it over if you want," Lusheng offered.

"Sure, but would you give me the highlights?"

"Of course. Looks like Mr. Hayden started his career at twelve—shoplifting, possession, drunk and disorderly, more shoplifting. The last one we've got in our records is a breaking and entering charge."

"When was that?" Hal asked.

"Well, hello, Inspector Harris."

"Hi, Lusheng."

"Date was June 15, 2004."

"Fredricks was murdered in April," Hailey said.

"Where was the B&E?" Hal asked.

"Oakland."

Two months after Fredricks was killed, but that wasn't a connection. A thousand crimes had taken place in that time frame. "Does it say what was taken?"

There was a moment of silence. "Some jewelry, a little cash. Looks like a smash and grab."

"Convicted?"

"He spent two weeks in and six months on probation. Looks like the stuff got returned too."

"Did Hayden live in Oakland?" Hal asked.

Lusheng hesitated. "Nope. Driver's license says San Francisco. Address on his jacket's in the city too."

Hailey looked at Hal, but he simply shrugged.

"There's nothing else?" she asked.

"Not that I can find. He would have turned eighteen four months after the B&E. Any other charges should be in the system."

"We already got those," Hailey said. "Thanks, Lusheng."

"No problem. Sorry it wasn't what you were looking for."

Hailey thanked him.

Hal leaned forward to hang up when he said, "Hey, Lusheng?"

"Yes?" he cooed.

"You have the victim's name on that file?"

"Hmm."

Hailey started to stack the papers on her desk.

"Ah, here it is," Lusheng finally said. "Last name was Blake."

Hailey froze. That was it—a connection. Finally.

"Blake?" Hal repeated.

"You know them?" Lusheng asked. "Donald and Patricia Blake? He was an editor on the local paper. They were out at a work dinner when it happened. Kids were at a neighbor's. House was empty …"

Hal and Hailey stared at the phone in silence. Donald Blake's family was murdered. Blake killed himself.

A year before that, their dead gunrunner, Jeremy Hayden, had broken into his house.

That could not be a coincidence.

CHAPTER 14

HAL GRABBED HIS jacket. "I'm going down to evidence to get the keys to Robbins's house."

"Should I come?"

He shook his head. "You go home. Keep your phone on you, and I'll call when I'm done." He took a few steps and turned back. "See what you can find out—"

"About Blake. I know. I'm going to talk to Ryaan Berry about Regal Insurance Group. She recognized the name when we talked the other night."

"Yes." He was jazzed. "There's got to be some connection to Regal Insurance."

*

Hal arrived at Hunters Point while it was still light enough to make the projects seem innocuous, especially from a distance. A series of blue and yellow faded blocks rose up around him, the buildings sitting high enough on the hill that it was hard to see their true state.

Hal figured that was in the design.

Aside from his house and the department, he'd visited

these buildings more than any place in San Francisco—a sad statement to his personal life.

And to the state of things in these projects.

When Hal turned off Third Street and onto Evans, the dampening light warned that night was closing in. He turned up Keith Street and passed two kids pedaling across the cracked blacktop, the bikes so small their knees nearly touched their chins. Farther down, a handful of others played hockey with loose chunks of asphalt.

This was one of the roughest neighborhoods in the Bay Area. The kids who grew up here had almost no chance of getting out. According to some statistics, more than a quarter of them wouldn't live to see eighteen.

Almost none lived with both parents. Some didn't live with any parents at all. Maybe half went to school, fewer regularly. Even Hal wasn't safe here. No police officer was.

He arrived at the building where James Robbins lived and looked around for the backup patrol officers who were supposed to meet him. He'd arrived first.

Robbins's mother had died of cancer two years earlier. His father was AWOL. He and his sister were in the care of a woman named Betty Parker, although Records showed Parker had a different apartment number than Robbins and his sister. Dispatch confirmed the car was en route, so Hal went to take a look around, maybe talk to a couple of Robbins's neighbors. He climbed the stairs to the third floor.

Smells of trash and urine filled his nose as he stopped at Robbins's door, the first unit on the west end of the building.

To the left of the door was a small patch of concrete

balcony, maybe three feet square, littered with trash, cigarette butts and bits of broken bottles. He walked to the edge and looked down at the street. The kids still rode their miniature bikes. The shouts of the hockey players rose up from below.

When he turned back toward the door, he noticed chalk drawings on the outside wall of Robbins's house, just a foot or so above the ground. Beneath them, the dirty patio had been swept clean of debris.

He squatted down and looked at a child's rendering of a cat or rabbit. The chalk wiped off on his fingers, so he assumed it had been done recently. A short piece of chalk was wedged in a crack in the wall.

He wondered about the artist.

At Robbins's door, yellow police tape sealed the scene. Along the hinge, the tape was pinched, as though the door had been opened. On the opposite side, someone had slit the seal to enter. He knocked twice, hard, standing against the wall beside the door and holding his thumb over the peephole.

The door groaned, scraping in its jamb, and then opened. A small girl stood in the hallway, loading books into a backpack. Her hair was in two loosely braided plaits, frizzy around her scalp as though she'd gone few days without restyling it. She wore a faded yellow T-shirt and jeans that were both too short and too big on her bony body.

"I'm just getting my books—" Her gaze shifted from the bag to his feet. She looked up and began to shriek.

Dropping the bag, she shoved the door closed with two hands. Hal held it open by putting his foot in its path.

"Help!" she screamed. "Mrs. Parker!" She ran back into the apartment.

A door down the hallway burst open.

"You get 'way from there. I'm calling the police," shouted a heavyset woman in a green flowered dress. Mrs. Parker?

Hal lifted his badge. "Hal Harris, ma'am. I'm an Inspector with the San Francisco PD." He turned toward her, his foot still in the open doorway, but she stepped back into her apartment.

"You ain't fooling me, mister," she shouted from behind the door. "Don't take but fifty cents to get you one of those badges."

Hal pulled his phone from his pocket slowly, showed it to her as he radioed dispatch. When he requested a status on his backup, he was told they were still en route.

He kept his back to the wall between Robbins's apartment where the girl was still hiding and the big angry woman down the hallway, not ready to turn his back on either one. "I'm here because of James Robbins," he said loud enough for both to hear. "He's confessed to a shooting that I don't think he committed." He waited a minute and added, "I need to get some answers, so I can prove he's innocent."

Mrs. Parker poked her head out from behind the door. "You the police, and you don't believe he did it?" She narrowed her eyes, pointed a finger at him. "Now I know you a fake."

"I'm not a fake, ma'am," Hal insisted, taking a quick glance into Robbins's quiet unit and feeling more than a little on edge. This was no place for a stranger, let alone a police officer without backup. Where the hell was the black and white? "Do you know James Robbins, ma'am?"

"Course I know him," she said indignantly. "Practically raise him and Tawny since their mama died." She waddled out into the hallway, pulled the door closed behind her, and keyed the two locks. Coming at him, she filled the hallway almost from one side to the other, and Hal pressed against the wall as she passed.

She looked into the Robbins's doorway. "You probably scared her to death, poor child. After what she seen." She stepped into the apartment, followed by the musty smell of malt liquor that might've been a few days old. The floor moaned beneath her. "Tawny!"

"What did she see?" Hal asked.

She looked Hal up and down, shook her head, and continued inside.

Hal searched the street for his backup. Nothing.

"I'm Mrs. Parker. Betty Parker." Then once she'd disappeared inside the dim apartment, she shouted back, "You coming in here or what?"

Hal radioed that he was entering the Robbins's unit and asked dispatch to please status his backup. They should've been there by now. Hal stepped into the apartment and shut the door, pushing hard as it stuck. He kept to one side as he moved down the hallway, back to the wall. The first room he passed was a bedroom, empty. "Ma'am," he called out. "Mrs. Parker?"

"We down here," she said from deep inside the unit.

"I need to know who's in the unit, ma'am. How many people."

"Ain't but the two of us," she said. "Me and Tawny."

She waved her arm and the heavy flesh of it swung back and forth behind her motions. "Come here, girl," she snapped.

The young girl emerged from the shadows. "Me," Mrs. Parker said, then turned to the girl. "And Tawny. Only ones here."

Hal kept his badge up in his left hand, the right resting on his holster. "Is James your brother?" he asked Tawny.

She nodded.

"You mind if I look around?"

"What you looking for?" Mrs. Parker barked.

"Nothing specific, ma'am. I'd just like to see the place."

She frowned and then waved at him. "Go ahead. Don't you touch nothing, though."

He nodded and backed into the first bedroom, carpeted in an ugly dark brown, a different shade from the dirty beige of the rest of the place. Remnants of the visit from CSU were visible in the black powder on the desktop and the small bits of numbered tape tacked to the places where they had removed evidence. Otherwise, it was pretty clean, especially for a kid's room.

Cleaner than his own.

A ratty blue and white striped comforter had been thrown back over the pillows in a lazy attempt to make the bed. A few clothes hung over a beat-up wooden desk chair. One of the chairs had a broken leg that had been repaired with duct tape.

This had to be James's room. The walls around the bed were plastered with posters of bands Hal had heard of from his sister's kids and some Sheila had listened to— Drake, Jay Z, Wiz Khalifa. On a small desk beside the bed was a small Bluetooth speaker. In the closet, old jeans and shirts sat folded in stacks on a long shelf, underwear and paired socks in bundles on another.

No new equipment, no fancy clothes—nothing that suggested Robbins had extra cash from running with Fish.

On the floor beside the bed lay a binder with a math textbook splayed open across it. Hal bent down, opened the binder, and flipped through pages of homework assignments. At the top of each was a grade circled in red: 8/10, 9/10, a 7/10, where the teacher wrote: "You can do better, James!"

James was a straight kid. Good grades, tidy. Behind the homework pages he found a test with an 87 written in red at the top. Hell, that was better than Hal had done in high school.

The floor groaned as Mrs. Parker came into the room, eyeing him suspiciously. "What you planting in here?"

"Nothing, ma'am." He nodded to the binder. "Looks like James is a good student."

"Course he is."

Hal moved past her, down the hall, and found a second bedroom, the girl's. He paused in the doorway. It was done in yellows, worn and faded.

Like James's, the room was kept tidy by someone who cared for her things, even if they were secondhand. In the living room, the girl sat on the floor against the wall, watching him as he walked into the kitchen area where a few dishes sat in the sink, rinsed and stacked.

On the refrigerator door was a photograph of Robbins and the girl. In it, she grinned widely, her front two teeth missing. Hal pulled the photo loose, turned around, and surveyed the blood spatter that covered the two couches and the walls behind them.

When he looked over at Tawny, she, too, was eyeing the wall.

Hal dragged a chair from the kitchen table and sat down.

Tawny pulled her knees to her chest, hugged them tight.

"Were you here the night your brother was shot?"

She looked up at Mrs. Parker, standing in the hallway.

Hal did, too, but she wasn't looking at either of them, her gaze somewhere on the ceiling, as though she was making an important decision. Mrs. Parker moved slowly into the room and lowered herself into a corner of the couch, as far from the blood as possible. "Go on and tell 'im, girl."

Tawny licked her lips. "I was outside, drawing on the wall." She paused. "With chalk—not paint or anything. The chalk washes off in the rain—"

"I saw it. A cat?"

She nodded. "Started out a bunny, but the tail got too long." She chewed on her mouth a moment.

"Who was here that night?"

"Just my brother and Fish."

"But someone else came later, didn't they?" he asked.

Tawny looked back at Mrs. Parker.

"You got to tell 'im all of it, Tawny. Ain't gonna help James to lie," the old woman said.

"I know your brother didn't shoot his friend," Hal said. "I need your help to find who really did."

Tawny looked at him. "James said not to tell."

"I can't help him unless you tell me."

"Go on, child," Mrs. Parker coaxed, impatiently.

Tawny looked at the couch on the far side of the room. Where her brother had been sitting.

"I was drawing when I heard a pop, like someone in a movie getting shot." She furrowed her brow. "But there weren't no screaming."

"Wasn't any screaming," Mrs. Parker corrected.

"They're always screaming in the movies when somebody gets shot." She glanced sideways at Mrs. Parker. "Plus, I saw the movie him and Fish was watching, and it didn't sound right—too quiet. It weren't—it wasn't a quiet movie.

"So, I stopped drawing and listened. It was real shots. I thought James would come out to get me. He always knew if trouble was coming. He was real careful about me since Mom—" Tawny blinked hard.

"Go on, girl," Mrs. Parker whispered.

"James always told me to get down on the ground when I heard shots, so I did. I heard someone coming down the hallway, and I thought it was James. But then the door stuck. James knows you got to pull down on the handle to get that door open. All his friends know it too. I stayed in that corner. The door finally opened and the man cussed loud. I didn't move one single inch."

Hal leaned forward, propped his elbows on his knees, and kept his voice steady. "Did you see his face, Tawny?"

Her eyes grew into dark saucers. "His face was turned. I saw his hands. They were real big. Way bigger than James's." She looked at Hal. "Big as yours."

179

Hal studied her, stood up. "You sure he was as big as me?"

She stared up at him. "I think so. He was real big."

Hal figured James was five-eleven. He made notes. Not many guys were as big as he was. Six-four tended to put you on the high end of the spectrum, unless you were talking about the NBA.

"He had some new shoes on too. Jordans."

Hal wrote that down.

"Black with red," Tawny continued. "Brand new."

"Besides the shoes and his hands, what else did you see?"

She tugged her lower lip. "He cut his hand when he came out the door." She looked at Mrs. Parker. "On that metal you always telling me to watch for."

"There's a piece of rebar sticks out of the cement wall over there. Must've called on it a dozen times. Don't anybody come fix things 'round here."

"Do you know how badly he cut himself?" Be a nice break if he ended up in a hospital. Hospitals kept records.

"He was bleeding some," she said.

Probably not bad enough for an ER visit, but he might've left some DNA.

"I didn't see nothing else," she continued. "He was dressed dark, and there's not real good light out there. I mostly draw in the dark till my eyes get used to it." After a few moments, she cocked her head and added, "I guess there was one more thing kinda weird."

"What's that, Tawny?" he asked.

"He clicked."

Mrs. Parker sighed heavily from the couch, and when Hal glanced back, she was asleep.

"What you mean, he clicked?" Hal asked.

She studied her hands.

"Tawny?" he pressed.

"Like he had a paperclip in his mouth. It clinked around his teeth."

Hal tried to imagine the sound. What would the guy have in there? A bullet? "You're sure it was in his mouth?"

"Yeah. It weren't like change in his pocket or anything. It sounded like he had something in his teeth."

How was he supposed to go about searching for someone with a clinking in his mouth?

A sudden pounding on the door made Mrs. Parker shoot upright.

"Police."

Tawny scurried to sit at her feet.

"Hang on," Hal said, motioning to her to stay seated. "They're with me." Pressed to one wall, he shouted down the hallway. "This is Inspector Harris. I'm already inside."

Someone pushed on the door. It stuck.

The thunk of a foot striking the wood, a sharp scrape, and the door swung open. Two patrol officers stepped into the open doorway, weapons drawn.

Hal stood in the hallway with his badge in one hand, the other clearly visible. "You guys are a little late."

The officers holstered their weapons. "We had a burglary in-progress on the way."

"You can go ahead and hang outside. I'll be out in a minute."

The guys went back out the door and, with some effort, shut it behind them.

"Where are you staying?" he asked Tawny.

"She's staying with me," Mrs. Parker said.

"I understand you're her legal guardian."

Mrs. Parker frowned. "I ain't illegal."

"But you don't live here."

"Like hell I don't." Mrs. Parker struggled to get off the couch. "Go on get your stuff, Tawny. We getting out of here."

"What about James?" Tawny asked.

"I'm going to talk to him next."

Hal led them out, past the uniforms and down the exterior corridor to Mrs. Parker's place. The sky was dark and the buildings were quiet now. It felt almost eerie. Mrs. Parker unlocked the two deadbolts, stuck a third key into the knob and opened the door, breathing hard from the effort.

He got Mrs. Parker's phone number and told them he'd call tomorrow. He needed to talk to James Robbins first.

The corridor was dank as he walked back toward the officers, assaulted again with the stink of rotting trash.

"We got another call," one of the patrol guys said.

Hal nodded, following them to the stairs. "Go ahead. I'm heading out anyway."

At the top of the stairs, he called Roger's cell phone. When Hal had taken Jim's letter down to the lab an hour earlier, Roger had still been there. He'd said something about a long night. Hal hoped he was still there.

"Sampers." The sounds of the lab bled through the

receiver—printing, people talking, the loud humming of one of the machines.

"It's Hal. I've got some blood at a scene at Hunters Project that might connect to our case. Any chance we could get someone out to collect it?"

"Text me your location, and I'll get someone right out."

"You're the man."

"You know it," Roger bantered back.

That made Hal laugh. Progress. They were actually making progress. He sent the address to Roger and started for the stairwell.

An explosion. A piece of cement stung his ear. The bullet sank into the siding behind him with a thump.

Hal dropped to the floor. The phone slipped from his fingers. "Damn."

He drew his gun as another bullet kicked up a chunk of cement over his head. A third brought the sound of shattering glass and screams from a floor above.

Hal didn't move. His heart hammered at his throat. A moment of quiet, then the gunfire erupted in a rapid rat-a-tat. He froze, pressed as close as he could to the wall of the balcony, trying to count the shots. Ten or maybe eleven. An automatic weapon.

Then, the firing stopped.

He studied the silence. The crunch of shoes on dirt. Someone walking.

On his belly, he crawled toward the stairs, hidden behind the cement railing wall.

The steps went silent.

Hal eased himself down the steps, still low behind the railing.

Above, someone yelled about a broken window.

Hal pushed through a pile of black garbage bags until he was pressed against the dumpster. His back to the cold cement, knees to his chest, he was protected on two sides.

Gun drawn, he listened, waited.

Cars hummed from the freeway. Someone's bass pulsed in the distance. Up the stairs, Hal's cell phone rang. The stench of sour milk, soiled diapers, and something like rotting limes emanated from the garbage bags. Hal stayed put, counting the beats of the music above.

The place was still. The sound of his own heart rose above the quiet.

Only when he heard the beautiful sound of shrieking sirens did his heart finally start to slow.

CHAPTER 15

HAILEY TUCKED THE kids in and stepped back into the hallway, checking her phone again. Nothing. Why hadn't Hal been in touch?

He was up at Hunters Point, at James Robbins's house. She hadn't heard from him, and it made her uneasy. She should have gone with him.

"Lock all the doors, Mommy," Ali called out.

"I will," Hailey promised her. "You're safe."

Hailey walked down the stairs and saw Jim and Tom Rittenberg standing in the entry hall, their heads leaned together, talking intensely. Tom looked better than he had. The cane was missing and he stood straighter than he had last time she'd seen him. Dee was good for him.

Dee walked in from the living room. Tom straightened up the moment he saw her. Her face flushed. She enjoyed the attention. Tom and Dee. It made sense. Jim patted Tom on the back as Dee opened the door for him.

How would Hal react to the fact that Dee was seeing Tom Rittenberg, the father of Abby Dennig?

How much closer could her personal life get to this case?

Dee followed Tom out the front door, and Hailey started down the stairs.

"Glad you're still up," Jim said. "I've got something for you."

Hailey followed him into the kitchen, where he poured himself a large glass of wine, offering her one as well. Hailey shook her head. Hal was over at Hunters Point, and she wanted to be sharp when he checked in.

These days, she had too many balls to keep in the air, and the alcohol didn't help.

Jim was drinking too much. He rarely looked drunk, but the recycling bin had more empty wine bottles than usual. The drinking was probably in reaction to something. Would he talk about it if she asked?

He pointed to a manila folder on the table. "Dee put this together for you. It's copies of all the media pieces she's collected—anything at all related to local politics, people I know. She's thorough."

The folder contained maybe fifty pages of print. Hailey set it aside to look at later.

"She also made a list of everyone who's been in the house. O'Shea asked for it, so I thought you'd like a copy." The theory would be that Jim's shooter knew the layout of the house. Which meant he—or she—had been there before.

Hailey flipped it open and scanned the names and addresses. At the bottom, Dee had written "UPS to deliver new computer" and "electrician—Liz looking for invoice."

"There was an electrician here?"

Jim drank from his glass. "Dee told Inspector

O'Shea she'd get the electrician information from Liz in the morning."

Hailey scanned the other names. She'd met so few of them. They were almost all here during the day—while she was at work and the girls at school. But what about in the hours between school and when Hailey came home? Had the girls met these people? "Any of them seem like possible suspects?"

"No." He swirled the wine around the inside of the glass.

The Chateau St. Jean bottle sat mostly empty on the table. She hadn't told Jim about Fredricks's finger. Why would she? She stared at the cork. "How do you buy that wine?"

"What do you mean—how?"

"Do you buy individual bottles? By the case?"

"We buy about six cases when it's released each year." He set the glass down. "Seems like this year I've gone through more than usual."

"It's been a long year."

He nodded without speaking.

"Do you know the name Donald Blake?"

He shook his head.

"You're sure. Donald Blake?" she asked again.

"I don't," he repeated. "Should I?"

Hailey stood, filled a glass with ice, and added sparkling water.

It was something Liz always bought—different flavors of water. This one was raspberry and orange. Hailey had actually started to like the stuff.

She sat at the table and fingered the wine cork. The

bottle on the table was now empty. "Was there something else you wanted to talk to me about?"

"Just the list," he said. He was lying, but she had no idea why.

"Seems like Tom and Dee are spending a lot of time together."

"They are," Jim said.

She studied his face as he drank from the glass. "Is that a good thing?"

"Maybe," he said.

Why would it be a bad thing? Because Dee was Jim's little sister, or was there something about Tom that worried him?

"Dee's always done exactly what she wanted, so it's not like we could stop her even if we wanted to," Jim said with a soft smile.

"Seems like you guys are close. She doesn't talk to you?"

"She doesn't. Our family wasn't good at talking," he admitted. "She's got her Valium when things don't go her way. I've got my drink."

They sat together in silence for a moment. Then Hailey said goodnight and headed up to her bedroom, the cork still in her hand.

She checked on the girls. Camilla slept soundly, on her back, her arms splayed, while Ali had curled herself into a tight ball, frown lines deep on her face. Hailey rubbed between Ali's eyes and watched as she relaxed. Her eyes opened.

"Mommy," she said, groggy.

"Yes, baby."

"Is Daddy still dead?"

Hailey bent down to kiss her forehead. "Yes, baby."

Her eyes fell closed again.

Hailey lay beside her, cupping the tiny form against hers.

A while later Jim climbed the stairs. A few minutes later came the creaking sound of water in the pipes.

Hailey rose from the bed and sat in the rocking chair in the girls' room, using the dim glow of the nightlight to read through the articles Dee had pulled. It was full of news of Abby and Hank Dennigs' deaths, but every article mentioned Tom Rittenberg. Dee had included policy articles and campaign news that related to the police or guns, but none of them were relevant to their case.

When the house was silent, Hailey crept back downstairs. She stood outside the door of Jim's office.

She never came to this room. Even when Jim and she spoke, they avoided this room.

John died in this room.

In certain light, Hailey swore she could still see the bloodstain on the floor.

The carpet was new, but the stain of John's blood was still there for her, burned into her retinas like a camera flash.

She left the overhead light off and turned on the small desk lamp instead. In the corner stood the old file cabinet. Hailey had assumed things would be filed alphabetically. Instead, the top drawer held all his campaign records—contributions, financials, media, literature, and speeches.

Inside large green hanging folders were thin manila ones. The media file contained eight or ten manila folders—*New York Times, Chronicle*, the *Washington Post*. She drew out the *Post* folder, skimmed through the pieces, and saw Jim's name mentioned in reference to a couple of bills.

The folder for the *Chronicle* was the fullest.

Hailey skimmed for Donald Blake's name but didn't find it on any of the bylines.

The articles were about politics. No mention of John's death, nothing about the recent shooting.

The lower drawers contained the bills Jim was working on and below that, employee files. She skimmed through the names, but none of them were familiar. Below that were things she didn't even look at—life insurance files, records for his Keogh plan, medical bills …

Hailey sat on the floor with her eyes closed. Jim had kept the letter from Nicholas Fredricks, so surely he'd kept other letters as well.

Where were those? There was no sign of them here.

Something Hal had said came back to her.

Why all this stuff was coming in the form of letters? Why not calls?

An anonymous call or email was infinitely easier than delivering a letter to the station.

Someone was bringing letters in without being noticed.

Could it be Jim? But what sense did that make? What reason did he have for leaking information he could have easily given them?

Maybe Jim had a safe somewhere. She sat in his chair and opened the single drawer in the center of his desk. Rows of pens, a couple of small notepads, paperclips, and binder clips in a shallow dish. No keys or codes. When she shut it, his computer woke up, and she jumped as the screen grew bright. She reached to turn off the monitor, but stopped. Jim would know she'd been there. She'd have to wait for it to go back to sleep.

When she sat back in his chair and saw a paperclip on the floor, she stooped to pick it up and noticed a hidden drawer under the desk. The drawer was small—maybe three inches deep and nine inches wide—and set all the way at the back of the desk. Hailey touched it, felt a small metal pull on its underside, and slid it toward her, cupping her hand beneath it in case it fell. Amazingly, the drawer slid all the way to the front of the desk and beyond a few inches. Just enough to see it was empty. Hailey pushed it closed again.

If anything had been in this office, Jim was smart enough to get rid of it. He had a shredder.

She glanced around the office for it. Under the desk, Jim's small wire trash can was empty. She looked beside the file cabinet and behind the door. Circled the room. No shredder.

Cabinets lined the wall behind the desk, the shelves filled with stacks of printer paper and boxes of stationary and envelopes. She eased the doors shut again and opened the next two. More office supplies. Behind the third set of doors, Hailey found the shredder, drew it out, and set it on the floor.

The bin was empty.

A fine, white paper dust coated the surface of the dark plastic, and a handful of tiny diamond shapes suggested it had been used, but how recently was impossible to tell.

Hailey lifted the shredder and peered down into the metal slats of the machine.

Nothing.

She flipped it over and saw a thin strip of paper caught in the bottom.

Her fingers were too wide to get hold of it. Using an unfolded paperclip, she pried the scrap loose. It was blank on one side, and the other side had only two letters, which read "ry," handwritten and photocopied. It could have come from anywhere.

Hailey put it on the floor to reassemble the shredder and imagined all the words that ended with "ry." Impossible to guess.

Someone's name? Harry? Mary?

Hailey returned the shredder to the cabinet and looked at the narrow wedge of paper again. It looked like there was a line after the *y*. Not a line, an exclamation.

She recognized the handwriting.

She knew what this was.

Still holding the tiny paper wedge, she shut off the desk lamp and ran up the stairs, avoiding the spots that creaked the loudest. Inside the small room she used for a den, she dug through her briefcase for the photocopies of the evidence. Beneath those was the page she was looking for—the article from the *Chronicle*.

She lifted the tiny scrap to the edge of the page they'd been sent.

"No source, no story!"

The scrap from Jim's shredder matched exactly.

Hailey sank back into the chair, willing it to be different, to see some clear distinction that wasn't there.

They were the same.

Jim had sent the police Donald Blake's article. Or he'd gotten one just like it and hadn't told her. And he said he didn't know Donald Blake.

Which meant Jim was lying.

With the scrap tucked carefully into a pocket of the bag, she booted up her laptop. Her phone vibrated on her hip. Hal.

"That took you a while," she said.

"Someone just shot at me."

"Hal! Are you okay?"

"I'm still out here. I've called for backup. They're en route."

"I'm on my way."

"Hailey—"

"Text me the address."

She ended the call, started up the stairs to wake Liz, and found her already halfway out her bedroom door. Since the girls and Hailey had moved in, Liz and Jim had turned the bed in their room around so Liz was on the outside, and she'd developed an almost supernatural sense for knowing when Hailey was coming.

"I've got to go in."

Liz followed her down the stairs, poking her head into the girls' room to check them as Hailey sprinted for the front door.

No text from Hal. When she called, it went straight to voicemail. The awful pit in her stomach formed as she called dispatch.

"His backup is two minutes out," they told her.

"Text me the address."

"Will do."

She would not think about everything that could go wrong in two minutes. She heard the buzz of the text from dispatch, checked the address and drove toward the projects. She counted to sixty, too fast to make a whole minute, and counted again. Then, she dialed.

Hal answered. "Hey."

"Shit," she cursed, letting the fear course out. "Damn it, Hal."

"Yeah," he said, breathless. "I know."

"You scared the crap out of me." Hailey heard the sirens. "I'm on my way. I'm almost at Cesar Chavez. Be there in ten minutes."

"Hailey, this place is—"

"Watch for my car," she said, cutting him off. She wasn't interested in being told it was dangerous. "And don't let those patrol guys go anywhere."

Ten minutes later, when Hailey turned off Third Avenue onto Evans and passed the closed down PG&E plant, red police lights shone in the sky like beacons.

Hal stood beside a black and white, arms crossed, talking to a patrol officer who took notes. She parked diagonally on the street, scanned the faces watching them in the dark, and slammed the car door harder than necessary as she got out.

She wanted to touch his shoulder, to hug him like a kid. Instead, she fought with her welling emotion. Since John, everything felt so much more dangerous. And what if these people had been targeting Hal? What if this was happening because of Jim?

If Jim did something that got Hal hurt …

Hal smiled. "You were asleep."

Hailey touched her head, the half-done ponytail loosed into a frizzy mane. "Maybe you could go a day this week without getting shot at."

The patrol officer looked at her. Hailey glared until he returned to his notepad and started asking questions again.

Where was Hal standing? How many shots were fired?

She stood silent beside him until she could hear the hiss of his breathing.

He was really okay.

Now she could be too. She forced slow, even breaths.

"We lose the shooter?"

"Think so. My bet—he was gone before the black and whites got here." Hal pointed down the hill. "Shots came from there, I'm guessing. First couple cleared my head, so he had to be shooting upward." More sirens wailed in the distance. "Makes the most sense, anyway. It's a straight shot to Palou down that way, then the freeway's only a few blocks."

"I probably passed him." Hailey nodded to the bystanders. "Anyone see anything?"

"Nothing yet."

"I won't hold my breath," she said. If the guy got away with shooting someone a block from the police station in the middle of the day, it didn't seem likely they'd catch him in the projects at night.

"Smart move."

Another patrol officer approached, clipping his radio back on his shoulder. "No luck."

"Think he's a local?" she asked. "He'd know where to hide."

Hal frowned. "Maybe, but not too bright about it. If he'd waited another minute, I'd have cleared the stairs, and he would have had a clean shot at me."

The thought was terrifying.

"Inspector!" an officer called from the hillside below. "You guys got to see this."

They walked slowly down the hill, watching their path for footprints or evidence. The dirt was strewn with garbage—broken glass and bits of paper and cardboard. It was impossible to tell what might have been useful. The tracks led down the hill and back up again, which meant the shooter came up and then went back down the same way. There were a million ways around that place—and any of a dozen paths would have eliminated a need to backtrack. Safer that way. The fact that he'd taken the same path suggested the shooter didn't know the area well. Probably not a local.

They stopped a few feet from a V-shaped impression in the mud.

"Christ," Hal said. "You know what that is?"

Hailey studied the footprints, the strange angle of the feet. The tread was heavier on the heels, sunken a couple of inches into the mud. The mud nearby was moist, but not soft. It held firm when she pressed a finger into it.

The firmness suggested that the shooter had not merely paused in that spot—he had planted his feet there.

The tight set of Hal's jaw told her he was thinking the same thing. "Israeli shooting stance," she said.

"Goddamn right," he whispered.

CHAPTER 16

HAILEY'S PHONE BUZZED as they left Hunters Point.

"I need a drink," Hal said.

She wanted to go home, but after bailing out on her partner the night Carson was shot and going out with the Rookie Club instead, she owed him. "Sure. Where?"

"Hanlon's?"

The cop bar. She would have chosen somewhere quieter, but it was Hal's call. He would be amped up—the adrenaline fading and the fear starting to settle in. She knew how this worked. "Hanlon's it is."

At the bar, Hal ordered a beer on tap and Hailey asked for the same, avoiding eye contact with the familiar faces. By this hour, the sober ones had gone home.

When they were served, Hal lifted the cold pint glass, took a few long swallows, and set it down, nearly empty.

"You okay?"

He didn't answer and lifted his hand for another. When the bartender came back with a full glass, he set two shots down next to it. Something amber-colored. Whiskey probably. A couple of officers from Sex Crimes

waved from across the bar. In the process, one of them—
an old-timer almost at retirement—stumbled and fell
back onto his barstool.

Hal lifted the shot, took a sip, made a face, and
nodded to hers. "You going to drink that?"

"I'll pass."

Hal held the shot between two fingers. It looked more
like a thimble than a shot glass as he tipped it down his
throat. He took a few more sips of his second beer, stood
up, and threw a twenty on the bar. "Let's get out of here."

Hailey looked at her full glass. She didn't need a
drink. "I'll drive."

He didn't argue. "You need to get home?"

Hailey glanced at the clock. Ten thirty. "I've got time.
I can take you first."

"I want to make a stop."

She watched him. "Where?"

"I'll show you." In the car, Hal dialed. "I need to see
if James Robbins has been released." When he hung up,
he said, "He's at CJ-nine." Robbins had gotten medical
release from the hospital jail ward and had been trans-
ported back to the regular city jail at the Hall. "Let's go
talk to him."

"Now?"

When Hal didn't answer, she drove them to the station and parked on the street. They entered the jail via the
steps where Dwayne Carson had emerged only minutes
before he'd been shot. The new city jail building had tiled
blue glass and a sleek, modern design. The architecture
would have been better suited to a library or a convention

center. No matter how attractive the building, it still housed criminals.

Hailey watched Hal from the corner of her eye, but she had no idea what he was thinking. The muscle in his jaw was working and the stiffness of his posture read as anger. But anger at whom? At her?

They showed their badges at the desk, checked their weapons, and took the elevator to the fourth floor where a guard led them to James Robbins's cell. Hal asked to be let in. After the door slid open with a long mechanical hum, he stepped past the thick iron bars.

The cell emanated a dank chill. Hal stood in the darkness, his expression unreadable. When had that happened? She used to be able to read Hal.

"You want in too?" the guard asked.

The intensity of Hal's expression made her wish she could stay outside, but she didn't have a choice. Hal seemed on the verge of lashing out. The cell door closed behind them with a low buzz.

Robbins lay on the bottom bunk, one knee up and one leg stretched out, a hand tucked under his head. His prison orange stood out in the darkness, and when the door clicked shut, the whites of his eyes flashed at her.

He sat up slowly, onto his elbows. Hal crossed to him in a single stride.

When Robbins had both shoes on the ground, Hal smacked him in the jaw.

"Hal," Hailey snapped, but her partner didn't turn.

Robbins rocked back, cupping his jaw. "What the hell."

"Get up," Hal ordered, balling his fingers into tight fists.

Hailey stepped forward.

Hal spun toward her, palm out. "Don't." His eyes were narrow, tight. He stank of beer. "I won't hurt him," he whispered.

She'd never seen him like this. What was it about Robbins that made him so angry? Or was it her?

James Robbins licked his lips, pressing himself against the cell wall.

"He's scared," she whispered.

"Please," Hal said.

She stepped away.

Robbins hovered tighter to the wall. "What're you doing in here?"

Hal grabbed his orange prison jersey, yanked it. The fabric ripped. Her heart pounded.

"Get up," Hal shouted.

The kid tried to duck out from under the bunk.

Hal grabbed his shoulder.

"Hey!" Robbins yelled. "Someone help me!"

From down the hall, another inmate shouted back, "Shut up, pussy!"

The guard didn't appear.

Robbins backed himself to the bars.

Hal leaned in so their chests were almost touching. Anger came off him like heat.

Robbins tried to catch Hailey's eye. Hal gripped the kid's jaw. "Look at me. Don't look at her. You're talking to me." Spit flew from his lips.

"What do you want?" Robbins asked.

"Tell me why you lied," Hal demanded.

Hailey sank against the hard cold bars. She thought of the scrap of paper she'd found in Jim's office. He was a liar. That made her a liar too. How would Hal react to that?

"I ain't a liar."

Hal dropped a fist into the top bunk. The springs yelped.

Robbins sank to the floor.

"Get up," Hal demanded.

He covered his face.

"Get the hell off the floor." Hal yanked him up.

"Hal," Hailey pleaded.

He let go, raised both hands in the air.

"Tell us about the shooting," Hailey said.

Robbins glanced between them, shook his head. "I didn't lie."

Hal gripped the kid's elbow and twisted the arm behind his back.

He pressed Robbins's face against the bars. She'd only ever seen Hal like this once before, right about the time that he and Sheila were breaking up. He'd been a mess. Edgy and mean, and for someone his size, it was scary, even for those who knew him well.

Even for her.

Then, one night they'd caught a guy who broke into his girlfriend's apartment and killed two women. Brutally raped one before killing her, then killed the other.

When Hailey and Hal entered the scene, the perp was high on coke and Grey Goose in his yuppie apartment. Hal let loose. He had the guy off his feet and against a wall, suspended by the collar of his expensive French shirt.

Hailey had talked him down. It was his career at stake, all the good he could do would be lost over one piece of shit. Hal had stormed from the scene, and she hadn't seen him until he showed up to work Monday morning.

He'd brought her a latte—his silent truce.

Robbins was nothing like that guy. He was a kid, and maybe an innocent one.

She put her hand on Hal's shoulder and he let go of Robbins, moving away.

Robbins huddled against the bars, giving in to the tremors.

"I went up to Hunters Point tonight," Hal said, his voice gravelly, hoarse. "I went to see where you live."

The kid's shoulders tightened toward his chin as though he could block out the sound.

"Someone shot at me."

Robbins sank to the floor, put his temple to the bars, and closed his eyes.

"You want to tell me what that's about?" Hal asked.

Robbins shook his head.

"Who shot Carson?"

He didn't open his eyes. "I did."

Hal lunged forward.

Robbins tensed for the strike as Hailey stepped between them. "We're trying to help you, for God's sake. Hal is trying to save you." The kid turned his head and opened his eyes, lifting his hand to his ear where his wound had begun to bleed through the bandage.

Shit.

"You know how many innocent people were up there

tonight, while some asshole was shooting at me?" Hal asked, his voice quieter, defeated.

Hal pushed a picture into Robbins's face. A girl—about Camilla's age—smiled at the camera. "How about her?"

Fear bleached the color from his face. Gone was any last bravado. "No."

Hal held the picture a few inches from Robbins's eyes. "Tell me who shot Dwayne Carson and the driver ..."

"Sigler," Hailey said.

Robbins's eyes filled with tears. "Where is she?"

"He asked you a question," Hailey said. "Tell us who shot them."

Robbins shook his head. "I don't know. I don't know who shot 'em."

"But it wasn't you?" Hal asked.

Robbins deflated. "No."

"I didn't hear you."

Tears streamed down his cheeks. "I didn't kill them. I never killed anybody, I swear."

"So why confess?" Hal asked.

Robbins sobbed. "Because he threatened Tawny. He called the hospital room and told me if I didn't confess to killing Fish, he'd come after her. Then, same guy calls back and tells me I gotta confess to those other guys too—I never even heard of those guys. What would I want them dead for?" He pulled himself to his feet, clutching the photo to his chest and blinked against the tears.

"You're willing to risk going to jail for murder?"

"I go to jail or they kill Tawny," Robbins barked. "Which would you choose?"

"Not all guys would have chosen to protect their sister," Hal said, backing off.

Robbins rubbed a hand over his face. "She ain't got nobody else."

"Who shot you?" Hal asked.

"I don't remember," Robbins said, his eyes open, clear. "I swear, I didn't see him."

"You got any ideas who the shooter might've been?" Hal pressed.

"Only one I can think is the guy Fish was working for. He dealt."

"Dealt what?" Hailey asked.

"Guns. Moved them for some guy."

"What guy?" Hal said.

Robbins shrugged. "I just know he's bad."

"How?"

"Fish was scared of him, and Fish wasn't scared of most people." Robbins's eyes grew wide and round. More tears spilled. He turned to Hal. "He got Tawny?"

"She's fine. She and Mrs. Parker went with the U.S. Marshalls. They're going to safe housing for a while."

Robbins wiped his face. "Oh, thank God."

Hailey stepped forward, touched his arm. "Robbins, come sit."

He walked the three feet to the bed as though it was a marathon and slumped down. The flimsy mattress bowed, and Robbins sank into the middle. "Christ, I thought he'd killed her." He looked up. "How long can she stay there—in the safe place?"

"As long as she needs to," Hailey said. She had no

idea how long they'd be able to keep her there. She hoped she wasn't lying. "We'll work it out," she said honestly.

"You know anything else about this guy? The man who called?" Hal asked.

Robbins shook his head. After waiting a minute, Hal walked to the door and called for the guard.

Hailey squatted beside the bed. "You're safest in here for now, okay?"

"And you're sure Tawny's okay?"

"I'm sure. But we've got to find this man. We'll be back in the morning to ask some more questions."

Fish must have been part of the same group of gunrunners that Carson was. He'd been eliminated just like Carson. Why? Because they'd seen something? Or someone? Sigler and Robbins—they were just collateral damage.

The guard opened the door.

"He's bleeding," Hailey told the guard. "If it doesn't stop within the hour, he goes back to the hospital."

The guard shrugged.

Hal stepped forward, scanned his uniform, and paused on his name tag. "It's your responsibility, O'Malley, if something happens to him. You got it?"

The guard didn't make eye contact. "Got it."

Hailey passed her card through the bars to Robbins. "Call me if you need to."

Hal was already halfway down the hall when she caught up. His eyes were red and his shoulders hunched, but the anger seemed to have dissipated—for now. Maybe it was the alcohol, but she suspected something else was going on. Behind the steel doors, the elevator lurched and moaned somewhere below them.

Hal jabbed his thumb into the button a couple of times and then punched the steel door.

"You want to talk about it?"

"You know what I do sometimes?"

Hailey said nothing. It wasn't that sort of question.

He leaned in closer. "I go down to the file room and pull John's file."

She stumbled away from him. Reached for the wall for support.

"I reread it every couple of months to see if something new jumps out at me," he went on. "The way we always did the Silverstein case. And the Delgado one. Martin. Szczygiel. Farr. Remember all of them?"

His face blurred in front of her face. The air was thick and hot. Hailey willed the elevator doors to open as the machinery groaned from somewhere deep in the bowels of the building.

Hal reared back, jabbed a thumb into his own chest. "I've checked that file out nine times. Harrison's had it six. King's checked it out. Marshall. O'Shea. Pretty much everyone in the whole damn department." He paused. "Almost everyone—but you know who's never once asked to see that file?"

The file. Panic clenched her lungs. She'd never thought to pull the file.

"Never once requested the file to her own husband's unsolved murder?"

She went for the stairs. Heard Hal slam the door open behind her as she started to run down the stairs.

"You!" he thundered. "You have never pulled John's file. Not one goddamn time."

Hailey tripped and caught herself, ran on. He was on her heels. She could not outrun him. What did she tell him? What reason had there been to read John's file? She was grieving, consumed with guilt for loving another man when her husband died. She had done all she could manage just caring for her daughters, keeping her job.

No. He knew her too well.

She should have pulled that file. She should have scoured every lead, every piece of evidence.

He grabbed her arm, his fingers searing the skin. "You want to explain that to me?"

Hailey twisted herself free, turned away, and kept running.

"Do not walk away from me!" he yelled and the echo exploded off the concrete walls.

Hailey turned back, shaking. "You're drunk."

She flinched at his hard, sharp laugh.

"The rest of them might think you haven't pulled it because you're too grief-stricken—too fragile—but I know Hailey Wyatt." He jabbed his trigger finger into his chest. "I know you."

She shivered.

"So just answer one question, Wyatt," he demanded. "One fucking question."

She stood firm, her hand on the banister.

His voice dropped into a whisper. He pressed his hand down on her shoulder.

"How the hell did John really die?"

CHAPTER 17

THE ANGER BURNED through Hal like electricity, sparking at the hesitation in her eyes.

The lies.

"He was shot," she said.

He shook his head. ·

"By an intruder," she said, a tremor in her voice.

"Bullshit." The pieces fell together in his mind. John Wyatt was not killed by an intruder. Hal pushed past her, slammed up to the front desk, and retrieved his service weapon.

How long had he known it? Months. How long had he kept himself from recognizing the truth? To protect his partner. His friend. Lying to himself and everyone else.

He was done.

She could go to hell.

Hailey followed behind him.

His car was at the bar, but he'd find another ride. He was done with Hailey Wyatt and her lies.

Someone called his name. Sheila jogged toward them. He felt a sudden tightness in his belly.

Crazy Sheila.

Crazy, *hot* Sheila.

Hailey stopped beside him, the lies between them like angry static.

Hal focused on his ex-wife.

She was a beautiful woman. Thinner than she'd been when they were married—maybe too thin. The same wide amber eyes smiled at him. That smooth, perfect skin.

"Sheila." Hal motioned to Hailey. "You remember my partner?"

Sheila nodded but her eyes remained on Hal. "I was hoping I'd catch you. They told me you'd called about a guy being held in the jail, so I took a chance."

"You caught me, all right," he said. A charge passed between them as she touched his arm. "You can go on home, Wyatt."

"You need a ride," she said quickly. "Back to your car."

He met her glare with his own anger.

"I'll give him a ride," Sheila cut in.

Hailey would hate that. How she would hate him walking away from her. And worse, walking away with Sheila. She could stew in her lies and her deceit. She had it coming. "Yeah. Sheila can take me."

Hailey narrowed her eyes at him. A slight shake of her head. Hal ignored all the signs. Knew that she was telling him Sheila was a bad idea.

He didn't give a damn what Hailey thought.

Sheila moved in beside him. "He said you could go."

"I'll make it home, Wyatt," Hal said, lacing his arm over Sheila's shoulder.

As Hailey walked away from them, her heels clacked

on the cement. Hal didn't look back. "I could use a drink," he said.

Sheila squeezed his arm in excitement.

Already, Hal felt the slow onslaught of regret.

No. He'd been shot at, held at gunpoint, lied to.

Damn it, he deserved a fucking drink.

They ended up in a hole-in-the-wall bar a few blocks from his apartment. Sheila was playing the game hard. She ordered shots of Patron to remind him of their honeymoon and paid for them with cash so that he wouldn't remember the credit she'd charged up in his name.

She bought the first three rounds. After that, he had a vague recollection of pulling out his credit card. They walked home. She was first up the stairs. Moving slowly, seductively, she swayed her hips to hypnotize him.

It worked.

He fumbled to unlock the door, carried her inside, and kicked it closed.

This is a mistake. He slid his tongue into her mouth, palmed her backside, and lifted her up. She kissed his neck and trailed her fingernails along his shoulders and back.

He didn't care. Not tonight.

He dropped her in the center of his unmade bed and unbuttoned his shirt, watched as she shed her jacket, her sweater, her bra …

His face against the creamy skin of her neck, he inhaled the smell of her—rose water on her skin and gardenia in her hair. Smelled it and remembered the night they'd met, the morning he'd asked her to marry him, the drive from their wedding to the coast for their honeymoon.

Redwoods and dense fern, the sky threatened rain.

Sam Cooke blasting from the radio, the two of them laughing. He pulled the memories in, wrapped them between his fingers with her hair, and fought to let go of James Robbins and Blake and Fredricks.

Let go of Hailey Wyatt.

Some time later, he slept. An empty, dark sleep without dreams.

CHAPTER 18

TREMBLING, HAILEY MADE her way to the car, clenching her jaw and fists, holding it all in.

Losing John.

Losing Hal.

Hailey revved the engine and squealed out of the parking structure, opposite from where she'd left Hal and Sheila.

God, she was an idiot. She had driven away the one person she could trust completely.

And now she was stuck living with a liar.

Who knew how much of what Jim had said was lies. How could she trust him about the night John died?

"I don't know." Jim had said, carrying Ali. The shaking. Liz screaming. Jim shouting.

Then, John. The blood.

So much blood …

At the intersection of Van Ness and Broadway, Hailey hesitated. Why did Hal have to push? Why couldn't he be more like Bruce?

Bruce didn't want the truth. He clung to the hope

that they would end up together. That meant letting her keep secrets. Bruce knew that.

Only Hal forced it. He had always been subtle. Until tonight. Now all the things she'd worried about since John's death—they were all out.

Because she had never pulled his case file.

Never even thought to pull it.

Hailey turned toward home.

She needed to confront Jim—to see his face and gauge how many more lies were behind the ones she knew about.

She was not playing along anymore.

The house was dark when she parked in front. She wondered if the confrontation might have to wait until morning. She held the scrap of paper from Jim's shredder and the draft of the newspaper article by Donald Blake.

As she came back into the hall, Jim came down the stairs, his bathrobe tied sloppily across his middle.

"Couldn't sleep," he said, rubbing his eyes.

She held the sliver of paper in one fist, the letter in the other.

"What've you got?"

"Evidence."

He slipped his hand into the pocket of his robe. "You want to go downstairs?"

She followed him into the den.

Instead of sitting behind the desk, Jim sat in one of the big armchairs, the one closer to the place where John had died. That was how she thought of the chair.

She stood in front of him.

"What is it?"

She handed him the article and watched as he scanned the byline and the note. Then he read the article as though he'd never seen it before. Convincing.

But he read too quickly.

"Blake. You mentioned him earlier."

"You've never seen that before?" she asked.

"Never." His eyes didn't waver. Nothing moved in his throat. He didn't fidget or look away.

She lay the shredded piece on the photocopy and slid it across the page until it fit like a puzzle piece over the full picture. "I found this in your shredder."

"My shredder?"

"The one in your cabinet, Jim. Blake's family was killed in gang fire. After he wrote this. The dead gunrunner broke into Blake's house. Dennigs, Wesson, Fredricks. You, Jim. It's all related."

John. Was it possible John was part of this too?

She'd worked so hard to push the night he died from her thoughts. And now, it was right there. They'd been fighting. Jim and John. Jim had called something bullshit. Horse manure. He'd said, "That's a load of horse manure."

She pressed her palm to the painful pulsing in her chest. How she wanted to take the girls and leave. But where?

"I didn't kill Nick."

Nick. "But you haven't told me everything. You know more about his death."

"I had no reason to hurt him," Jim said. He didn't deny it. He did know more than he was saying.

She was done with him. "Don't bother trying to

convince me. From now on, Jim, don't bother. I'm going to tell Hal. All of it."

"All of it?" he repeated. The reference was to John. Not trusting herself to speak, she only nodded.

Dee appeared in the doorway. "You guys okay?"

"I need to go to the station for a bit," Hailey told her.

"Liz is asleep," Dee said. "I've got work to do, so I'll be up for a while."

Hailey didn't want to leave the girls. But she didn't want to wake them either.

"I can work in the kitchen in case someone wakes up," Dee said.

"I'll be back in an hour or two," Hailey said. "Are you sure you don't mind?"

"Not at all. I'll be up twice that long working on a budgetary proposal."

"You should go to bed, Jim," Dee told him.

Jim frowned but didn't argue. Instead, he padded toward the stairs.

Hailey forced herself to turn and leave.

As she drove down Broadway and through the tunnel, driving faster than she should have, she watched her rearview mirror. The tears welled up, burning in her eyes. She needed to talk, to let it out. How long had she held it all in?

As she made a left on Powell Street, the sobs came in a rush. She swiped at her eyes to clear her vision. How much she wanted to confide all of this in someone. Suddenly desperate to tell it, she turned again on Green and, when she was sure there was no one behind her, turned onto August Aly.

"I didn't kill Nick," Jim had said. No outrage at the implication that he was involved. No shock at the accusation. He had known she thought it. So why not tell her what else he knew? If he wasn't involved, who was he protecting? Dee had been in love with Nick. Surely he would want to find the person who'd killed the man she loved.

Parked in front of Bruce's building, she dialed his number.

"I'm downstairs," she said. "Will you come meet me?"

Quiet on the line.

Silence.

"Uh—" he finally said.

"I'm downstairs."

"Yeah," he said, clearing the sleep from his voice. "I can't."

"You can't—" Hailey gasped. "Oh. You're not alone." Then there was a woman's voice in the background, groggy, close to the phone. Curled against him.

"Are you okay?"

She didn't answer. Why was she surprised? He'd been with other women before. But after John's death, he'd promised they would be together. That he would wait for her to be ready.

"Wyatt?"

Still, she couldn't bring herself to speak.

"I'll see you tomorrow, okay? We can talk in the morning."

"Don't bother." She slammed her palm into the wheel, dropped the phone, and punched the dash. "Goddamn it!" The car shook beneath the weight of her anger, and she screamed until the sound stabbed in her throat.

The door of Bruce's building opened. He came out in jeans and a Cal sweatshirt—the same clothes he threw on after they'd been in bed together.

She revved the engine and peeled from the curb.

It wasn't Bruce she needed.

It wasn't Jim.

It wasn't even John. Bruce had been right about that. Her marriage with John hadn't been working.

Hal. It was Hal she couldn't lose.

She drove back down Broadway, the tears drying on her cheeks as her cell phone buzzed on the seat. Bruce. She didn't answer.

Not ready to go home, she went to the only other place she could think of. The station was quiet when she arrived, strangely calm. She parked in back, took her gun from the glove box, strapped on her holster, and got out of the car.

Music blared in the hallway of the basement. The door to Records sat open.

A lab tech stood at a counter, typing on a computer, bobbing her head in a way that should have made typing impossible. She had beautiful dark skin and amber eyes. Hailey recognized her from the other day, when Hailey had been pacing around the lab, waiting for the results on the prints from the button and from the letter Jim had received when he was shot. How much had changed since then. She'd trusted Jim then. She and Hal had been okay.

Hailey thought of Sheila and hoped Hal wasn't still with her.

The tech turned the music down.

Hailey showed her badge and introduced herself.

"I remember you from the other day," the tech said. "I'm Naomi Muir."

"I've got something I need to run against existing evidence. If you can tell Roger I left it for him?" Hailey pulled the cork from her pocket and handed it to Naomi.

"We're not testing for prints?" Naomi asked.

"No. Wine. I want to see if this is the same vintage as the one we've got in the Fredricks' case." Hailey gave her the case number, and Naomi wrote it on the outside of a paper sack, dropped the cork inside, and taped the top closed.

"You the contact?" Naomi asked.

"Tell Roger to call me as soon as he can. Only me."

Hailey had never made a request like that. Every piece of evidence always went to either her or Hal. It was always who was available first. What would happen if Roger questioned it? Or if Naomi didn't make it clear?

If Roger told Hal …

She'd have to come clean sooner than she'd planned. Either way, Hal deserved answers.

And she deserved the repercussions.

Naomi took down the instructions, confirmed her cell phone number, and put the bag in the plastic bin headed to the lab. As Hailey left, Naomi turned the music back on.

"Who is that?" Hailey asked.

"Velvet Underground," Naomi said. "Cool, huh?"

"Very," Hailey agreed, though she wasn't sure if it was cool or awful.

The door to Records was locked, so Hailey rang dispatch and asked them to page the on-call officer. When the officer showed up, he stank of cigarettes. He shivered and rubbed his hands together in the cold, foggy night air. "Always happens the minute I get outside."

"Sorry, Simon."

"No worries, Lady Wyatt. Who you here for?"

Hailey looked into the room, the metal shelves she'd stared at so many times, the case boxes she'd pulled and studied, created and added to. Closed. Left unclosed.

Simon cleared his throat and Hailey looked up.

"John Wyatt," she said.

Simon stepped backward, whistled, and spun on his heels. He took a couple of steps and began to skate down the cement floor. Heelys. She didn't know anyone still wore those.

Simon set a box on the counter, opened the book, and had her sign it out.

"You okay, Lady Wyatt?"

Hailey nodded.

"You take it easy now."

She nodded again, carried the box to the elevator, and rode it up to the fourth floor. Walking toward Homicide, she prayed she could get to one of the interview rooms unseen. The department was silent. She went straight to the far interview room and locked the door.

Sitting in a cold steel chair, she stared at the case information. The file number was printed on the front: H, for homicide, and the numbers 5987513.

Below that, John J. Wyatt.

She stared at the unopened box. His clothes would be inside. The slug they'd taken from the wall where it had sunk three inches after exiting his back, between the thoracic vertebrae T4 and T5, the shot a through and through. Entered the lower left side of his chest, punctured his lung, nicked his vena cava, and exited through his spine.

Photos of the scene, of him on the table.

The autopsy.

Before the funeral she'd opened his shirt to see the Y-shaped wound that Shelby Tate had so carefully restitched on John's chest. The red puckered stitches were purple and blue on the edges where the yellow thread bound them.

The blood had been cleaned off.

The pictures of him at the scene would be worse. Gory. Blood was everywhere. On the floor, his clothes, on all of them. Blood on her hands from trying to stop the bleeding.

Then, on his face when she'd held his cheeks and kissed him goodbye.

Her clothes would be inside the box too. The blouse she'd been wearing, her slacks.

Reports. Diagrams.

She could handle this. She had to.

The worst would be the pictures, but they were images she knew.

Images that followed her into sleep, and into waking, every day.

Hailey cut the seal on the box and pulled off the top. A thick brown folder sat on top.

She would do what she should have done a year ago. What she had forgotten to do. No. She had known this file was here. She had chosen to ignore it.

Because ignoring it was easier than reliving that night.

And now she had no choice. She had lost her partner. She had lost her best friend. She had to find a way to get him back, to make this right.

She took out the folder and set it on the table. She would read the entire file on John's death from page one.

CHAPTER 19

AT FOUR IN the morning, Hailey was still sitting in the empty interview room, mapping trajectories across the copies of the crime scene drawings from the file.

John was six-foot.

According to the autopsy report, the gunshot wound had an upward path of approximately fourteen degrees.

If John and his shooter stood close, the shooter was someone about John's height. The gun would have been held at chest level, aimed up slightly, raised toward the heart. Increase the distance, and maybe the shooter extended an arm.

Then, the angle might've flattened for someone his own height. There was no stippling around the wound, so the gun wasn't fired closer than twelve inches. If she took into account the blood spatter and the angle the slug made in the wall, there was a way to figure it out, but the measurements were complicated.

Using a small metal protractor and an old ruler on the photos, she couldn't be exact. On top of the poor tools, Hailey had never been good at math. In theory, she understood how this was supposed to work, but she couldn't do it. Not alone. Not without help.

She wanted to go over to ballistics and have them enter it all into the computer, run it. She wanted to fast-forward through the time it would take to have answers. Answers to questions she had waited more than a year to ask.

Nowhere in the file did the investigators make any supposition as to how tall the killer was, or how far away John had been from the bullet. But those details changed everything.

An intruder.

An average male.

Jim had requested the police leave their family out of it. For the sake of the grieving mother and the grieving wife, he had said. For the fatherless children. "For me. For all of us. Get what you need, ask your questions, and let us be."

The police had done that. Of course they had.

Senator Wyatt had asked.

They'd gathered evidence and talked to everyone who'd been there.

But the police only talked to everyone who had been there *in Jim's version*. In that version, Liz and the girls had been upstairs, getting ready for bed. Jim and Hailey were in the kitchen. John, alone, was in the study when the intruder had found him, shot once, and ran.

In Jim's version.

She closed the files and took her copies, returned the box, and went home.

Hailey would have to ask for help, something she

should have done over a year ago. Right now, the only answer she had was maybe.

Maybe it was Jim.

Maybe Jim had shot his son.

Dee was at the kitchen table when Hailey got home—now in her pajamas—working on her laptop. Printed spreadsheets covered the table. She removed her reading glasses and rubbed her eyes.

"The girls okay?"

"Not a peep. I looked in on them about an hour ago. Sound asleep."

"I love watching them when they're sleeping."

"They are precious. I used to babysit John when he was their age."

Hailey wondered if Dee had imagined she would have a family. If she'd planned one with Nick Fredricks. Maybe Hailey could find a way to ask.

She wondered how the evening had gone with Jim. Had they talked about Nick? No one knew them both better than Dee. "How did Jim and Nick get along?"

"They were both stubborn men with strong opinions, so they butted heads a fair amount." Dee closed the laptop. "I heard your conversation earlier. It isn't my business, but I want you to know that Jim and I were together when Nick was killed. But even if we hadn't been, Jim isn't a killer. He barely survived what he did to Dottie."

"Nick knew about that."

"I told Nick," Dee admitted. "Jim hasn't forgiven me for that."

"Nick used it in a letter to threaten Jim, just a few months before he was killed."

"I was cross with Nick for using that information," Dee admitted. "It wasn't appropriate. Nick sometimes had a different perspective on how to make things happen."

"You think maybe Nick did that to someone else and got himself killed?" Hailey asked.

"I think it's possible. I still think about it, even after all these years. Tom pointed it out the other night—I'd somehow ended up talking about Nick's death again. I'm sure it drives him crazy."

Did it bother Tom to hear about Dee's lost love? Would he be threatened by something so far in the past? Hailey thought of Bruce, the other woman. Was he still threatened by John? It would make sense. She could no longer recall all the things that had driven them apart. John's flaws had vanished in death. How could Bruce compete with that?

"But Jim didn't have anything to do with Nick's death. We were standing together when we got the news. I hadn't seen Jim that upset since Dottie."

Did that mean he wasn't guilty? Maybe. In twelve years, Dee had to have asked herself that question over and over. If she believed Jim might have been behind Nick's murder, surely she wouldn't be here, living in his house.

But even as Hailey closed her eyes to go to bed, she felt like she didn't know Jim Wyatt at all.

*

She arrived at the station at eight the next morning, after a sleepless night. In her notebook, she'd made lists of places she and the girls might stay so that they could get out of Jim's house. Already, she'd put in a call to the woman who used to watch the girls when they lived in Berkeley.

Twice before she'd left the house, Bruce had called. Twice he'd sent text messages.

She'd ignored him.

Marshall's door was closed when Hailey arrived, and she walked past, straight to her desk. Hal's coffee cup wasn't on his desk, but she didn't see him in the department.

As her computer booted up, Marshall's door opened. He peered out, his face angry.

He pointed to Hailey, curling his finger to beckon her in. Silent Marshall was bad news. Much better to hear him yell or curse. Anything but silence.

Hal sat in one of the old wooden chairs across from Marshall's desk. The other was vacant. Marshall pointed to it and she sat.

Hal held his head in his hands. Hailey started to feel sick.

What did Hal do?

Marshall ran his finger under the rim of his collar, took the knot in his fist, and pulled it loose. Then he twisted his hand under it to undo the top button. All the while, he stared at her. "Harris came in this morning to request a transfer."

"A transfer?"

"He wants a new partner."

Hailey felt a blush spread across her cheeks.

"Isn't that right, Harris?" Marshall pressed.

Hal lifted his head, sat up straight, and nodded. "That's correct, Captain."

"You know about this?" he asked her.

Hailey shook her head, couldn't find her voice.

"You're okay with it?"

No. Of course she wasn't okay. How could she be? How could Hal ask for this? How could he not give her a chance to explain? She studied Hal. The same Hal from last night. His expression was angry, but flat. Unreadable.

Marshall launched himself from his chair. "Somebody better start talking," he barked.

Someone outside his office dropped something. It broke. A string of curses followed.

"This isn't reality TV or a fucking soap opera. You don't just come in here and tell me you 'don't like your partner.'" He strung out the final words, using the mocking tones of someone whining. "You'd better have one hell of a reason."

Hal sat up. "I have reason to believe Inspector Wyatt hasn't been forthcoming about our recent cases. I can't have a partner who lies, Captain."

She felt as though Hal had struck her.

Marshall knocked his chair to the back wall and leaned across his desk. "You said that, Harris. But it doesn't mean shit until you tell me what you're talking about."

Hal shook his head and looked down.

"What about you, Wyatt? You want to explain what he's talking about?"

"I'm not sure, sir." She searched for a story, something harmless to confess. This was her reputation, her career.

"You're not sure," Marshall snapped. "So I'm supposed to get IA up here so we can dick around for the next month with microscopes up our asses?"

Nothing made Marshall angrier than the idea of

having Internal Affairs in his department's business. He pounded his fist on the desk, turned his back, and kicked the chair. It bounced off the wall and landed on its side.

He pressed both palms flat on his desk and lowered his voice. "I am not breaking up this team unless one of you has formal charges to bring against the other." He sighed and looked at each of them in turn. "You are my best team. This Dennig case is all over the goddamn papers. I've got City Hall and the chief on my ass twenty-four seven to solve this thing. Hell, even the mayor is calling from Sacramento. What do you want me to tell them? 'Sorry, Harris and Wyatt aren't getting along?' Do you have any idea what kind of shit storm that would cause?"

Marshall pulled his chair back beneath him and sat down. "Either of you got something to say?"

Hal shook his head.

"No, sir," Hailey said.

"Then, get out of here."

They both rose, but Marshall stopped Hailey. He waited until Hal had left the room and closed the door behind him.

"If you're holding something back, Wyatt—any-thing—I'll see that you can't get a job writing parking tickets in the Tenderloin. You hear me?"

"Yes, sir."

"Get the fuck out of here."

Hailey left. Just a few steps out of Marshall's office, the door slammed behind her, glass rattling, the captain cursing behind it.

Hal wasn't at his desk. Hailey sat, numb and shaky. Hal was ready to turn her in.

He was like family.

Had been like family.

Marshall's door flung open and he came out. His second button was undone, his tie gone completely. "We've got a one-eighty-seven at the Bank of America Center." Another murder. He pointed to Hailey. "Hedge fund manager." He looked at a piece of paper. "Guy's name was Harvey Rendell, runs Rendell Funds. You and Harris are on it. They found the same kind of button with the anti-NRA slogan. Get over there now and keep the connections under wrap. I want to know what the fuck's going on before the press does."

He walked into the center of the department's desks and turned a full circle with his hands on his hips. "Where the hell is Harris?"

"I'll find him." Hailey texted Hal with the details and retrieved her purse from her desk drawer.

Marshall waited a minute, and when Hal didn't appear, he shook his head, mumbled something, and walked back toward his office. "I want an update in an hour," he said before slamming his door again.

"Haven't seen him like that since the press caught Krantz boozing on the job," Kong said from his desk.

"Don't ask."

Hal was waiting in the hall. He dangled a set of keys casually and didn't meet her eye. How long could they go on like this? She tried to find a way to open the conversation.

He started down the hall. "I'm driving."

She followed him, but he was moving fast. He entered

the stairwell ten feet ahead of her. The door closed before she could reach it.

When she stepped into the dank, cement stairwell, Hal was already a full flight down.

He made no attempt to let her catch up.

CHAPTER 20

THE CAR RIDE was unbearably silent. Hailey was desperate to make amends. But how?

What could she offer Hal? He'd already said he didn't want to work with her.

She'd always been the one the others envied. How many people complained about lousy partners? She'd never had that with Hal. They'd always had a strong friendship, as well as mutual respect. They'd always had such easy synchronicity. He'd been her best friend, and then her family.

Hailey considered calling Jamie. They'd known each other since they were rookies, and the sex crimes inspector was both sharp and empathetic. But she'd been through enough. What Hailey needed was a sounding board, but how could she talk to anyone when there were too many things she couldn't say?

Too many secrets she had to keep.

Traffic was backed up because of the rain, which fell in sheets as they made their way, lights flashing, toward the Bank of America Center across town. Hal honked to hurry the particularly slow drivers out of his path.

One guy in a five-series Mercedes flipped them off, and Hal blared his horn.

"You're going to write him a ticket? Do we have time for that?"

"Asshole flipped off a cop."

One asshole to another.

If things didn't change between them, a transfer would be the only option. She wanted nothing to do with Hal when he was this angry. And he obviously didn't want anything to do with her.

A few blocks from the department, his cell phone rang. "Harris," he barked.

Hailey could tell from his expression that it was Sheila.

"I can't talk now," he said. "It was." Pause. "No, I mean it. Can I call you later?"

She saw the shame in his face. Damn it. He'd slept with her.

Would he have done that if he hadn't been so angry with her? Why should she care who he slept with?

But she did.

Not because she wanted to be with Hal. It had never been like that. But because he was the only adult on the planet she trusted.

He doesn't trust you.

That was on her.

When he hung up, Hailey turned to face him, searching for the right thing to say. The anger etched into his cheeks and brow shut her down before she could say a word.

He flipped on the radio and changed the channel by jabbing his thumb at the buttons as traffic crept forward.

A few minutes later, Hal grew impatient and turned on his siren so that people moved slowly out of his path. Traffic thinned out as they crossed Market Street, and the more speed they gained, the calmer Hal was.

Hailey felt angrier.

Hal had actually asked for a transfer. No one did that. It was career suicide—for both of them.

He wasn't entitled to know everything about her life. She didn't know everything about his. His father had been accused of accepting bribes, and Hailey had never asked Hal to defend his father. Never pressed him.

It was his business, not hers.

Now he had the Captain watching them. That was screwed up. God, she needed old Hal back.

They needed to break the awkward silence. "Hal."

"What?" he snapped.

"Please Hal," she tried again, her voice softer. "We need to talk."

"I got nothing to say."

"You're behaving like a child," she said. Immediately, she wished she could take the words back.

"Sorry I'm not up to your standards."

"Shut up, Harris. Just shut the hell up."

"Don't you—" Hal barked back as Hailey's cell phone rang. An East Bay number.

They both stared at it. Hal shrugged.

"Wyatt," she said, half expecting to hear Marshall, even though the call was coming from the wrong part of the bay.

"This is Bert Tomaso from Oakland PD, calling on Donald Blake."

"Thanks for calling back, Bert." Hal looked over, eyeing the phone. "I'm here with my partner, Hal Harris." The words came out a little rougher than she'd planned.

She punched the speaker button and held the phone between them.

"Hi, Hal," Bert said.

"This is Bert Tomaso from Oakland PD, regarding the shootings of Donald Blake's family," Hailey told Hal. "Bert. We're here."

"Sorry I didn't call sooner. We've had quite a week over here."

"Sixteen gang-related shootings in three days," Hal said. "I read about it."

"Yeah. A real mess," Tomaso sighed and Hailey realized she hadn't seen a paper in almost a week. "I hear you guys are working something related to the Blake family murders."

Hailey told Tomaso about the case, and Hal added that they'd learned Blake and his wife had been victims of the B&E committed by the dead gunrunner, Jeremy Hayden.

"I don't know anything about the B&E, but I still think about that murder case. You guys have one of those? One that won't leave you alone?"

"I've got one of those," Hal said. "A personal one."

"The Blake family. Wife and kids," Hailey said, cutting him off. "They were killed July of 2013, right?"

Hal shook his head. "August 2nd." Of course he'd remember.

"Right," Tomaso said. "Good memory."

"We got a copy of the file," Hailey said, "but we wanted your take on it."

"There's a lot that's not in the file, so it's better we talk."

"What do you mean?" Hal asked before Hailey could.

"Between you and me, Blake's car was forced off the road," Tomaso said.

"Forced off the road? You mean, before the shots?" Hal asked, pulling to the curb so he could give the call his full attention.

"Right," Tomaso said. "My theory is that two or three cars worked together to run the Blakes into the neighborhood where they were shot."

"Was the theory that—" Hailey started.

"You think Donald Blake was a specific target," Hal asked, cutting her off.

"Him or someone in his family, absolutely. My captain didn't agree. Didn't like what that would've implied. Better that we don't get people thinking they might be kidnapped off the highway and shot. Know what I mean?"

"He still there—that captain?"

"No," Tomaso said, the relief obvious in his voice. "Long gone."

"You were saying?" Hailey prodded. "About the car."

"Right," Tomaso continued. "The damage to the car corroborated my theory, and I had a homeless who witnessed it. Said it was a black car, that it tapped the bumper while another tan one rode alongside."

Her breath caught. "A witness?"

"Had," Tomaso said. "She disappeared two days

later. No trace. Her cart, all her stuff was there, but she was gone."

Homeless rarely abandoned their belongings without a fight.

Hailey sat back against the seat.

"Did you ever find the car that hit them?" Hal asked.

"Nope. Never found anything. I did some research on Blake, though, while he was in rehabilitation. Some shitty irony for a guy like that."

"And Donald Blake is also deceased?" Hal asked.

"Killed himself," Tomaso added. "Broke into the salvage yard where the police kept the car—the one his family was in when they were shot. He douses the car in gasoline, gets into the driver's seat, and lights it on fire."

"They sure it was Blake in the car?"

"Wasn't easy, but they ID'd him by a dental bridge. It's the worst case I ever worked," Tomaso added.

Hailey imagined a man so desperate that he'd lit himself on fire. It was awful.

"Damn," Hal said. "Anything about Blake stand out during the investigation? Any reason he would've been a target?"

"Not really. He worked in DC—low-level jobs mostly. He spent his free time running with a group that organized protests to push for gun control, but nothing that tied to any Oakland gangs."

The description reminded her of Fredricks, but Fredricks died in 2004. Blake would have been barely out of college then. Had their paths crossed?

"They lived in your neck of the woods for a while," Tomaso said, "then moved back to the East Bay."

"Right. We talked to the paper."

"You read his stuff?" Tomaso asked.

Hailey thought about the drafted article they'd received. "A little."

"He wrote almost exclusively about guns and gang violence, a lot about the problems over here."

"You think he was a target because of what he wrote?" Hal asked.

"No idea," Tomaso confessed. "I couldn't make it fit. Tried every damn thing, followed every trail—his colleagues, family, past jobs, everything. I wish I could be more help."

"No. This was useful," Hailey said. "Thank you."

Hal drove up California Street, crossed Battery and Sansome, caught the tail end of a yellow light at Montgomery, and stopped at the entrance of the Bank of America Center.

A uniformed security guard stood at the top of the driveway and told them to circle and enter on Bush Street. He was white-haired with a thick accent—Eastern European maybe. Hailey was bad with accents. Hal was good with them.

But he wasn't talking to her.

Hal flashed his badge, but the guard shook his head. "You've got to enter on the other side."

Hal swore under his breath and circled the block. Another guard, younger, with no accent—except maybe a trace of Jersey—asked for Hal's ID and studied it carefully.

These guys worked for the building, so the extra security wasn't for the murder scene. "Something going on in the building today?" Hailey asked.

"Standard since 9/11."

When the guard returned the badge, Hal drove down into the belly of the building and parked in a spot marked "Loading and Unloading Only."

A young guy jogged out of the small valet box. "Excuse me. You can't park there."

Hal stepped out of the car and flipped open his black badge. Then he tossed the kid his keys.

The kid fumbled and dropped them to the ground.

"Better not scratch it," Hal warned. "Belongs to the police department."

Hailey passed the guy as he picked the keys carefully off the ground and carried them to the small glassed-in guard's shed.

Hal was already walking into the stairwell when she entered the building. She followed him up to the mezzanine where they rode an escalator to the lobby.

At the entrance to the elevator bank was yet another guard who pointed them to the main desk to sign in.

"We don't have this kind of security in the damn jails," Hal muttered as they opened their badges for the guard at the desk.

"We're heading to a homicide scene on thirty-one," Hailey told him.

The guard nodded, took Hal's badge, and wrote down his information in slow block letters.

"You take down the information for the paramedics when they head up to save some guy having a heart attack?" Hal asked, the edge in his voice making the guard halt.

"I haven't heard of any heart attack today, officer." He passed the badge back and reached for Hailey's.

"Rendell Funds?" Hal said when he was done writing.

The guard pointed down the hall. "For thirty-one, take any of the elevators in the middle bank."

Hal frowned. Hailey knew he was thinking about the thirty-one floors he was about to ride up.

She walked past him, punched the button in the bank, and waited until the orange light lit. Hal got in behind her and stepped to the back of the box. As the heavy sway of gravity sank in her gut, Hal made a small, suffering groan behind her. She didn't turn back, instead watching the yellow lights above the door click off the floors until they stopped on thirty-one with a lurching halt.

Two uniformed officers stood in the hall, talking. Across the floor, a set of double glass doors read Rendell Funds in large, blue block letters.

"The building's on rollers," one of them was saying. "If there's a big quake, the whole thing just slides around."

The other one looked around. "I don't want to be up here when that shit's going on."

"Better than the whole thing breaking in half. That's what would happen without the rollers."

"One of you should be inside," Hal barked.

Both stood at attention. "There's an officer inside, Inspector."

"Then go back to the station. Go do something else. Don't sit up here fucking around," Hal mumbled, walking past.

"He doesn't like heights," Hailey explained, shrugging apologetically at them.

A length of yellow crime scene tape stretched across the top of the doorway. Hailey ducked beneath it, past a brass plaque on the wall beside the door that read, "Harvey Rendell, Rendell Funds."

Inside, Roger Sampers was heading up the evidence collection. His bald head and hairless face looked a strange shade of yellow under the office's halogen lights. A moment later, he crossed to her. "I got the cork."

Hailey saw Hal in the other room.

"Talk later?" Roger said as though sensing her unease.

"Yeah."

Hal watched them.

Roger stooped to talk to a tech collecting evidence around the secretary's desk with a red Dirt Devil.

Hailey joined Hal beside the corpse.

Rendell sat in his chair, his head lolling back, mouth open, eyes closed as though he were sleeping. He was a huge man—close to three hundred pounds.

Shelby Tate was taking photographs.

"Hey, Shelby."

"Hailey, good to see you. Been missing you at our dinners."

"I'll get back one of these days," Hailey said.

"I hope so."

"How did this guy die?" Hal interrupted, looking annoyed at the two of them.

Shelby gave Hal a sideways glance. "Secretary thought it was a heart attack until she saw the bottle."

"Bottle?"

Shelby nodded to the table where a plastic evidence

bag sat on the desk. Inside was an orange pill bottle, empty.

No prescription sticker on the outside.

"He had a pill caught in the back of his throat. I think it was Halcion," Shelby said.

"Halcion—that's—"

"A heavy narcotic," Hal said with almost the same tone he'd used with the officers in the hall.

Shelby raised her eyebrows and turned to store her camera in a gray canvas bag.

"I was going to say it was the same stuff used on the Dennigs," Hailey said.

Hal didn't acknowledge her. "How do you know he didn't OD?" he asked, turning toward Shelby.

"Well, it was meant to look like one," Shelby said, unzipping the body bag. Two paramedics lowered the body into the bag. "He was smothered, actually," Shelby went on. "Heavily drugged first. Maybe he wasn't dying fast enough."

"Or maybe the perp figured it was going to take more Halcion than what he had to kill the guy," Hailey said.

Hal looked down at the huge man. "Like maybe the killer had never seen Rendell before?"

"Maybe."

"Where's the secretary?" Hal asked, looking around the room.

"We sent her out for a cup of coffee," Roger said, walking back to them, glancing at his watch. "She was screeching too loudly to get anything done. She should be back here soon."

"You sent her out for coffee?" Hal said.

"I sent her out with one of my people. I'm not an idiot, Harris."

Hal nodded, stepped back. "Of course not."

Hailey put some distance between her and Hal as they watched the lab techs work the room. Soon, they'd be able to look around, but Roger guarded his crime scenes like a sentry, and he insisted his team do the initial sweep without interference.

Plenty of crime scene leads had been ruined by the nasty business of evidence chain of custody. Evidence had to be tracked from the initial scene through a multi-step process. If you overlooked anything, then the evidence might become inadmissible during the trial. When the investigators wanted their man convicted—and they all did—they knew better than to interfere.

"You guys can start with the files," Roger said after a few minutes. "I still want the area around the body clear."

Hailey and Hal snapped on latex gloves and moved to opposite ends of the room, starting in on the file cabinets. The first drawer she opened was client files, beginning with "T."

Each had a white label with the first and last names of the client, an account number, and a date that Hailey assumed indicated when the account was established. Tanner, Mark and Christine, had been clients for three years. Inside the file were records of trades, deposits, and withdrawals. Each page had been signed by Rendell. The file also included check stubs from disbursements and copies of client deposits.

From the looks of it, Rendell kept meticulous records. The older files were bigger. One from 2000 contained trade confirmations that were fifteen years old. "This guy kept everything."

"Here too," Hal said. "Don't usually see these guys hang onto stuff longer than the law requires."

"Even that's sometimes a stretch," she said.

"Why keep them?"

"Don't know. The IRS requires you keep records seven years, but the statute of limitations for prosecuting criminal charges is usually longer," Hailey added, feeling some of the familiar rapport return between them. "Better to dump everything right at seven than risk having something farther back getting used against you."

The two worked in silence for a few minutes, until Hal called, "I've got something."

He held a file marked with Abby and Hank Dennigs's names. "Filed under 'R.' Her maiden name. There's one for Tom Rittenberg too."

He set the file on the top of the cabinet and let it fall open. The page on top was dated November 9, 2010. He flipped through the stack and turned to the back as Hailey watched over his arm. The last page was dated January of 2004.

"Nothing since 2010?"

He went back through the middle of the file again. "Doesn't look like it."

He pulled the pages out of the folder. Maybe two inches of paperwork, but the faded bottom of the green hanging folder was worn, its perforations looked stretched to three inches or more.

"Someone cleaned it out."

"We'll need to collect anything in the garbage and the shredder," Hal said to Roger.

Roger nodded. "It's already done, and I've got someone trying to find out where the trash goes from here. If it's not at the dump yet, I'll get it."

Naomi Muir stood in the doorway. "We found a safe out here."

"Let's call someone in to break it," Roger said.

The partners continued searching the cabinets, working in silence for almost fifteen minutes.

"Hailey," Hal said, almost a whisper. He drew the file out, set it on the cabinet between them, and held his palm flat on top of it. His hand covered almost the entire front surface. Between his fingers, she saw the name on the file—Wyatt.

"Oh, Hal," she whispered.

Hal moved his hand from the file. The first page was a copy of a check for twenty thousand, written last month and signed by Jim.

"I'm so—"

Hal returned the page to the file, his jaw tense as he slammed the file closed. "Maybe Marshall will give me that transfer now."

Hailey tried not to flinch. "Maybe he will."

Hal walked away, and she pressed her forearm against the cold metal, checking her phone while her thoughts raced. She was alone now. She couldn't trust Jim, and she had alienated Hal. Bruce was with someone else. She could do this alone. She needed to find a place for the girls. To keep them safe.

No word from the girls' old babysitter. They'd be out

of school in a couple of hours, and she still had nowhere to take them.

"You guys probably want to come have a look at this," Roger called from the other room.

Keeping distance between them, the two followed Roger through the outer office and into a small adjoining kitchen. The freezer door was open. Cold smoke billowed out into the warm room. The freezer was empty, except for two trays of ice.

On the kitchen table a small blue plastic box was laid out on a sheet of plastic, its lid open.

Inside were a half dozen of the buttons.

Without looking, Hailey knew they read "Wage Peace, Not War." Roger lifted a plastic sandwich bag from the box.

The plastic was fogged from the freezer. Whatever was inside looked vaguely like a cork.

Hailey found it hard to swallow.

Shelby entered the room, and they all stood over Roger as he opened the bag. Hailey leaned forward and looked in. It wasn't a cork. It was the tip of a finger.

"Jesus Christ," Shelby whispered over her shoulder.

"Or Nicholas Fredricks," Hailey said.

Hal nodded, staring at the frozen finger. "That would be my guess."

CHAPTER 21

WATCHING ROGER PACK up his team, Hailey started to get antsy. She didn't want to talk about that cork over the phone, and Hal was watching her now. She'd have to follow Roger out, make an excuse to leave Hal.

She would have to lie.

Again.

She'd tell him as soon as she was sure. She swore to herself. As soon as she was sure the girls were safe.

"I'm going to head out if that's okay," Hailey said. One of them had to stay and wait for the safe breakers, but it wasn't going to be her.

"Where to?" Hal asked. He gave her his full attention. Arms crossed, leaned against the wall.

"Picking up the girls from school."

"You'll be back?"

Roger walked out.

Hailey started past Hal.

"You coming back?" he said again, louder.

She didn't stop. "I'm not sure. I'll have my phone."

Only one officer stood in the hallway now. "You can probably go," she said. "Check with Inspector Harris."

"Harris," he said. "He's the—"

"The big guy. The angry one."

The officer nodded but didn't make a move. Maybe he figured it was better to stay put rather than deal with Hal.

Smart choice.

Hailey caught Roger at the elevator. The tech, Naomi Muir, was with him. The two of them discussed evidence priority on the ride down. As the elevator settled on the ground floor, Hailey inhaled deeply.

Roger was going to have questions too.

She wouldn't ask him to lie for her. If the cork matched, they'd get the information to Kong and O'Shea. They could get a subpoena for Jim's house and collect their own cork. Jim had at least half a case of the wine left.

"I need to speak to Inspector Wyatt a moment," Roger told the tech, turning towards Hailey.

"I'll take the evidence and meet you at the van," Naomi offered.

"It'll be only a few minutes," he added, waving over his shoulder.

Hailey and Roger walked slowly across the lobby toward the door to Kearney Street. Rain fell in a light mist. Roger looked longingly outside.

Gearing up to deliver bad news, maybe.

Hailey held herself still.

It wasn't like him to avoid a conversation, which meant he was struggling with something. She and Roger had always worked well together. She respected him and he her. Or at least, he had.

"I'm sorry if I put you in a bad position," she said.

He sighed. "What's going on, Hailey?"

"I'm chasing a theory. About Jim Wyatt."

"Your father-in-law?"

"Yes."

"The corks are the same," he said.

"How certain are you?"

"Very," he said. He touched her arm.

She nodded, grateful that he didn't say it, that he didn't try to console her with words.

"Clearly it's the same wine," he continued. "We know that from the cork design. St. Jean has up to eight red varietals, depending on the year. If you're dealing with the same varietal, then you get into vintage differentiations, which can be enormous, as well as some minimal barrel distinctions within a single vintage. Those are less obvious but still present. But I tested the two corks and the wine on each is from the same varietal, the same vintage ..." He paused. "It's possible that the two bottles even came from the same barrel, but I can't be certain."

The same barrel. Jim was involved. For all the times she'd thought "maybe," now it seemed clear. He wasn't a killer. She couldn't believe that. But he wasn't innocent either.

Hal had been right.

"How many bottles does a barrel hold?" she asked.

"A barrel is sixty gallons so it holds twenty-five cases, three hundred bottles."

"Twenty-five cases," Hailey repeated.

"Assuming the bottles are bought by the case—I don't know the percentages on that because the distributors sell them as cases, but most stores sell them individually."

Jim bought them in cases.

"It's the 2010 Chateau St. Jean Cinq Cepages," she said.

He nodded and rubbed his eyes.

"So the wine is the same varietal, same vintage, but we're not sure about the barrel."

Even if it wasn't the same barrel, they were talking about one wine. One specific vintage. The wine Jim drank most nights. Even if he drank only three bottles a week, he would go through one hundred and fifty bottles a year. They would surely come from different barrels, just by chance.

Somehow Jim was at the center of this thing.

"Right," Roger agreed. "For one thing, it's impossible to tell how much the wine was affected from being in the coffin. I assume quite a bit of mold was present."

"There was," she said.

"I wouldn't testify to them being the same wine." He paused. "At least not based on the chemistry of the samples. The cork samples tell a similar story. It's real cork, from a cork tree—there's a move now towards man-made material for corks—" He stopped, waved his hand. "You know all that."

Hailey nodded. Endangered cork trees.

"The nutrients in the soil will create variations in the cork even from trees as close as six or eight feet away—some within a single tree."

Hailey looked away, dreading what he would say.

"These two samples come from the same tree," Roger said. "The same vineyard would get corks from the same place, so again there's still a possibility that those corks came from two different barrels of wine. Even if they're both from the same barrel of wine, that fact doesn't necessarily link them to a single wine drinker."

She thought it did. She felt sure of it. "Is there anything else we could test? To be sure?"

"Not one hundred percent. Not from the wine or the corks. There was one other thing that suggested the same source."

She waited.

"Both cork samples showed an odd angle of wine absorption."

"What do you mean—absorption?"

"A tiny bit of wine gets into the cork—it's very slow and very minimal, but you do find minute samples of wine that are absorbed over time."

"From storing them on their sides."

"Right. People who know wine store the bottles horizontally."

"These were stored like that? On their sides?"

"Actually, what's interesting is that both of these cork samples came from bottles stored at a slightly declined angle—that is, more declined than ninety degrees."

Jim's bottles were stored in a dank, cement room in the basement, a room that reminded her of a prison cell. It was no larger than five by five, and the door was made of thick oak beams, a flat iron bar across the top and bottom and a heavy iron ring to pull it closed.

Hailey had always wondered where it had come from, what castle—or maybe what dungeon.

Hand-carved alder racks lined the walls of the wine cellar, each bottle cradled and each neck supported at the same angle. One that was pointed down—maybe five or ten degrees more than ninety.

"The same angle on both," Hailey repeated, feeling the finality of the words.

"Are you okay?" Roger asked.

"I will be." She glanced across the lobby, thought about getting home. "I've got to go now."

"What do I do about the cork?"

A woman in a suit stepped out of the elevator and glanced over at her, then away. Something in her stride reminded Hailey of how she saw herself—strong, focused. Suddenly, Hailey no longer felt like that woman. "Tell Hal."

"What?"

"Tell him. Call and tell him about the cork. He'll know how to handle it."

"Don't you think it should come from you?"

She looked at Roger, at the furrow of his naked brow. She didn't think Hal would stop being angry at her long enough to listen. "Not this time."

"What's going on with you two?"

Hailey didn't answer.

"Are you okay, Hailey?"

"I'm fine." The answer came too quickly. Roger didn't push.

"You want me to tell him that you said to call him? So at least he knows you weren't keeping it from him?"

Hailey shrugged again. It wouldn't matter.

It was too late.

CHAPTER 22

HAL WAS NO idiot. Hailey had gone after Roger.

The way she dropped everything, the urgency in her voice, the way she evaded his questions—he could still read her like a book.

Add that to the list of stuff she was keeping from him.

His anger was like an acid, burning through everything he came across. After twenty-four hours, it had started to burn through itself. What remained was disappointment, betrayal. He needed to go for a run—to sweat—but he was stuck at the scene where their best evidence required a forensic accountant.

One named Tiffany was already at work on Rendell's books. Arriving in jeans and a button-down white shirt, her hair in a ponytail, Tiffany looked about twelve.

"It was my day off," she said before making herself at home at the secretary's desk.

"We'll need to go through all the books, but right now, I'm most interested in his payroll," Hal told her. "I need to locate someone who worked here. Home addresses and contact numbers would really help."

Hal paced the worn blue carpet in front of the desk

and stopped to stare at a panoramic photograph hanging on one wall, the only art in the room. Maybe four feet long and a foot and a half wide, the image was of a mountain range he didn't recognize. Jagged, sharp mountain peaks cut into the red-orange sky of sunset. The tallest mountain looked like a shark's tooth, hooked to the left.

"Tetons," Tiffany said.

"What?" Hal asked.

"The mountains—they're called the Tetons. Big one is the Grand. In Jackson." When he didn't respond, she added, "Wyoming. Great skiing."

"Never been skiing," Hal said.

"You ought to. It's awesome."

Hal studied the mountains. Nothing about skiing seemed awesome, only cold. But what did he know? He'd never been closer to Lake Tahoe than Sacramento.

Hal sat in an uncomfortable metal-framed chair opposite Tiffany.

"He kept good books on some things. Client funds are all clearly denoted, as are payables. But, there's no payroll system."

"Maybe it's on another computer."

"But there are no records of payroll deductions in his books. He'd have to denote them somewhere."

The secretary didn't work for free.

Hal hadn't seen her yet. They'd taken her for coffee, to calm her down. Why weren't they back yet? "Damn it. How is it possible to have employees and no payroll?"

Tiffany shrugged. "There are lots of ways to do payroll."

"What do you mean? He had to pay his secretary. Where are those entries?"

"I think he paid her. It just doesn't look like Mr. Rendell believed in the traditional W-2 system," she explained. She swiveled the monitor toward him and pointed to a line item for $32,000. "Twice a month, he took out big chunks of cash."

"He paid his employees in cash?"

"Looks like it." She scrolled down the page, pointed to another debit for $28,000 two weeks prior, and then another debit farther down for $40,000.

Hal came around the desk as she clicked through the records. "It's just about twice a month. The twelfth and the twenty-eighth last month." She brought up the calendar on her phone. "Twelfth was a Wednesday. Twenty-eighth, a Friday."

She scrolled through the numbers, jotting them on her notepad. "No real pattern in the last six months. Can't tell if the secretary makes fifty thousand a year or a hundred and fifty. And other employees—" She shook her head.

"He pay anyone?"

She nodded and launched a program called Sage Pro. "Like I said, some of the accounting is really good. Phone bills, cell phones—two cell phones." She looked up.

"Maybe one for him and one for the secretary?"

"I'll get the numbers." She scrolled down. "There's a printing service—probably does prospectus mailing and stuff." She nodded to the screen. "Lease expense is here, his credit card." She double-clicked. "He's got it itemized. Meals and entertainment, travel."

"Where did he go?"

"One ticket to New York on this statement. Stayed at Trump Tower." She closed the Visa information and continued down. "Here's a company listed under security—Security Specialists. Maybe that's where he got his employees." She opened up the account detail. "He paid them $60,000 a couple months ago."

"How far back do the credit card records go?"

"As far back as he's been entering the data." She went back to the check register and dragged the scrollbar up to the top of the page. "Looks like he started in October of 2014, so he's got records for almost two years."

"What about before that?"'

She shook her head. "No way to know without taking the computer in and digging around. Nothing in the file cabinets?"

He gestured to the laptop. "Mind if I look?"

"Be my guest."

Hal took the mouse and scrolled through the register. The first large transaction was in the amount of $72,000. November 10, 2014. "What is that?"

"Cash withdrawal. No details." She glanced up at him, eyes narrowed. "Why? What does it mean?"

"What day was November 10th?" He paused. "In 2014, I mean."

"It was a Monday. Why?"

"The Dennigs—" She nodded, waiting. "They were murdered on Tuesday, the 11th."

His phone buzzed. Sheila. He silenced the phone and slid it into his pocket.

He was angry he'd slept with her. He knew better. He hadn't been that drunk. There had been plenty of time to change his mind.

Worse, he'd taken her to the Tempest, just two blocks

from his house. That bar was his refuge. Now she knew where to find him.

At least he'd had the sense to wear a condom.

This morning, after she left, one of the kitchen drawers was open, and his set of spare keys was missing.

The professional safe breakers arrived, jerking Hal back to the present.

He retreated into the hallway to escape the noise, his head still pounding. Rendell's secretary came off the elevator a few minutes later, followed by one of Roger's techs, who looked exasperated.

"Miss Riley," Hal said, stepping forward. "I'm Inspector Hal Harris."

The tech gave him a brief nod of acknowledgement and stepped back onto the elevator.

"Call me Tammy," the secretary said, her cheeks pale, the skin a flawless cream except for the small, round spots where she'd applied a glittery blush. Her brown eyes were lined in black, and her mascara had melted into the space under her lower lashes and in the corners of her eyes.

"Can we talk for a few minutes?"

Her gaze skittered toward the door, and she whispered with a hiccup, "Is he still in there?"

Hal nodded. "He'll be coming through soon." When she gasped, he added, "He'll be in a bag, though." She nodded and backed to the far corner of the elevator lobby, where she glanced lovingly at the Smith Barney doors as though she'd always wished she worked there instead of for Rendell.

"We didn't find any employee files in the office," Hal said. "Were you the only one he had working for him?"

She shook her head and dotted her eyes again. "There was one other."

"In the office?"

"No. Well, he came in sometimes but not very often. Harvey couldn't stand having him here, so he was mostly in the field. That's what Harvey called it, 'the field.'"

Hal opened his notebook. "What was his name?"

"Gordon." She paused to think. "Gordon Price."

"Why didn't Harvey want Price in the office?"

"He was sort of conspicuous—if you know what I mean."

Hal shook his head. "I don't."

The secretary flushed, looking at the floor, away from Hal. By conspicuous, maybe she meant black.

"And he had this annoying habit of flipping his retainer around his mouth. It would click against his teeth. Drove Harvey crazy."

"A retainer," Hal repeated. Clicking. Tawny Robbins had said the man who shot James and his friend clicked. "You have an address for Mr. Price?"

"I think I can find it."

"Excellent."

Hal entered the empty lobby, Price's address in hand. In one corner was a sign for the stairs—a stick figure walking down a crude drawing.

He didn't have time for thirty flights of stairs. He had a man with a retainer to find.

Inside the elevator, Hal pushed "L" for lobby, then closed his eyes.

CHAPTER 23

HAILEY LEFT ROGER with questions. She couldn't face them, or the answers she would have to give. Not when she should have been asking them all along. Why hadn't she demanded more answers from Jim? She'd taken so much for granted.

No wonder Hal was so angry.

She caught a cab on California Street and gave the driver her address, asking him to please hurry.

She still had time to get home, pack a bag, and get to the girls' school before the release bell.

She dialed Jim's line at the house. Dee answered, but Hailey didn't make small talk. She had about forty-five minutes before Liz and the girls arrived at the house. "Is he there?"

"Yes," Dee replied. "Hold on."

A moment later, Jim came on.

"You know Harvey Rendell?" she asked.

"I do. He's a fund manager."

"He's dead."

The driver glanced into the backseat.

Jim made a funny sound, something in his throat. "Dead?"

Dee spoke in the background, and Jim snapped at her. "How?" he asked.

"Someone fed him Halcion and smothered him."

"Halcion? Isn't that—"

"Same thing the Dennigs got." Before Jim could speak, she added, "You're a client."

"Yes." The word came out in a hiss of breath, an admission. The deflation in his voice was a concession, and she'd push it as far as she could. "So were the Dennigs and Colby Wesson." Hailey paused a beat to let that sink in. "They're all dead, Jim. And you haven't been honest. You're involved in this somehow."

"Of course I'm not."

"You were invested with Rendell. You got a button. Someone shot at you. That's no coincidence."

"I'm insulted that you would imply—"

"I don't care if you're insulted," she said, cutting him off. "If I were you, I'd be less worried about your ego and more concerned about ending up in prison."

She ended the call before Jim could say anything more, staring out the car window at the houses she'd passed a thousand times. Not all the homes were mansions—two thousand and three thousand square feet, but they cost millions of dollars. Three, five, eight million. Inside lived investment bankers and high-priced attorneys, people who made seven figures each month.

How had she lived here this long?

She would find a place where people like her lived.

Real people.

As often as possible, Hailey took the girls out of her in-laws' neighborhood, away from the San Francisco mansions, and brought them down to the new theaters on Harrison Street or the old ones down in the Marina, winding their way back through neighborhoods where she hoped to one day afford a place of their own.

The girls didn't need this much. Hailey could give them enough on her own.

Her phone buzzed. *Jim.*

"I referred clients to Rendell," he told her. "I don't think that's a crime."

The cab passed a house that had once belonged to Danielle Steel until she'd moved up a few blocks to one three times its size. Now some lowly surgeon owned it. "Did you refer Wesson?"

"I don't know Wesson. I don't know what's happening here, Hailey. I honestly don't."

"But?"

"Rendell supported my campaign."

"You mean in exchange for referrals to his hedge fund?"

He paused and then uttered a sigh. "Something like that."

But Rendell wasn't just looking for any referrals. He had targeted people who were closely involved in the manufacture and sale of guns. Why? And what about the hedge fund had appealed to those people? "Why did all the gun guys support the hedge fund? And why would you? You've always been for stricter gun control."

Jim's chair creaked. She imagined he would have his free arm extended out over the armrest, his hand relaxed at the wrist, his feet stretched out in front of him, legs crossed at the ankles.

After a particularly long day, John had sat like that too, oftentimes, holding a scotch in one hand. It was one of those habits passed from father to son, so that being with Jim meant being with John's memory too. "Rendell liked the gun guys, as you call them. It's why he asked to meet Rittenberg in the first place. Rendell networked through the NRA. I just made the introductions."

"Not *just,* Jim. You invested too."

"For a while, I did."

"Not just a while." There was a brief break in the line as Hailey added, "Recently."

"Hailey?"

"I'm here." Hailey listened to the silence on the other end, wondered what he was doing. "You sent him a check for $20,000 last month. He's got a copy of it in your file." No clicks, no breathing. "Jim?" The cab pulled behind a garbage truck, blocking the driveway.

"I'll get out." She paid the driver. "Jim?"

"Yes. Sorry," he said, his voice almost a whisper. "Can I call you later?" he asked.

"Jim, this is serious. People are dying and you're involved."

"I am not," he said, the same stern voice he used to stop the girls when they ran through the house or played too loudly. Then, his voice softened, the volume dropped. "I will call you back."

"You can try my cell phone, but I'm heading to a scene."

"I'll call you." The worry in his voice was unmistakable.

It made her worry for herself, for the girls. Out of the cab, she pulled her purse strap onto her shoulder and hurried to the sidewalk. Rain fell in heavy drops from the oak trees above. Under the loud hum of the garbage truck engine was the whisper of water rushing in the grate at the curb, streaming under the streets from the hills above, racing toward the Bay.

She prayed Liz would be out. This was the time of day when she normally did her errands or met a friend for lunch. She was in a garden club and had a standing bridge game. Then, she would pick up the girls from school and spend the afternoons catching up on household tasks so she could be home with the girls after school.

A horn honked from the street as a tan Taurus pulled into the shallow driveway.

Hal.

She felt overwhelming relief. They would work through this.

He hadn't given up on her.

A blond head appeared in the window.

Not Hal.

Bruce.

He raised his palm in a wave, rolled the window down.

Hailey stopped at the car and glanced at the street. Liz might be home. Anyone could show up. "What are you doing here?"

"Hal told me you were picking the girls up and coming home." He looked up at the house. "They here?"

"You talked to Hal?"

"Yeah," he said. "I had a long talk with Marshall too."

Marshall. Hal's transfer request. Bruce was internal

affairs. He wasn't here about whatever woman he was sleeping with. He was here about Hal. She had to pack a few things, go pick up the girls. "I can't do this now, Bruce."

"You don't have a choice."

Her stomach washed with anger. "I have a choice."

"Your captain called me, Hailey."

"Did he?"

Bruce nodded slowly.

"And did you tell Marshall that you can't handle my case?" she asked. "That it's a conflict of interest because we used to sleep together?" She drew out the words "used to." She and Bruce were over. Living with Liz and Jim was over.

Being partners with Hal was probably over too.

Bruce cracked his door open.

Down the street, an engine revved. "Don't."

A blonde drove by in a convertible Mercedes—cherry red—her hair held back by a Hermes scarf. Hailey recognized the style because she had one just like it in her own closet, one she'd never worn.

"Why don't you sit down for a minute so we can talk. I'll make it quick," Bruce suggested. "Or we could go somewhere else."

"I don't have time." She checked the time on her phone. Forty-five minutes before the girls were released from school.

"A minute," he repeated, reaching out to touch her.

She pulled out of his reach. "One minute."

As she came around to the passenger side, Bruce leaned across to release the door handle. She sat on the cool vinyl seat. The car smelled of pine air freshener and a male smell—deodorant or aftershave. But it didn't smell like Bruce's—at least not the one she knew. She had the urge to lean in and smell him.

But he was with someone else.

Maybe Bruce changed his scent for whoever he was with now. She felt sick.

How long had it been going on? She was cold. She didn't care. She did, but she couldn't. She needed to focus on the girls, then the case. Keep them safe and save her job.

"What did Marshall say?" she asked.

Bruce shifted sideways in the seat. "Can we talk about last night first?"

"There's no need."

"We need to clear the air. About us."

"There is no us, Bruce."

"We need some time alone, just the two of us." He ignored her words. He did that when he didn't like what she said. He always had. Why hadn't it frustrated her before?

"It's been a minute."

"You're angry about last night."

"No. I was … surprised, but I'm okay. Really."

"It wasn't anything serious. Just a woman I sometimes spend an evening with …"

She stopped him. "It's not because of last night. I'm glad you have someone, Bruce. Really, I am. You deserve it."

And it was true.

How many times had she left Bruce and gone home

to John, wishing Bruce would meet someone? That he would force an end to the relationship so that she didn't have to?

"Why are you doing this, Hailey?" He leaned forward and lowered his voice. "John is dead. Nothing is going to bring him back."

Hailey looked at Bruce, at the narrow slope of his nose and the wide arc of his brow, his green eyes, the lips she'd felt a hundred times.

It wasn't there.

She didn't feel it anymore. Not the same way. "I'm sorry."

He tensed. *He has a right.* He'd been patient, waited.

It didn't change anything. She didn't want to be with him. Not anymore. "Maybe we should talk later."

"No." He blew out his breath.

She ran her nail down the crease in her pants, traced the tear-shaped drops from the rain. "I need to go."

"Marshall thinks you know something about John's death."

Her fingers froze. Her throat tightened. "What?"

"Hal Harris thinks your father-in-law might've been involved."

Her mouth went dry. "Involved in killing his son? His own son?" She fought to swallow. "That's outrageous."

Damn Hal. Damn him. She fumbled to open the door.

Bruce grabbed her shoulders, held her. "Wait."

She twisted to free herself. "Let me go." She couldn't talk about this, couldn't face him. What could she say?

She knew Jim had nothing to do with John's murder. At this point, it was the only thing she *did* know.

"Hailey, wait. Please wait."

"I can't, Bruce. I can't." Hailey loosened his grip and took hold of the door handle.

And cracked the door open.

Glass shattered.

Gunfire exploded from behind. Hard pellets struck her neck and head. She dropped to the floor in front of her seat and fumbled for her weapon.

Tires squealed on the asphalt.

She released the safety and ducked out of the door. Using the car as a shield, she aimed where she'd heard the tires. A long set of skid marks trailed away from the house—ten, maybe twelve feet.

The car was gone.

"Shit." She dug through her purse for her phone. That bullet had almost hit her. They weren't aiming at Bruce. They were aiming at her. "I'll call for backup."

She looked at Bruce, still sitting in the driver's seat. He didn't move. His eyes were wide, stunned. His hand clutched his neck. His face went white. His pupils ballooned. The left was larger than the right. "Bruce?"

She crawled across the seat to reach for him. Gripped his hand, fingered his neck.

His hand went limp in hers. Darkness pooled in his palm, dripped between their fingers. "No! Bruce!"

His eyes fell closed, and his entire body went slack.

CHAPTER 24

IF HAL WAS going after Gordon Price, he needed probable cause. A retainer wasn't going to be enough to make an arrest.

Ideally, they could match Price's DNA to the rebar outside James and Tawny Robbins's apartment.

But this wasn't *CSI*.

DNA took weeks. He'd have to settle for some of Gordon Price's fingerprints in Rendell's office. He called the lab for Roger.

"You just missed him," the tech said. "He was here almost twenty hours and went home to get some sleep. He left a report for you—results on some cork."

"Must be from Fredricks," he said.

"I've got no idea. I didn't work it."

"That's okay." The cork could wait. Right now, he wanted to get his hands on Gordon Price. "I'll come by for that later. I'm calling on the scene from today—the Rendell murder."

"Yeah, we're working that one now."

"You have any hits on prints?" he asked.

"Yeah—Naomi's working that. Hang on."

There were a series of clicks and then a pause before someone else picked up. "This is Naomi."

"Hey, it's Hal. You doing prints from the Rendell murder?"

"That I am. About halfway through."

Hal circled the back of the station and turned into the parking lot driveway, his wipers squeaking against the dry glass. "You find a match to a Price? Gordon Price?"

"Hang on." There was a pause and Naomi started listing names. "Tammy Myers."

"She's the secretary," Hal said.

"Darryl Strong, Mitch Jackman, Thomas White, Angel Desantos …" She stopped and whistled. "Here we go. William Gordon Price. That the one?"

"That's him."

"Nice clean set on that guy," Naomi said. "He was there recently."

"That's just what I needed. Thanks."

"No problem, Inspector."

Hal drove from the lot, dialing Hailey's number from habit. He ended the call, hoping it hadn't rung on her end, and made a call to dispatch to request backup at Price's apartment. They had to move now, in case Price decided to run.

"Tell them to wait a couple blocks off," Hal said. "I'll radio when I'm there. Don't let them proceed without me." Hal turned on his lights and blared the siren as he raced toward Price's apartment.

In the department Taurus, the lights were hidden under the passenger's sun visor. Even with the visor down, the reflection of blue and red on the windshield always made him dizzy. Hal spotted Price's street, pulled to the curb, shut off his lights. Halfway there, his phone buzzed. A text from his neighbor Ken. *Sheila's here breaking shit.*

Damn it. Talking to Sheila was the last thing on his list. One damn day without a call—not even twelve damn hours. His cat. Poor Wiley was probably terrified.

Hal texted back. *Would you get Wiley?*

Already did.

Thx.

Sheila would have to wait.

The patrol car drove past.

Hal radioed for his backup car and told them to stay put. It was early still, a little before six. Price might not be home. If he was, they didn't want to spook him.

On either side of Price's tired-looking duplex were two single residences that had been totally rebuilt. Maples and birch trees lined the curbs. The landscaping on the south side of Price's was elaborate—a bushy English-style garden like in the magazines Sheila loved.

Sheila. *Christ.*

His radio crackled as the officers awaited instruction. Hal told them to hold their position while he walked past. He, at least, was in civilian clothing. If Price saw the patrol officers, he might make a run. Hal didn't want a chase, especially since Price had access to guns.

Hal walked past, taking note of which door entered unit B—Price's. His was the south unit. Hal circled the house, taking note of the overgrown side yard and the windows that faced it.

Through the one full-sized window was a room with a futon, extended. Sheets were in a crumpled ball in its center. Along the far wall stood a low, cheap white dresser, and next to it, a shiny, black beanbag, covered in discarded clothes. Jeans, blue button-down, socks and boxers lay scattered on the floor.

Scattered change and slips of paper peppered the surface of a dresser, along with a few bottles—beer and a tall clear one that was maybe vodka or gin. Hal couldn't see the label. Nothing like a wallet or keys to confirm whether or not Price was home.

Farther back was a frosted window, high off the ground. Bathroom probably.

In the back was a second door with a glass square in its center. Like the bathroom window, this one was also patterned to let in light but little else. Hal saw no motion on the other side. Exit points—front door, back door, and the two windows: bedroom and bathroom. Four exit points and only three officers.

Hal rounded the other side of the house, which he figured belonged to apartment A, because lace curtains covered the windows and overgrown ferns hung from macramé hangers hooked into the ceiling.

On the street, Hal crossed to the patrol car.

Hal introduced himself to the two officers. "Not sure this guy is home. Supposedly, he has a thing for working nights."

"So it might be about breakfast time for him."

"Here's hoping," Hal said, leading the way back to the duplex as he explained the layout. They grew quiet as they approached.

"Ting," Hal said, addressing one. "You cover the back

door. I'll ring the bell." Hal glanced at the other officer's name tag. "Bard, you watch the side windows from here."

If Price fired, it would be Hal's third gunfight this week. He wanted this guy unaware. "Take it real slow, guys. I don't want him to come out shooting."

Ting went to the back of the house. Hal counted slowly to fifteen. Then he nodded to Bard and rang the bell.

No reaction from inside. Hal rang again.

There was a faint click, like a door opening. Then came groans from an old wood floor. The sounds grew closer.

"Who is it?"

"I'm looking for Gordon Price."

"Why you looking for him?"

"I've got some questions."

"Price ain't here," the voice said a moment later. "You'll have to come back later."

There was a short pause, and Hal thought Price might be waiting to see if they would leave. A few seconds later, he heard the distinct slapping sound of bare feet on the hardwood.

"Running!" Hal shouted, jumping over the banister past Bard. As he started around the house, he turned back. "Stay there!"

Hal ran to the large bedroom and stopped. Moving slowly, he leaned across to look inside. The overhead light shone in the room, but otherwise, it looked the same as when he'd last seen it. He moved toward the back of the house and had almost reached the corner when he heard Ting shout, "Freeze!"

Ting held his gun drawn on Price, who stood in a

pair of navy plaid underwear, his hands in the air. Hal was pleased to see that they were empty. Even better, one was wrapped in a white bandage. Hal thought immediately of the sharp piece of rebar outside the apartment of James and Tawny Robbins.

"Place your hands on top of your head," Ting directed as Bard joined them.

"What the hell is this about?" Price demanded. He made a sucking sound and a retainer filled the front of his mouth, before he flipped it and bit it back into place.

"You worked for Harvey Rendell?" Hal asked.

"I've worked for a lot of people, man."

"Thirty-first floor, Bank of America Center," Hal said. "He pays in cash. We found your fingerprints in the office."

"Sounds like I've been there, then. I'd have to check my records."

Hal had him and he was going to savor it. "How about Hunters Point? You done some work up there, lately?"

Price's gaze narrowed, but he said nothing.

"How'd you hurt yourself, Gordon?"

"I cut it working on my car."

"Sure you did." He turned to Ting. "Let's escort Mr. Price downtown. I'll meet you at the station."

Price started to squawk, but Ting cut him off. "You heard the inspector. Move nice and slow."

He took a couple of steps and stopped, looking down at his shorts. "You going to take me in like this?"

"We'll get you some pants when you're in the car," Bard told him. "Move out of line and we can take you downtown in your skivvies. Break up the routine. Right, Ting?"

"Damn straight."

Hal blew out his breath.

Every cop needed takedowns like this one. Easy, straightforward.

Seemed like they happened less and less.

Hal watched the officers put Gordon Price in the back of the patrol car. While Bard went back in for clothes, Hal called the station about getting a warrant for Price's place.

He took a few minutes to savor the relief. It was the first time in this case he'd made progress without getting shot at.

Now, he just had to handle Sheila.

CHAPTER 25

HAILEY WOKE TO a piercing bleat. The hospital. She jumped from the chair. A painful crick pinched her back from sleeping in the chair.

Across the room, Bruce lay motionless. Tubes ran into his nose, an IV in his arm. He looked fragile, sick.

The sight made her nauseous, terrified.

Above him, the machines hushed and beeped. His chest rose and fell softly beneath her hand. The room went quiet. Then, the bleating noise again. The heavy drum of her pulse trumpeted the pain in her back.

She punched the red call button.

"Yes."

"Something's wrong. The machines—" She felt help-less, sounded helpless. "I need a nurse. Right now."

A heavyset nurse with tight red curls entered the room. The freckles were so dense across her cheeks that she had tan skin with white dots rather than the other way around. Abby, her nametag read.

The bleating had stopped again. "Something was beeping."

"Looks like the pulse ox slipped off," the nurse said,

lifting a small black clip and replacing it on Bruce's index finger.

"Was that the beeping sound?" Hailey asked.

"Shouldn't have been."

The bleating started again. Hailey searched the screen above Bruce's head, trying to make sense of the lines and numbers.

"It sounds like a phone," the nurse said. "That ring—I think it's your phone."

Hailey's cell phone sat on top of her purse, on the floor beside the chair. Three missed calls from Hal. Hal had called. What did that mean? Did he forgive her?

She was afraid to call him back.

But she would. Eventually.

Thank God the girls were safe. Dee had taken them to a hotel for the night. Hailey had wondered what they'd think about going with Dee, but Camilla had sounded ecstatic on the phone, and all Ali could talk about was ordering room service and watching *Kung Fu Panda 3*. Dee had booked them in a suite at the W—probably nicer than any room she'd ever stayed in. They would have a blast. And be safe.

That was one less thing to worry about.

The nurse shifted Bruce's head on the pillow and checked his breathing tubes and blood pressure monitor.

When she was done, she turned to Hailey and put her hand on her arm. "He's doing well."

"I'm sorry about calling you in here," Hailey said. "I guess I'm sort of out of it."

"It's no problem. Let us know if you need anything else. Dr. Schwann should be in again in a few hours."

Baker had performed the six-hour surgery to remove the bullet, which had struck only a fraction of an inch from Bruce's fifth cervical vertebrae.

Instead, it had punctured his right lung and done damage to some nerves. Chances were there'd be no permanent damage, but no one would know until he woke up.

"He will wake up, though?" Hailey had asked.

"We have no reason to believe he won't," Baker had told her after the surgery. "There was no cranial injury. His vitals are good." He must have seen her looking at Bruce's breathing tube. "A little extra oxygen, that's all. We'll remove it once he's awake."

"So, we just wait?" Desperation filled her voice. Jim had been shot. Then Hal at Hunters Point. Now Bruce. That bullet was meant for her. She had just gotten off the phone with Jim only moments earlier.

How could that be coincidence?

Dr. Baker nodded. "We just wait."

"Did you retrieve the bullet?"

"We couriered it over to the San Francisco police lab," he said. "Standard protocol for shootings."

"You didn't happen to notice anything odd about it, did you?" she asked.

The doctor frowned, shook his head. "I'm not into guns myself."

"Of course." She was disappointed. She wanted answers. She wanted them this minute. What was she hoping for?

For the doctor to hand her a connection between the gun used to shoot Bruce and the one used to shoot at Jim.

To confirm it was the same shooter. It had to be, didn't it? And what did it really matter? Knowing the same gun had shot both men didn't get them any closer to a suspect.

Nothing short of a copper jacket etched with a name was going to help.

When the resident came by at midnight, Hailey asked why Bruce wasn't awake yet. How long would it take?

"The bullet struck close to the spinal cord, so there's always the chance of paralysis."

"Paralysis." Bruce could not be paralyzed. Not after John. Not while sitting in front of her house.

"Sometimes it's just the shock to the body," the doctor added. "We have to wait and see."

Hailey was still waiting.

She stood in the middle of the room and felt the weight of the last year come down on her.

John's death. Jim's shooting. Hal's distrust.

The girls.

Ending things with Bruce minutes before he was shot by a bullet that was meant for her.

Hailey began to sob. She sobbed as she hadn't since the days after John's death. Let herself fall apart.

Only when her phone buzzed did she fight to calm herself.

Jamie Vail.

Hailey answered. "Hey."

"I heard," Jamie said.

"It's four in the morning," Hailey said.

"I know. I always wake up at this hour."

"Lucky you."

"It's amazing what YouTube videos you can get

sucked into in the middle of the night." Jamie paused as if waiting for a reply. "Do you want company?" she finally asked, the joking aside.

In the days after John's death, Hailey had struggled with needing to be alone and never wanting to be alone. Not that she'd had much choice—the girls had been glued to her. "I don't know," she admitted.

"You want to talk about it?" Jamie asked.

"It's a royal shit storm, Jamie."

"You're talking to the right person, then. I've lived through a few of those."

Hailey drew the chair to Bruce's bed and held his hand as she told Jamie about Hal's request for a transfer and Jim's shooting.

She told Jamie everything she had intended to tell Hal.

Then, she told Jamie about the conversation with Bruce—that he had come on official business. And soon, Hailey was telling Jamie all of it—about going to his house and finding out about the other woman, about breaking up with him minutes before he was shot. "I was breaking up with him."

"You didn't get him shot."

"He has to wake up, Jamie. I can't lose him, not after …"

"He's going to be okay."

"I know it's the middle of the night, but I hope they're in the lab working on this."

"Roger's there."

Hailey sat up. "He is?"

"He had the team working on matching the tread marks from the street."

"They find the casing?" Hailey asked.

"No."

She exhaled. "Who's working it?"

"A team out of CAP, but I don't know who."

Crimes Against Persons would process the scene as an assault. Unless he died. Then, the case would get routed to Hailey's department.

How soon would the shooter realize he got the wrong person? How long before he came after her?

She couldn't think about that now.

"Go get some sleep," Hailey said.

Jamie promised to touch base in the morning and hung up. Hailey slipped her phone in her pocket and stood beside Bruce.

The bristle of the day's growth on his jaw was rough on her fingers. She raked her hands through his hair as she had countless times. It fell, thick, across his cheek, and she brushed it off.

She pressed her face to his. "I love you. I'll let you go. Just wake up, okay? Come back."

She sank back into the chair. If she called the lab, she would only be pulling Roger away from the work. He would text if he made any discovery. She couldn't imagine calling him at four thirty in the morning.

Hal. He was the guy she'd call at four thirty in the morning.

She looked at the missed calls.

Hal had so many questions. Where would they begin?

She drifted off and woke later to the sounds of people

arguing in the hall. Hailey sat up and rubbed her eyes. She expected the doctor.

When the door opened, it was Hal who entered.

The anger in his face was gone, and relief poured over Hailey as she started to cry. "Hal."

CHAPTER 26

SEEING HAILEY'S FACE took Hal back to the day John had died. The awful tightness in his throat, a burning in his eyes.

He glanced at Bruce Daniels, lying in the bed. His neck bandaged, the machines, the IVs. The look in her eyes as she watched him.

He rubbed his eyes with one hand, stretching his thumb across the bridge of his nose. "Damn."

Hailey was scared.

She couldn't have been taller than five-three, the size of his ten-year-old nephew, but she was a force. Hal had never thought of her as small. She was the size of her intellect, her power. It was immense.

Often, he felt small. He'd never been comfortable around small women, feared the fragility.

Curled into the chair beside the bed, she could have been the patient. Tiny. Frail.

She stood and swept her palms over her hair as though to tame it and pull herself together. Then, her gaze drifted to Daniels and her expression crumbled.

It hurt to watch.

And there it was. Another secret she'd kept.

"Since when?"

"Almost two years," she said, her voice cracking. The tears fell faster, her breath coming in gasps.

He closed the distance between them, wrapped an arm around her, and pulled her, easily, against his chest. He looked down at the top of her head, felt the sobs against him, and said nothing.

Hal had met the doctor in the hallway. He would be in to check Daniels soon, but he didn't have a lot of good news.

Daniels should have been awake.

The longer the coma, the lower the chance of coming out of it.

Why was Daniels at Wyatt's house in the middle of the day? A partner should have known.

Hal had requested a few minutes with Hailey before the doctor came in. Maybe he could get her out of there. Just for a while.

Hal held her, fighting his own welling emotion. He'd only seen her cry a couple of times—both right after John's death. It had been awful, seeing her like that. But this felt so much worse. Like he was part of it. Part of her pain.

A few minutes later, a knock sounded at the door, and they both looked up as the doctor came in, followed by two others. Hailey stepped away from Hal and moved to the bedside.

"Let's go get some coffee, Hailey."

She shook her head. "I can't."

Hal grabbed her hand. "He won't be alone. We'll be right back."

She was trembling and whispering "no," but Hal held her arm tightly and pulled her toward the door.

In comparison to Bruce's room, the hallway was bright and loud. Hailey halted midstride, blinking and watching the activity at the nurses' station. Phones rang and a line of metal charts clinked against each other as nurses passed by to take one out or slide one in.

One nurse, a white guy almost as big as Hal, filled in a wall-sized grid on a white board. Third from the bottom was "B. Daniels." In the next box was the attending physician, the one Hal had met. Baker. Next to that, a bunch of letters he couldn't understand—some sort of acronym.

He pulled on Hailey's hand, not wanting her to try to decipher the board. The nurse directed him to the cafeteria.

He saw the elevators and paused instinctively. Hailey kept walking.

"Stairs," she said.

Her pace was slow. She yawned, barely raising her hand high enough to cover it. They passed a series of rooms. A game show played on a TV—*Wheel of Fortune* or maybe *Jeopardy*.

The patient was maybe seventeen. On his head was a metal halo attached to his skull with long pins. A woman adjusted his covers, though they were straight already, like she just needed something to do with her hands. She had the same expression in her eyes that he'd seen in Hailey's. *Please don't let something else go wrong.*

They reached the stairwell, and Hal pushed the door

open. Hailey stepped inside and stopped, looking around as though she remembered the place.

The last stairwell he'd been in with her was at the jail, the night before he'd asked Marshall for a transfer. This one was bright. Windows lined one wall, and it smelled clean. Hailey made her way to the steps and then turned, and sat.

"Aren't you hungry?"

"No."

"How about some coffee?"

She shook her head again.

"Shakley's awake," he said. Hal had gone to the hospital to see Shakley earlier, after he'd parted ways with Hailey at the Bank of America Center.

"He's going to be okay?"

"Better than okay. He's meeting with the police artist this morning to create a composite of his shooter."

Fresh tears trailed down her cheeks.

"He said it was a white guy," Hal added.

"I saw his face. I told you."

"And I believe you …" Hal moved to sit beside her, but she put a hand out to stop him. "You should go."

"I'm not leaving," he said firmly.

"You have to."

"Did you see him?" She wiped at her tears. "That happened because of me."

Hal shook his head, stepping forward again.

"Don't."

"That did not happen because of you."

"Yes, it did," she said. "I let it happen. Somehow, I let it happen."

"How?" Hal asked.

Hailey shook her head.

"Come on, Wyatt. You're the most honest cop I know. Who are you protecting?"

She rose and started to climb the stairs. "You have to leave, Hal."

Hal caught up and took hold of her shoulders, turning her to face him. "I'm not leaving."

She looked angry now. "I'm telling you to leave."

"And I said no," he shouted. His voice echoed in the stairwell. "Who are you protecting? John? Are you protecting John? Because he's dead, Hailey. You don't have to protect him."

She broke through his grip, starting up the stairs again. "Don't talk about John."

"Is it Jim, then? Why are you protecting him? He doesn't deserve your protection."

She said nothing, sinking onto the steps.

He watched her, the hesitation as it almost came free. He knew she needed to tell it. "Where's Hailey Wyatt? Where is she? Your husband died. He was shot, but this isn't about him. It's about his father, a man who belongs in jail. If John were the kind of man I think he was, he'd agree. He'd help me. Why the hell won't you?"

Hailey dropped her head in her hands.

The anger in him burst. She'd held this secret too long. It was wrecking them. It was wrecking him. He had to know. Damn it. She had to tell him.

"What about the girls? Is this the legacy you want to leave them with? Because I know what that's like, Hailey.

I know what it's like when the only thing anyone wants to remember about your old man is that he was crooked."

How could Hailey turn her back on the truth?

What would make her do that?

Why would she protect Jim Wyatt? How could she after all the lies? He had to have been involved. He didn't buy that it was Hailey's mother-in-law, with her lace doilies and her floral teacups. If she'd shot her son, she never could have hid the secret. It would have eaten her alive.

How many times had he studied that file? Most of the window glass had been found in the room, but a few shards of glass fragments lay on the ground outside. Someone had broken the window from the outside to make it look like the shot came from there.

Hailey held her arms against her midsection. As though protecting herself. She'd done that when she was pregnant, rubbing at her belly.

Pregnant.

Hal staggered back. His hands fell from her shoulders. "Christ." He knew. He raked his hands across his scalp. "It's the girls," he whispered. "You're protecting the girls."

Terror made her brown eyes black. She started to speak. Stopped. Started to stand, but didn't move. She shrank as though a box was closing in around her.

Hal sank onto the stair next to her and set his elbows on his knees. Above them, a door opened. Shoes clicked on the cement steps. Another door opened and it was quiet again. Hal hid his face in his hands, filling his lungs with deep breaths.

In. Out.

"I'll give you Jim," she whispered.

He waited, listening.

"But if you take him down, you take me too."

Why hadn't he realized sooner? She was protecting her girls. Of course she was. But why hadn't she told him? Him of all people. They could solve it if only she'd trust him. God, he was sick to death of holding it in, of pretending. He steeled his breath, pressed his hands into his knees.

"Was it Camilla or Ali?"

Her eyes went wide. Her hands pressed to her chest as though she couldn't breathe. "No."

"Ali," he guessed. Camilla was too old. It would have come out. But Ali had been only four, almost five, when John died. "Ali shot John."

Hailey leaned into the wall and cried. Silently. Streams of tears that she let drip off her chin and nose.

"How?" He sat on the stair, giving her space.

He didn't yield. "How?"

"Oh, God. She can't ever know. She can't ever remember."

"It's me. It's just me," he whispered.

And then she began to talk, to tell the story. "It was Jim's gun. He gave it to John because of the threats at the DA's office. He was teaching John to use it. Ali was bored—" She caught a sob. "—Liz was taking Camilla to a show, and Ali wanted to go, so she went into Jim's office. He and John started talking, got distracted ..." She paused. "I heard them arguing from the kitchen. But they did that a lot, Jim and John." She met his gaze. "It wasn't loaded. Jim swore he'd checked it, and John would've too. I'm sure he would have."

He hadn't. If it hadn't been loaded, John wouldn't be dead. One moment of oversight, a little carelessness—that was how it happened.

"Ali turned the barrel toward her dad. He reached for it—to take it away …"

There had been so much blood in the crime scene photos.

She touched her hand to the back of her neck, the place where John's wound would have been. Had she watched him die?

He gave her time, and after a moment, she went on. "Jim came out of the room, shouting. He had Ali in his arms." She looked up at him. "His only child was on the floor, dying, and he took her out of there, didn't want her to see it."

He couldn't imagine what Jim had gone through, leaving a dying child. He pictured his own father. The photos he'd seen of his murder. Rubbed his eyes.

"Can you imagine that? Can you imagine leaving your child to die to save Ali the agony of seeing it?"

"I'm so sorry."

"I got to him, but the bullet grazed the jugular. It was too fast."

Her eyes clouded. Her stare went flat.

"Christ, Hailey."

She looked at her open palms. "There was too much blood. I tried, but …"

She had spent the last year trying to save her child. Lying to her bosses, her partner. To everyone. Avoiding that file, because she already knew who killed John, and the reality was too painful to relive.

Why hadn't he seen it?

"Do you know what John said, lying on the floor?" The words came out as a whisper.

He didn't think she'd told this story to anyone. "Tell me."

The sun shifted across the windows beside them. Hospital windows. Another man shot, another man who might die. And Hailey, swallowing her guilt now, as she did then, until it choked her.

In the months before her husband was killed, she'd been with another man. In love with another man.

Tears streamed down Hal's face. He wiped his palms across his cheeks. "What did he say?"

She leaned against him then, her head on his shoulder, her voice barely audible. "He said, 'Make sure they're okay. Take care of her.'"

Hal wrapped an arm around her, tears still falling down his face.

"The intruder story was Jim's idea, but I went along with it," she said. "I won't have her growing up thinking she killed her father. I don't care what happens, Hal, but it won't be that." She pulled back and smoothed her cheeks with the flats of her palms.

"Is that why you're protecting Jim? Is he blackmailing you with this?"

"No." Her response was adamant. It was the truth. Hal should have known, but the days of being sure were gone.

"But you're protecting him. Why? Because he might try to use the truth against you?"

"I don't know," she said. "He's hiding something, but he didn't shoot himself." A moment later, she said, "He didn't kill—" She halted. "I don't think he's capable of this."

"Does Bruce know—"

"No," she said quickly. "Nothing. Not about John or this stuff with Jim. He knows nothing." She glanced at her hands. "I was breaking things off when he was shot. Since John's death, I can't—" She wiped her face again. "It just wasn't going to work."

Death had changed the way Hal remembered his father. His stubbornness and the occasional rages had sunk below the surface of his hearty laugh and the joy he took in Raiders football, his job, his kids. The ugly disappeared, and it became hard for Hal to remember why he and his dad hadn't always gotten along. He struggled not to blame himself for all the shortcomings in their relationship.

Hailey was doing the same. No live man could compete with the perfect ghost.

Bruce Daniels didn't have a chance. "Did he know? That it was over, I mean?"

In response to the question, she winced.

"You told him? In the car?"

"He probably knew before," she said. "But yeah. I told him it was over." Her hair fell forward as she whispered, "Then, someone shot him."

Hal pushed the hair from her face to see her eyes. He wanted to say something, to tell her she could trust him.

He would be here.

Before he could speak, she straightened her shoulders and sat up. Her walls rose again. "You have to do what is right for you, Hal. I'm not asking for any favors, but I'm going to protect Ali and Camilla with every last breath. Nothing matters more to me than them."

She started to stand, but he grabbed her hand, pulling her back down to the stair. "Hailey."

"I choose them. I always will. No matter the cost."

"I'm on your side, but you have to come clean with me."

She shook her head. "You can't be on my side, Hal. You have to fight for the law, for what's just."

"You *are* just. You *are* the law. That's enough for me."

Above them, a door opened, and the hinges cried in high-pitched moans like someone raising the dead.

A chill ran through Hal, but he kept hold of his partner.

"I've got your back, Hailey," he whispered. "I swear I've got it."

CHAPTER 27

THE DOCTOR WAS still in Bruce's room. It seemed like hours had passed. Years.

"How is he?" Hal asked.

Hailey had been too terrified to ask. Now she steeled herself for his response.

"He's responding to stimuli, so I am still very optimistic," Baker said. "I've requested an MRI to be certain we're not missing an injury." He closed the chart. "Other than that, we have to wait."

"When will you do the MRI?" Hailey asked.

"As soon as we can get him scheduled. We'll probably have results by noon."

Noon was hours away.

Hailey's phone rang from her purse. Her home number. "Hello?"

"Mommy," Ali said, and Hailey was relieved to hear the small voice. "We stayed at a really fancy hotel. They left us milk and cookies before bed, and we had waffles for breakfast."

"That sounds like so much fun."

"It was," Ali agreed. "Now Dee's taking us to school, and I wanted to say I love you."

Hailey fought not to cry. Her baby. Every time she heard Ali's voice, she prayed her daughter wouldn't remember what happened the night John died. That she wouldn't realize what she'd done. "I love you too, Ali. So much."

"Are you with the bad guys?"

Hailey's eyes stung. "No, sweetie. Right now, I'm with the good guys."

Hal smiled and followed Baker out of the room while Hailey spoke to Ali, then Camilla. Finally, Dee was on the line. "Everything's okay?" Hailey asked.

"It was great," she said.

"Thanks for taking them."

"No problem. We had fun. Don't know if you've ever had a pajama party at a hotel before …"

"I haven't," Hailey admitted.

"Well, you'll have to try it."

"Thank you, Dee."

"It's nothing. Is your friend okay?"

"I think he's going to be," Hailey said.

"Good. We'll catch up later."

Hailey ended the call and held the phone to her chest. She had to be there when they came home today. She needed to hold them, to smell the dirt and raspberry shampoo, the coconut lotion Camilla loved.

Hal poked his head in. "We've got until noon to get caught up. We should go."

Hailey nodded and gathered her things. Before

leaving the room, she touched Bruce's hand. Reassured by its warmth, she followed Hal out to the car.

They stopped for breakfast burritos at a place called Millie's in between the hospital and the station. While they ate, Hal told her about arresting Gordon Price. From a medical exam, the wound on Price's hand appeared to be a match to the rebar at James Robbins's house.

Same blood type too.

DNA would come later. Now, they had to hope that Price started talking. The DA had issued a warrant to the funeral home for the payment records on Fredricks's burial. Hal had sent a patrol officer to stand over the funeral director until he coughed up those records. He also had Naomi Muir researching Regal Insurance. Hailey had almost forgotten about that.

Roger had mentioned the cork to Hal, so Hailey explained the comparison the lab was running between the cork they'd found in Fredricks's casket and the one she'd taken from the house.

"Where's the cork now?"

"I had Roger give it to Kong to book into evidence."

Hal set down his burrito and wiped his fingers. "This thing is circling Jim."

"I know. You've known that for a while now."

"What is his relation to Donald Blake?"

"If I had any idea, Hal, I swear I'd tell you."

She was afraid the moment would be awkward, but Hal laughed. "I know you would," he said.

Her cell phone rang again. The lab. "Wyatt," Hailey answered.

"It's Roger. Where are you?"

"Hal and I are just coming from the hospital."

"How is he? Daniels, I mean?"

"Still in a coma," she said.

Hal watched her.

"I heard," Roger said. "I'm sorry."

Just like John's death. Why did people apologize for tragedies? Only fourteen hours in, and she was already sick to death of the condolences.

She pushed the speaker button and set the phone between her and Hal. "Hal's here too, Roger. What've you got?"

"We struck gold."

"We could use some of that," Hal said.

"We got a partial print off the inside of the blue box—the one with the severed thumb." The couple behind Hal turned to stare. Hailey lowered the volume.

"Who's the match?" Hal asked.

"Guy named Marty Schrauder."

Hal looked at her, and Hailey shook her head. "We don't know the name."

"There's no history on Schrauder—only a driver's license. It's why we didn't catch it yesterday. But last night, we ran all the prints through Sacto."

"All registered California drivers," Hal said.

"Right," Roger said.

"Who is he?"

"Schrauder is a nobody. No credit cards, no bank accounts. Only a driver's license."

Hal started to talk, but Roger cut him off. "Hold on. This is the gold—Schrauder's prints also match someone in the *Chronicle*'s employee database." Roger paused a moment for effect.

"The *Chronicle*," Hailey said. "That would be—"

"Donald Blake," Roger interjected.

Hal slapped the table and the folks behind him almost jumped up from their table. "Blake."

Blake wasn't dead. They ID'd him by some dental work. A bridge, Tomaso had said. He had planted it on another body. Faked his own death.

"And," Roger went on. "I just got a call from O'Shea. Officer Shakley's police sketch matches Blake too."

"Blake isn't dead," Hailey said out loud, the reality sinking in.

"There's more," Roger said. "Schrauder has a registered firearm. A .38—same caliber as the bullet shot at the senator and the one that hit Daniels."

"You have an address on Schrauder?" Hal asked.

"Yeah. I've got it right here."

Hal wrote it down and stood. "You want to take that?" He pointed to her plate.

She had barely touched her burrito. "No."

"Let's go get this guy."

"I'm ready," she said.

It was time to put this case to bed.

CHAPTER 28

HAL PROMISED HAILEY they would go back to the hospital at noon. She wouldn't have left otherwise. She needed the break—as much for her sanity as for their cases.

As they walked to the doors, she kept a look out over her right shoulder. As though she was waiting for them to call her back. To tell her that he'd woken up.

Or that he was dead.

Shivers raked down Hal's neck. Not yet. Daniels wasn't gone yet. He had to believe this one would work out.

Hadn't she been through enough?

At the entrance to the stairwell, Hailey straightened her shoulders. Hal wanted to say something encouraging—or distracting—but they'd already talked so much today, so much more than they'd ever talked in one sitting. He couldn't think of anything else to add.

Walking down the stairs, he realized he was exhausted, his emotions raw.

The air was cool and moist without the rain. A breeze caught in the collar of his shirt and circled his neck. He slowed to savor a moment in the fresh air and noticed Hailey was not beside him.

She had stopped, staring back at the hospital. He waited a few feet behind her. When she faced him, she forced a smile.

"Breeze feels good," he commented. Something to break the silence.

"It does."

From the car, she called the house. She spoke to her mother-in-law. Her tone was friendly, informal, but not intimate. He remembered the day they'd come to the hospital with Cameron Cruz. In the car that day, Hailey had sat in the backseat. She'd been on the phone to Jim.

"Girls okay?" he asked.

"Yeah. They're at school for now."

"You nervous?"

"We're ready for our own place," she said.

"Anything I can do to help?"

She shook her head.

She was alone with small children. He had no idea how complicated it was. At least when his father had died, his mother's children were grown. How angry he'd been with his mother when she'd told him she was going to L.A. to live with his sister. "You don't understand, Hal," she'd told him. "Someday you will."

He had disagreed. He'd told his mother he would never understand. Maybe he'd been wrong.

With the radio off, the car was awkwardly silent. He resisted the urge to fill the car with vacant noise, and then wondered why he felt the need to keep talking.

He was thankful for the distraction when his cell phone rang. Not Sheila. Even better. "Harris," he said.

"O'Shea here. Calling to tell you Price made his call." They were still holding Price as a suspect in Rendell's murder because of the prints found in the fund manager's office. The DA wasn't ready to file charges, but O'Shea had been hoping for some solid evidence against him in the deaths of Dwayne Carson, the driver Griffin Sigler and the kid in Robbins' apartment, Kenny Fiston. Not to mention the attempted murder of James Robbins. That would be enough to change the DA's mind. So far, no luck.

"And?" Hal punched the speaker button. "Price made his call," he muttered to Hailey.

"He called an attorney, but you're not going to believe who it is," O'Shea continued.

"Martin Abbott," Hal said.

O'Shea sighed. "Good guess."

"Yeah," Hal said. "I'm kind of psychic about attorneys. What did Abbott say to our Mr. Price?"

"Actually, Price wasn't calling to talk to Abbott."

"I thought he called Abbott's office."

"He did," O'Shea said. "Turns out Gordon Price's mother is the main receptionist at Abbott's office."

"Price arranged for Carson and Robbins to get Abbott's business card," Hailey said.

"And then his mother took their calls. She told Gordon Price when they called. Then, he could follow up on whether or not they were released from jail."

"That's the theory," O'Shea continued. "Now we've just got to get Price to admit it and tell us why he would have wanted them dead. Or maybe the question is who hired Price to kill them."

"You bring the mother in yet?"

"Not yet, but we've got a couple of uniforms on her," O'Shea said.

"Listen, Sheaster," Hal started, buttering him up with the nickname O'Shea loved. O'Shea swore someone had given it to him in the academy, but those who graduated in his class said it had been O'Shea's own invention. "Don't let Price go anywhere. Not until I get back there. Last guy who called Abbott ended up dead in front of the station. Didn't make it a full block. You hear me?"

"Loud and clear, my friend," O'Shea agreed. "Maybe by the time you're back, he'll be ready to talk."

"Here's hoping." Hal ended the call as Hailey was typing on her phone.

"Oakland PD got us a warrant for Blake's house. I've got directions. Head to the bridge."

Lights flashing, Hal crossed two lanes of traffic to make a right on Bryant and head to the onramp for 80 eastbound toward the Bay Bridge. Even at midday, traffic backed up as it narrowed down to four lanes on the bridge.

As they crossed over Treasure Island, Hailey drew something from her purse. The *whoosh* of her inhaler was faint, but unmistakable.

"You okay?"

She nodded.

Blake lived on Harrison Street, in Oakland, in a section of street almost directly under highway 80. Off the exit, they came around a curved ramp and ended up a half block from his house.

Blake had faked his own death so that he could orchestrate this whole thing. But what did Abby and Hank Dennig have to do with the people who had killed his family? Were they killed because they were in the gun business? The same as Colby Wesson?

Did Blake figure out that the guns that killed his family had been made by Wesson's company and distributed by the Dennigs? How in the world could he have known that?

And it still didn't explain why he shot at Jim or Hal or her ...

Hal turned right at the next corner and made a U-turn, parking in view of Blake's front door. They waited in silence for the Oakland black and white.

Hal pulled his bulletproof vest off the backseat and strapped it on, putting his jacket back over it. Hailey did the same, moving a little more slowly as she fiddled with the straps. She wore a man's vest because the women's were cut short, leaving the abdomen exposed. The man's vest was heavier, and the straps were built for wide shoulders. She complained that they bit uncomfortably into her narrower ones.

The black and white arrived about fifteen minutes later and did its first pass as a drive-by before circling back around and parking in front of the house, blocking off the driveway. Two officers emerged from the car, each with his hand on his weapon.

By law, he and Hailey had no jurisdiction here.

Guests only, they stood on the street while the Oakland officers approached Blake's door.

The officers knocked twice. "Schrauder!" they called, referring to him by his new name, which Hal hoped might make Blake less violent than hearing his real name.

"Police!" An officer pounded a fist on the door and then stepped back. Both remained carefully shielded by the doorframe. Hal had the strong sense that Blake was in there. Still, the apartment remained quiet.

Hal scanned the street for civilians, but it was empty. This was a working neighborhood, and at this time of day, most people would be gone. If they needed to talk to Blake's neighbors, they would have to come back later.

The two officers spoke into their radios and circled the house. Hailey started walking. Had made it two houses down when the two officers returned to the front of the house.

"We've called for backup," one said. "They should arrive within a few minutes."

Hailey started to speak, but Hal nodded.

"Okay," he said and stepped back so that he was in her path, turned and led her a few steps down the sidewalk. "Soon."

There had been a time in their partnership when they had controlled their anger under the most difficult circumstances. Unflappable, she'd called them, although on occasion he was known to let his anger get the best of him.

Now, though, the anger came from her.

A second car arrived some twenty minutes later.

Detectives, both men. They were older—late forties,

early fifties—it was hard to tell. They could have been younger. Police officers didn't age gracefully.

The one on the passenger side was heavy in the middle and wore a dark suit, the pants belted across the widest part of his girth. With a bald head and round dark eyes set deep in a doughy face, the big guy looked like Humpty Dumpty. It looked weird to see a man with a huge gut hanging over the top of his pants, but it looked stranger to see pants belted across the gut.

The other detective was Latino and lean—maybe five feet ten, though his curved shoulders made him seem shorter. He had a head of dark, thick hair, but around thin lips and a narrow, flat nose, the beard and mustache were gray.

The two men gave Hal and Hailey a passing glance before approaching their officers. The four huddled while the patrol officers made motions at the house.

Hailey sighed.

After a few minutes, the thin detective reached into his pocket and drew out a folded piece of paper.

The search warrant.

"Finally," Hailey said.

The two detectives approached, the big guy arriving first—his belly eight or ten inches before the rest of him. Both men looked directly at Hal, so he introduced his partner, then himself.

Hailey ignored the slight, reached out to shake hands. "You've got the warrant," she said, skipping the small talk. "Can we go in, then?"

"Soon as we clear it."

"We'll be waiting," she said.

The front door opened under the pressure of a boot and the officers entered, the older two right behind. Hailey and Hal held their weapons drawn at the base of the stairs. A few minutes later, the big guy called them in. "All clear."

Hal remembered the sense he'd had that Blake was in there. He'd been wrong. What had made him think Blake would be there?

Just before entering the house, he glanced over his shoulder and scanned the street. Caught the eye of the detective doing the same. No Blake.

The detective with the big gut put one of the patrol officers on the door in case Blake showed up.

Inside the front door was a long hallway. It was empty, the wood floor worn and stained in a dark path maybe fourteen inches wide, right down its center. Hal knelt and stared at the dark path without touching it, wondering if it was wet. He drew a glove from his back pocket, pulled it on and scratched the surface of the wood.

"It's just old," the big guy said. "Foot oil over lots of years does that. There was probably carpet here once."

Hal opened his mouth to respond when he heard Hailey. Not a word. A choking sound.

Hal sprinted down the hall, weapon drawn.

Hailey stared at the living room wall.

Gun dropped to her side, she wrapped her left arm across her middle. In front of her, a strand of red yarn ran across the length of the room. Taped along it were printed black and white photographs.

Hal holstered his gun and scanned the first photograph. A man and woman stood beside a dark convertible

Mercedes. The man, pictured in profile, reached for the door. The woman faced the camera.

It was Abby Dennig.

"It's him."

"Yeah," Hal agreed, glancing around the room. "But where is he now?"

CHAPTER 29

THE PICTURES IN Donald Blake's house were as eerie as the worst crime scene photos Hailey had seen. They captured mundane tasks—images in which the subject never looked at the camera.

Abby loaded her car in front of the marina Safeway.

Hank Dennig talked on his cell phone in front of his office.

The camera was their stalker. The images might have been weeks or days—or maybe hours—before their deaths.

Did the victims see the photographer?

In one, Abby pushed her young daughter on the swing. Her brow creased, Abby had turned her head in the direction of the camera, though it hadn't caught her eye.

Had she sensed that she was being watched?

Donald Blake had taken pictures of the Dennigs and another man she didn't recognize—both times outside a house. In the first image, the man she didn't recognize stooped to pick up a newspaper off the curb, wearing a pair of pajama bottoms and a robe, open to display his bare chest, the belt hanging loosely around his waist. In the second, he wore dress clothes. A briefcase sat on the stair beside him, a stack of mail in his hands.

Then, there was a close-up of a car with no plates, parked in a garage that looked like it was part of the same house. Hailey squinted at the fine print around the plate.

"What does that say? Around the license plate?"

Hal leaned in, careful not to touch it. "Elk Grove Buick-Pontiac-GMC." Looked up. "Where the hell's Elk Grove?"

"Up near Sacramento," the detective with the gray beard said. "I was up there two weeks ago."

"Wesson," Hal said.

"So Blake killed Wesson," Hailey said.

"And probably the Dennigs," Hal added. "He's got a registered .38, which was the caliber used to shoot Jim and Bruce, so it's likely he was responsible for those shootings too."

"He didn't kill Jim."

"Right," Hal agreed. "But he hit Shakley and killed the gunrunner, Jeremy Hayden."

During the sting. Had Blake meant to merely wound Jim and miss Hailey? If he was the one using the Israeli shooting stance, he was a good shot. He wouldn't have missed. "What about Carson and the driver?"

"I think Price shot them."

"Why? Price worked for Blake as well as Harvey Rendell?" If Blake was avenging the death of his family, why hire it out? And why kill a couple of street kids with guns? It was unlikely that any of these San Francisco kids were related to the Oakland shooting that happened three years ago.

The kids who shot up Blake's family would be in their twenties by now. Many of them would be in prison or like Jeremy Hayden—dead. Had Blake killed them too?

But the kids involved in the guns in San Francisco were not the kids who shot Blake's family. Not likely. Gangs stayed in their own neighborhoods. They didn't go shooting up neighborhoods across the bay.

Hailey and Hal were quiet.

"Let's hope something here gives us some answers," Hal said.

Hailey moved down the images.

She wanted to reach the end, to see Jim's face, if it was there.

The next images were of Harvey Rendell. He wore a different suit in each—four separate days, at least. In two, the dark façade of the Bank of America Center showed behind him. In another, he stood in the door of a restaurant where she'd eaten a few times—a small, wonderful French place John had liked called Le Central.

Hailey scanned the background, half expecting to see someone she knew. Lace curtains obscured the other patrons. The specials were handwritten in white chalk on a large blackboard that leaned against the glass beside Rendell, who held a cell phone to his ear, staring at his feet.

"Check this out," Hal said, pointing to a large color photograph on the wall behind the red yarn.

The image had been framed with a thin black plastic frame, like a college kid might use to put up a poster. Almost that large, the photograph was grainy and out of focus, the file not high enough resolution for the enlargement. The backdrop was deep blue with swirls of white—like wispy thin cloud cover—a photo studio backdrop. In the center of the image, Blake sat with his wife on a small, plush, burgundy bench.

Hailey recognized the reddish-brown beard. She's seen this man before, running from the building where they'd found the gunrunner, Jeremy Hayden, dead in the closet.

Blake looked happy in the photograph. A child stood on either side of him and his wife—a young girl in a blue pinafore beside her father, and a boy in a blue sweater and khaki pants beside his mother. Mrs. Blake held a third child in her lap. The infant wore a white one-piece outfit that made guessing its gender impossible.

Blake held his palms flat on his thighs, as though he was about to stand, or was struggling to hold still. Each of them was smiling. Only Blake wasn't looking at the camera, his gaze sideways. He wore the crooked smile of someone crazy in love.

Hailey stepped back, Blake's expression a reminder of her own loss. The mug with John's face was the one image of John that Hailey looked at regularly.

Images of John were everywhere in their home—pictures of him from infancy and youth. School photos—team shots of little league baseball and the high school basketball team—lined the hallways. There were pictures of him with his high school and college friends, at their wedding, and with the girls.

They dotted the walls, topped the bookshelves, glowed from the desktop.

In the days after his death, the images had stopped Hailey like painful shocks. Walking from the bedroom to the bathroom was an assault. The girls stood and stared at the pictures in which John held them. Liz had made each girl her own collage, ones that still sat beside their beds, each filled with memories of their father and them.

There was a time when Hailey considered asking Liz to take some of them down, to store them for a bit while the initial pain eased. But for all the agony the images caused her, they seemed to provide solace to Liz. Hailey had learned to gaze past them, over them, through them—anything to avoid meeting John's eyes.

Hailey couldn't imagine how painful it would be to look at her entire family after she'd lost them.

It would have made her crazy.

Maybe that was what it had done to Blake.

Hailey glanced back down the row of images—the Dennigs, Wesson, Rendell. How were they involved in the deaths of Blake's family? There were no pictures of Officer Shakley or Jeremy Hayden. Were they just accidental victims?

Missing, too, were Carson and the driver, as well as Kenny Fiston and James Robbins. Perhaps Gordon Price shot them, not Blake?

"What the hell is this?" Hal squinted at a yellowed newspaper article framed beside the family portrait.

Hailey read along with him.

Frank Littick is charged in the murder of six-year-old Dorothy Williams, known as Dottie. The shooting occurred Thursday sometime after dark in the Rodger Young Village. Littick was found passed out in his Quonset hut, heavily intoxicated.

The murder weapon, a German Luger that Littick claimed he took off of a dead Nazi, was found in his possession. Littick, back from duty only nine weeks, will be formally charged next week. His two children, a boy, aged 7, and a girl, aged 5, have been taken from his custody and sent to live with family in Pennsylvania.

"Quonset hut?" Hal said.

Dottie. Blake knew about Dottie.

Was that why he'd shot at Jim?

Hailey focused in on the name Frank Littick, the smudged edge of the newsprint around the last letters of the name.

Jim and Dee had taken their aunt and uncle's last name when they were adopted. That name was Wyatt. They were originally Jim and Dee Littick. John's last name would have been Littick. Her name would have been Littick too.

She felt cold shivers at the thought.

"Oh, shit." The voice belonged to the heavyset detective. "You guys had better get in here."

Around the corner, the series of photographs continued. A gasp stuck in the back of her mouth.

An image of Jim, standing on their street.

At the base of the stairs to the house—the place where Bruce had been shot just yesterday.

Hailey covered her mouth. "Hal."

Hal didn't answer, his attention on something else.

She couldn't draw her gaze off her father-in-law. A

worried look on his face, Jim gripped the banister in one hand, his case in another.

Coming home.

Two stairs above him, looking back, was Tom Rittenberg. Not the jovial Tom she knew. The grief she'd seen was gone too. In the photograph, anger tightened his face until she barely recognized him.

Hailey studied the small check print on his tie, tried to remember if she'd seen it before. His suits were almost all dark, and for the most part, they looked the same to her. She hadn't paid attention.

"Hal," Hailey said again, tearing her gaze from the image. Why was Rittenberg so angry? Was it a coincidence that Blake had captured this image, or was he pointing a finger at Tom Rittenberg as well?

Hal watched her. The detective and one of the patrol officers did too.

"What?"

She started toward the next images. Hal grabbed her arm, held her at a distance. Alarmed, she pulled away from him and pushed past to see the other photos. She had to know.

She cried out, falling back from the images.

Hal caught her, moving her against the solid wall.

Her legs shook. Her knees wouldn't hold her. Her pulse trumpeted in her temples. The other officers talked, their words overlapping Hal's until all the voices swarmed around her like hornets. "No. No!" she screamed.

"You have to sit," Hal said. "Come sit." The words didn't make sense, though she understood them.

"Should I call an ambulance?"

"She needs air."

Hands gripped her shoulders, her arms. A palm pressed to the small of her back. She couldn't walk past. She had to see.

She pulled herself free. Studied the three images.

The first was of her standing in front of the Hall at the press conference, her chin cocked up. A sliver of Marshall was visible on the other side of her—his shoulder and part of an arm, fingers on the microphone.

In the second, Hailey was in the lobby of the Bank of America Center, talking with Roger.

When she looked at the third, an animal noise burst from her throat.

Hailey, standing on the street outside of Jim and Liz's. She was turned sideways, holding a bag of groceries in one arm and two small backpacks in the other.

It was a few days old. Three or four maybe.

Trailing behind her were Camilla and Ali. Camilla was climbing the stairs with her back turned. But Ali had stopped.

She looked directly into the lens of Blake's camera.

CHAPTER 30

NO ONE ANSWERED at the house.

Liz didn't pick up her cell phone. Jim's office said he and Dee had already left for the day. Dee didn't answer her cell. Neither did Jim.

The image of Ali's face filled Hailey's head with every blink.

Her girl's face on a killer's wall. Would he kill her child? Or was it a reminder that she was a target?

If Blake had arrived before Bruce had pulled into the driveway … She would be dead.

Her children would be orphans. Like the Dennigs' children.

Now the Dennigs' tragedy circled her like a vulture on the scent of rotting flesh. How easily it could be her …

She felt sick. With trembling hands, she punched redial again and again, praying for a real voice.

Liz didn't always carry her phone. It often sat overnight in her car, ran out of battery. This wasn't unusual.

They didn't always answer the home phone. Jim and Liz didn't grow up in the generation where everyone was expected to be accessible at any time. Plus, it was three o'clock. Liz would be on her way to pick up the girls. This was normal.

Please, let it be normal.

Hal gripped the steering wheel in both hands and drove faster than she'd ever seen him. Lights streaked across the underside of the tunnel as they passed over Treasure Island. Sirens howled in their ears, making conversation impossible. She couldn't talk.

She dialed the phone, and in the seconds that lapsed between calls, she watched the road.

Hal didn't have to honk. Somehow, cars just cleared the way.

His phone rang. "Harris."

She heard someone talking.

"Is it about Blake?" she asked.

He shook his head. "Hang on, Ryaan. Putting you on speaker." Hal set the phone on the seat between them. "Hey, Ryaan, can you repeat that first part—and maybe talk a little slower?"

"Yes. Okay," Ryaan started, breathless. "The forensic accounting group has been digging into Regal Insurance. We hit pay dirt."

"We're listening."

Hailey stared at her phone. The blank screen. They were still in school. For the next ten minutes, they were safe. She tried to focus on what Ryaan was saying.

"Hank Dennig and Colby Wesson were both beneficiaries of large claims on policies. Both had insured weapons stolen from their facilities. And get this, they were covered for multiple losses. Dennig had two different claims for stolen weapons. Colby Wesson had three—all paid out in full, all in the eighteen months before they were killed."

Dwayne Carson had told Hal that Regal did this to him. Like it was a name.

"Carson said 'Regal,' but who did he mean?" Hal asked, clearly thinking along the same lines. "I assume Regal's a big company."

"It *is* big, but guess who is a 51 percent stake-holder in Regal Insurance Group?" Ryaan continued. "Tom Rittenberg."

How often had Tom been at the house lately? At her house, near her daughters? "Dee is seeing Tom. They've been going out," she whispered to Hal.

"There's more," Ryaan said, not hearing her. "Rendell had a lease on a secured storage area down by the airport. Guess what's in there."

"Guns," Hal said.

"Exactly."

"Guns Rendell bought, or the ones that had been stolen from the Dennigs and Wesson?"

"We've got a team on the way down there now, but we're guessing we'll find some of those stolen guns in storage. Which explains why none of them hit the street until now. After the Dennigs and Wesson were killed, Rendell sat on them until he thought it was safe to start moving them again."

"Dennigs and Wesson stole their own guns, collected the insurance on the loss, and then resold them on the streets for profit?"

"That's the theory," Ryaan said. "Blake finds out about the insurance fraud and the resale of the guns—probably to the same kind of street kids who killed his family. In his mind, these guys—and anyone who invested in Rendell's hedge fund—are responsible for the death of his wife and kids, so he's targeting them." Ryaan was quiet a beat before asking, "Hailey, you there? You're quiet."

"That's good work, Ryaan," Hailey said, fear tight in her throat.

"Yeah," Hal added. "Thanks for the call. Keep us posted."

"Will do."

Hal ended the call, as a chime rang from Hailey's phone. *Early release,* the screen read.

"What?"

Hailey didn't realize she'd made a sound. "The girls."

"Hailey. What's wrong?"

"Today was early release. At the school."

"What time?"

"Two thirty."

He glanced at the clock on the dashboard, their eyes met there. It was three o'clock now. The girls were out of school.

They'd been out long enough to be home.

"Maybe Liz took them on errands," she whispered.

Hal nodded, licking his lips.

How often did Liz take them on errands? Half the time?

No. Less than that.

They had a schedule. Some days they stopped on the way home. Liz had a day in there for ice cream, and a day she went to the butcher.

Today was Thursday, but Hailey had no idea what that meant. What did they do on Thursdays?

"Who knows if Blake would go there," Hal said.

The house was where Blake would go looking for Jim, for her.

"Hailey," Hal said, making a quick right-hand turn and heading for the bridge. "We're going to go to the house. We're going there now." He turned on the sirens. "It's going to be okay, you hear me?"

She shook her head and looked at the phone again. Dialed Liz, then Jim. Then tried Dee again.

After two rings, the line clicked open. "Dee?"

Voices in the background. A woman's voice.

Not Dee's, but perhaps Liz's.

"Liz? Dee?"

A man barked, "Shut up!"

"Dee?" Hailey asked again. A girl's cry echoed somewhere in the background. She felt it in her marrow. "Dee!" she shouted. Shaking, she glanced at the screen.

The call had ended.

"Camilla," she sobbed. "I heard her voice."

God, no. Not them. Not her girls.

Hal snapped the radio off the dash. "I need all units at Broadway and Pierce. Possible 2-2-1 in the home of James and Elizabeth Wyatt."

A 221, a person with a gun.

"And a possible 4-1-7 boy Henry. Proceed with caution. Inspector Wyatt and I are en route."

Hostage situation. An armed man had her children.

Hal honked at a car and blew through the tollbooth, darting through traffic as he raced across the Bay Bridge.

Blake was already there.

Dee, the girls, and Liz and Jim probably too.

Would he shoot all of them?

"What if he kills the girls—"

"He won't," Hal said. The radio beeped, and Hal answered the call.

"Backup's at Sacramento and Franklin," dispatch said. "ETA is two minutes."

Hailey didn't breathe.

"The girls are inside." She grabbed his arm. "They're inside, Hal."

"Hailey Wyatt's kids are inside that house," he said into the radio.

"Okay," dispatch said. "I'm letting everyone know."

Gone were the call codes, the professional tone and words. She was one of them, and there was a murderer in her house.

With her kids.

"Stay strong, Hailey. You stay strong for them," Hal commanded.

Trembling, she hit redial. Prayed she'd get an answer. Hear Dee's voice.

The call went straight to voicemail.

She dialed the home line again. Then Liz.

No one answered.

They reached the crest of Franklin Street and raced toward Broadway. Cars swerved to the right as Hal barreled through the intersection, honking over the blaring siren.

If something happened … She would die … *No. Do not think that way.*

Help me. Please, God, help.

As they turned left on Broadway and crossed through the first intersection, the flashing lights became visible at the house. Three patrol cars, an ambulance with its back cracked open, paramedics at the ready. Above them, the leaves on the oak trees flickered in the light and a soft wind.

Hal parked at a diagonal and jumped out, leaving his door open. He ordered a patrol officer to set up a periphery at the bottom of the stairs.

Hailey had hoped the sight of the house might bring some consolation, but instead, she felt distinctly ill.

She sprinted up the walkway. Hal was right behind her when they reached the stairs that led to the front porch. A group of task force officers in black jumpsuits and Kevlar vests stood against the banister that led up the stairwell. Under dark helmets, it was impossible to tell one from the other.

Marshall barked into his radio. "Report on your position." His face was tense, worried. He was never in the field. He was here for her.

Marshall believed Blake might kill her family. That's why he was here.

"In position," Cameron said across the radio. "You tell Hailey that we're going to get them out of there."

"Please," Hailey whispered.

"Who's inside?" Hal asked.

"Don't know yet. I'm waiting for another specialist to access the neighbor's roof. Hope to have surveillance from there."

"I need to go in," Hailey said.

"No," Marshall said. "No one goes in."

She trembled. Her heart felt like it would explode. "I'm going in there."

His radio crackled, and they all silenced. Marshall pressed the radio to his ear and adjusted the knob so Hailey couldn't hear.

Keep related parties out of the loop.

She'd done it with the families of victims dozens of times.

Her pulse filled her insides, beating like something giant and swollen up her neck, throbbing through her back. Her breath wheezed. Her inhaler was in her purse in the car. Tears stung in her eyes. "You can shoot me then, Captain. Camilla and Ali are in there. I *am* going in."

"She's right, Marshall," Hal said. "You can shoot me, too, but we're going inside."

Marshall only nodded.

Hailey watched as Hal unholstered his gun and released the magazine, pulling the extra magazine from his holster. He nodded at Hailey. "Full."

Marshall reported into the radio that the two inspectors were about to enter the house. Hailey froze. What if she got them shot? What if waiting was better?

But she couldn't. She couldn't be out here when they were in there.

She drew her own weapon. Checked her ammo.

The task force captain stepped forward. "At least let me put a wire on you."

Hailey reholstered her gun and took her jacket off, moving quickly. Focusing on the girls, hoping they could feel her.

Mommy is right here.

Hal and the captain threaded the wire under her vest, clipped it to the inside, and zipped her back up.

When it was done, Hailey drew her gun again. She met Hal's eye, and together they climbed the stairs.

They reached the front door just as the first two shots erupted.

CHAPTER 31

HAL TOOK THE lead, Hailey on his heels. He unlatched the front door and crept into the quiet hallway. Listening to the silence, he scanned the dim entryways, trying to remember the layout of the house.

The house was huge, the furniture centuries old and perfectly kept. It had felt like a museum back then. Now, the place was dank and cold and smelled faintly of gunpowder.

He tried to pretend it was just another crime scene.

But this was Hailey.

She was *his* family.

Hailey at his back, Hal cleared the front rooms. When they were cleared, Hailey waved the task force down the hallway to the kitchen at the end. To the left a wide wood staircase doubled back on itself as it rose to the second floor.

The den door was closed. The room where John had died.

Hailey pointed to it.

She would not lose the rest of her family there. Hal would take a bullet before he let that happen.

The task force spread out to clear the rest of the house.

Three went up the stairs, two into the kitchen. One squatted low against the wall across from the den door. The last remained with Hal and Hailey.

The dark wood door opened part way. The room was dark.

"Hailey," came a woman's voice.

Hal shifted forward.

"Only her," the woman said, her voice cracking. "Or he'll shoot."

Hailey stepped forward.

"I'll be right here," Hal whispered, grabbing her arm. "You need me in there, you just say one of the girls' names."

Hailey nodded.

He didn't want to let her go. But he had to. He couldn't do this for her.

As soon as she entered the room, the door closed.

Hal sprinted out the front. "I need access to Wyatt's wire. Now!"

CHAPTER 32

THE DEN WAS pitch black, the window shade drawn and closed. The room smelled of a men's cologne and something sweeter, floral.

Behind those smells were gunfire, and the dirty penny scent of blood.

The hard muzzle of a gun pressed into her skin below the Kevlar vest.

Hailey froze, glancing at the closed blinds. No chance Cameron could get a view inside the room through those windows. No shot from outside was going to save them. It was up to Hailey.

"Drop your weapon," came a muffled voice.

She drew the weapon from her holster. The gun at her back rattled against the backside of her pelvic bone. The grip was lower than she'd expected. Below her vest.

He knew about the vest.

Or, he was smaller than she'd thought.

The voice, too, had come from directly behind her rather than above. Blake had seemed larger in the photographs, but maybe he wasn't. Perhaps she could take him right here.

"Now," the voice commanded, and she heard the low voice crack. It wasn't a man's voice. Who was holding that gun?

"Mommy," Ali whispered.

A wave of fear crashed over her. She turned toward her daughter's voice.

A hand yanked the gun from her grip. She managed to release the magazine. It dropped on the carpet with a dull thud.

Impatient for her eyes to adjust to the dark, she scanned the room for the girls. A cry came from the far side of the room, but Hailey was afraid to call out. She thought it was Cami, but what if it wasn't? What if Cami didn't answer?

What if something had happened to her?

"Liz? Are you here?"

"Mommy?" Ali's voice called again.

"Baby."

There was scrambling behind Jim's desk. Dark shapes shifted.

Hailey stumbled toward them in the dark.

"Don't move!"

Hailey spun toward the familiar voice. The overhead light came on, blinding her.

Jim sat at his desk, the others huddled behind him. He looked annoyed, rather than scared. But the girls looked afraid. Why didn't Jim?

Hailey turned.

Back pressed to the door, a pistol in her fist, was Dee. The gun in her hand was Russian. Behind her, a body lay on the floor. His face lay in profile, the full reddish-brown beard of the man she'd seen leaving the crime scene in the Tenderloin a week ago. He was the man in the photograph—Donald Blake.

"Dee, why are you pointing that gun at them? The girls are back there."

She didn't answer. The gun didn't waver. Hailey studied the gun, confirmed the make. "A Makarov," Hailey said for the wire.

Dee looked at the gun blankly. Like she didn't know what kind of gun she was holding. Didn't know that the gun in her hand had killed more people than any other in history.

Millions of Jews executed by Russian soldiers. The terror climbed under her skin like a burn.

Dee adjusted her grip on the gun awkwardly. It was not her gun. Whose gun was it?

Did Jim still own a gun?

Even after John was shot?

Tom Rittenberg had been the director of the NRA. He would own a Makarov.

On the floor, Blake's hands lay open, empty. Blood had soaked through his shirt onto the carpet. A foot— maybe two—from where John had died.

"Dee, you don't want to hurt them."

"Like hell I don't." Her teeth were bared, her jaw clenched. The gun lifted higher into the air as if she was taking aim. "He got them killed—all of them."

A Makarov magazine held seven bullets. Dee had shot off two, which left five bullets remaining. She could still kill all of them.

Dee. The night she'd run into Dee in the hall. She'd

been lurking there, listening. The way she talked about Nicholas Fredricks. She'd lost the love of her life. Was that why she was doing this?

Hailey fought to stay calm. She'd never seen Dee out of control. She had no idea what she might be capable of. Take stock. Move slowly.

"What happened, Dee?"

Dee said nothing.

"I'm going to check Blake." Hailey dropped to her knees and felt for a pulse. She wasn't sure if Dee would stop her, but she didn't. Dee's focus on Jim was unwavering.

"He's dead." As she got to her feet, Hailey checked along his waistline.

No weapon.

Hailey saw the butt of the gun at Dee's waist. It looked like a revolver.

"I shot him." Dee didn't take her eye off Jim. "He was going to kill me. I didn't even see it coming, but Tom was right. Blake was going to shoot them, and then he was going to shoot me."

Tom Rittenberg. He was behind this. Would Dee believe Hailey if she told her about Regal Insurance? About Tom's piece in the guns?

Or would she decide Hailey was a liar, too, and shoot them all?

"Thank you, Dee. You saved the girls." She wanted to say their names but she was afraid Hal would take it as a sign to come in the door. She had to create a diversion first, get Dee focused somewhere else.

"But the girls are scared now, Dee. Remember the

pajama party—the fun you guys had at the hotel? You don't want to hurt them. You need to put the gun down."

Dee shook her head. "I can't put the gun down. That's what he said. Whatever you do, don't give up your gun." Tears streamed down her face.

She had to be talking about Tom. Tom had put her up to this. It would be perfect for him—with Blake and Jim dead and Dee in jail or killed in police crossfire, Tom Rittenberg could walk away, a free man. If Jim survived, he would be able to tell the police how Tom had recruited them to invest in the hedge fund. His testimony could help put Tom in prison for the rest of his life, and then some. "Dee," Hailey said. "Talk to me."

One of the girls cried out. Liz hushed her.

Jim's expression tightened and filled with fear. Jim knew his sister better than anyone. What did he think she would do?

In the harsh den light, her skin looked mottled. There were sunspots and freckles across her nose and cheeks that Hailey had never seen. Dee had always been made up. The front of her shirt was pulled from her pants where the gun had been shoved in. Her hair hung in frizzy strands.

How long had her eyes been so red and puffy? Did Hailey miss that? How sick she looked.

"Blake's whole family was killed," Dee whispered. "But he blamed Tom when he should have been blaming those street kids with the guns." She bared her teeth and turned to face her brother. "And people like Jim who killed to hide his secrets, to protect his political ambitions."

"I know about the guns that were stolen and sold on the streets, Dee," Hailey said softly. She let a beat pause.

Kept her voice low. "I just found out. We'll make this right. Let the police do it, Dee."

"Donald Blake wrote about the gun violence—just like Nick did—and Jim went after him. Sent those street kids after him."

"I didn't," Jim said. "I never—"

"Let me help you," Hailey said, speaking over Jim's denial.

"This isn't about you," Dee whispered, drawing Hailey's attention to her eyes. The pupils were small, the whites bloodshot, and the irises the same gray as wet concrete.

"You should've stayed out of it. It was about him." Dee waved the gun toward Jim. He tensed as the gun moved through the air. Liz and the girls crouched on the floor, partially hidden behind him. But if Dee shot and missed Jim, the bullet could easily hit one of them.

"But he bought you off." Dee waved the gun at Hailey again. "Whatever he did to buy you. It's what he does. Buys people. He tried to do that to Tom too, but it didn't work."

"You have to believe me. Tom is a liar," Jim said.

"Shut up!" Dee shouted, firing a bullet over their heads.

Jim flinched.

Ali and Camilla screamed. Liz shrieked.

The bullet sank into the sheetrock.

"It's okay," Hailey said. "We're okay." She had been here all along—under this roof every day. Hailey had overlooked her. She had focused on Jim's part in all the deaths—the cork from his favorite wine vintage, the connection between him and Nick Fredricks, his invest-ments with Rendell's hedge fund—but she had never once looked at Dee.

Dee aimed the gun back at Jim. "Do not say another word. You said Nick was a liar too. You're the liar. You, Jim!"

"Dee, please," Liz pleaded.

"You, too, Liz. Not another word. You should've known what he was doing—where he was investing your money. You were too busy ironing your white linens to know that your husband is a killer."

Liz's crying was muffled.

"We can put him away," Hailey said. "He'll go to jail."

"Jail's too good for him." Dee choked on a sob. "He deserves to die for what he did to Nick."

"I don't understand, Dee. You told me Jim was with you when Nick died," Hailey said.

"He was," she snapped. "All these years, I believed him when he said he had nothing to do with it. Twelve years and Nick's killer has been right under my nose."

Hailey edged closer, but Dee was focused. Hailey wouldn't make it to the gun before Dee could fire. Her only choice was to keep talking. "Why do you think he killed Nick now?"

"I heard it. Tom has it recorded. Jim said he'd pay four hundred thousand dollars if Nick was dead."

"Please, Dee—" Jim started to speak.

"Don't, Jim," Hailey warned.

Jim clamped his mouth shut. He gripped his hands together as though praying, his eyes pleading with his sister.

The gun trembled in Dee's hand.

"Tell me, Dee. Tell me about the order to kill Nick. Is Jim talking to Tom in the recording?"

Dee nodded.

"Why didn't Tom take it to the police?" Hailey asked.

Dee's eyes went wide. "Tom never thought Jim was really involved—it came up when we were talking. I told him how you and I talked about how Nick and Jim used to fight. That was when he figured it out."

Hailey felt like she'd been punched. That conversation in the kitchen—a chance interaction for five minutes. Dee had mentioned that Jim and Nick used to get into it over politics. Hailey had made some stupid comment, something about how she could see Jim doing that. Could that tiny interaction have led to this?

No. Tom Rittenberg caused this. He was setting Jim up to take the fall, using Dee as his weapon. He preyed on her heartbreak, on the death of Nick Fredricks. Tom Rittenberg, who was a fifty-one percent shareholder of Regal Insurance. He was the one who benefited. The payout to Dennig and Wesson for the lost guns showed as a huge loss on the books, one he made up by selling the guns on the street. The resulting cash more than made up for the loss on the books and he didn't have to pay taxes on a dime of it.

"Dee, I need to tell you something, and I need you to listen to me."

"You're not talking me out of it. This goes back too far. I've waited too long. He should've gone to jail when he shot Dottie. Dad should never have taken the fall for that. If he hadn't, I could have stayed with him and mom."

Hailey couldn't do it. The risk was too high. Telling Dee that Tom Rittenberg was a liar was only going to push her over the edge.

How long had Dee been hovering at the edge?

How had Hailey missed it? How had Jim?

Go back to the talking. "How did you meet Blake?"

"He read all Nick's work," Dee said. "I keep a website up with everything he ever wrote." Her smile was a mixture of sadness and rage.

Just then, the office door rattled.

Dee swung and put a bullet through the solid wood.

Liz shrieked, and the girls began crying again.

Liz hushed them.

Jim clutched his hand over his heart in a pained silence.

No sounds from outside the office. Would she have heard something if Hal had been standing on the other side?

If someone out there was shot?

She breathed slowly. "It's okay, Dee."

Dee had always been the calmest of the Wyatts— so controlled. Now, her eyes sparked in fury. Rage set her mouth in a straight, hard line, flushed her cheeks. Hailey couldn't read her next move. Should she close in, or create distance?

Dee moved to the wall as though she required propping. Had she been drinking? Jim had once made a comment about Dee's Valium prescription. The other night, Hailey had seen Dee take two pills in the kitchen. Maybe she had Valium in her system. But the gun didn't shake. She didn't look drunk or drugged. She looked ready to shoot them.

She was down to three bullets. Still enough to kill the girls.

"You could have just let us go, Jim. We were going back to Cornell. We were going to get married. You killed him. You killed the man I loved!" Dee raised the gun and fired.

The girls screamed.

Jim howled.

Hailey sprang toward the girls. "Camilla! Ali!"

The white fabric of Jim's shirtsleeve began to stain red.

Dee spun toward Hailey's movement. The gun level at her head. The door flew open.

Hailey dove sideways.

A shot fired.

She fell in slow motion. Hot, then cold. Screaming. More shots.

Then, silence.

Hailey opened her eyes and saw the ceiling. Hal's face.

The room exploded in noise.

Shouts, commands. Crying.

Hal gripped her shoulder. He wouldn't let her sit up.

"My girls," she said, the word catching on her emotion.

"They're fine," Hal said.

Hailey shook her head. His hand was on her face.

"I promise they're fine."

"Girls!"

Then, they were there. Beside her. Her beautiful girls.

Two men hovered over her. White jumpsuits with red. Paramedics. Hal gripped her hand, made room for them.

Hailey reached up and touched their faces. Ali's,

Camilla's. The skin like velvet—like silk and honey and everything perfect and good.

Heaven.

Pressed the furrow from Camilla's brow and followed her worried gaze toward the spot of stinging pain on her shoulder.

"Just flesh," one of the paramedics said, pulling a length of medical tape from a roll with one.

"It means I just need a Band-Aid," Hailey told the girls.

"You're going to need a big Band-Aid, Mommy," Ali said.

Hailey nodded and turned to the paramedics. "Sure. Give me a big one."

Hal disappeared from view. When he returned, he helped her sit up. Propped against the wall, Hailey held Ali in her lap and Camilla tucked under her good arm.

She could have stayed there forever.

CHAPTER 33

MOVING GINGERLY AROUND her sore shoulder, Hailey poured two fresh cups of coffee and returned to the conference room where Hal paged through photographs and documents taken from Donald Blake's home. She set a cup in front of Hal, who grunted.

The two girls were asleep on a cot in the corner of the conference room, their heads in opposite directions, their feet curled in the center. Hal had brought them here while Hailey got patched up.

She had checked herself out of the hospital against the doctor's advice. Hal's too. With a nasty flesh wound across her shoulder, she could have used a night in her own private room to rest up, but she wasn't going to miss the opportunity to finally close this case. She needed to see it through.

Hal hadn't been to sleep yet. Typical Hal, when he got focused on something. Already, he had the pieces of the puzzle mostly put together. Tom Rittenberg had been arrested and Roger and his team were collecting evidence from his house and office. They'd already confirmed that Rittenberg was the owner of the Makarov Dee had. Roger's team found it listed on an insurance policy. His prints were also on the stock.

Jim was still in the hospital. He would survive. That was a good thing. The Wyatt family didn't need any more deaths. But Hailey was done with him. He would be charged with impeding an investigation, at the very least. Who knew if he'd serve any time.

Hal had spent much of the night collecting evidence from Dee's room and Blake's house. Among her things, Dee had the taped conversation between Tom Rittenberg and Jim about Nicholas Fredricks. "I'll put it this way," Jim had said, sounding much younger than he did now. "It would do wonders for my career if Nick Fredricks wasn't around." There was a muffled, scratchy voice. Then Jim began again. "It would be worth four or five hundred thousand, for sure."

The lab was running tests on the file. She wanted to believe Rittenberg had edited the recording to make it sound as though Jim were hiring a hit on Nick Fredricks.

But she wasn't making bets on anything surrounding Jim.

Whatever Jim's involvement was, he didn't pull the trigger. They had already confirmed that Jim was with Dee for a campaign fundraiser at his home the evening Nicholas Fredricks was killed.

Even if he hadn't pulled the trigger, Jim Wyatt likely got Nick Fredricks killed. Hal suspected Tom Rittenberg saw it as an opportunity to manipulate Jim.

And it seemed to have worked.

The forensic accountants would take weeks to dig through the records, but already, they had confirmed that

Jim didn't start working with Tom Rittenberg until after Fredricks had been killed. So far, Dee had refused to roll over on Jim. Once she had learned the truth about Tom Rittenberg, she'd clammed up entirely. They might never get evidence against Jim from Dee. For as much as she obviously loathed him, she depended on him too. He was the only constant in her life, for better or worse.

There were still some pieces missing, some they may never understand fully. Blake had photographs of Hank Dennig meeting with Jeremy Hayden, their dead gunrunner. Hayden appeared to be delivering a bag of cash, likely from the sale of the stolen guns. Hal thought Hayden was probably the hedge fund's primary connection for selling the guns on the streets.

Hailey sipped her coffee and watched as Hal flipped through the documents from Blake's house.

"Why didn't Blake just bring this all to the police?" she asked. "It would have been enough to open an investigation."

"I think he was too far gone for that," Hal said, pushing a black composition notebook toward her. "Take a look."

Hailey reached out, gasping at the pain in her shoulder.

"You shouldn't be here," Hal commented. For the nineteenth time. "But I know you won't leave," he added before she could respond.

She slid the composition book across the table and flipped it open. The pages held collages of photographs— some in color, some in black and white. Some were photocopies of the same images she'd seen at Blake's house. Most images had been cut so that only their faces remained.

Blake's family.

Page after page after page of their faces, the photographs

overlapped and turned sideways and upside down. On one page, his wife's face created an X across the page. On another, his son's was an O. There was no pattern, no message.

Hailey felt like she was drowning. The tightness in her chest, the difficulty breathing. She'd lost John, almost lost Camilla and Ali. And Liz.

Liz too.

After everything that had happened at the house, Liz had to be medicated. She was spending the night at General so the doctors could keep an eye on her.

Jamie Vail was coming to pick up Camilla and Ali in a few hours. They would stay with her and Tony for a couple of days. Jamie's adopted son, Zephenaya, was thrilled to have other kids in the house. And Tony planned to keep them home from school—all three of them—so that made it especially exciting. Zephenaya had been through his own trauma. It might be good for the kids to have some time together.

Hailey had always been amazed at how openly kids talked about things adults buried.

She turned through the pages of Blake's journal, where he had written out his wife and children's names hundreds—maybe thousands—of times.

"He was heartbroken," she said.

The door opened and O'Shea poked his head in. "James Robbins is here to view the lineup, and we've got Gordon Price ready in interview two." He caught Hailey's eye. "Good to see you all in one piece."

Again, Hailey looked to Camilla and Ali. She wasn't in one piece—not since the day Camilla was born. Being a mother meant part of your heart walked around outside your body. "I was lucky." *I am lucky.*

Hal rose from the table. "You want to interview Price with me, Sheaster?"

"Damn right, I do."

Hal and Hailey hushed him simultaneously as the girls shifted in their sleep.

"Sorry," O'Shea whispered.

Hailey left the conference room door open so she could hear the girls if they needed her. James Robbins waited in the viewing room.

O'Shea and Hal gathered the lineup. Robbins rubbed his hands together and bounced on the balls of his feet.

"They won't be able to see you," Hailey told him.

"It's not that," he said, pausing momentarily. "I'm afraid I won't recognize him. What then?"

"We'll have to get him another way," Hailey said, shrugging.

His eyes widened. "What about the safe house? Can we stay there—if I don't recognize him, I mean."

"Of course," Hailey reassured him. Hal was working to place James and Tawny Robbins in witness protection. Hal would make it happen. He related to James Robbins. A young black man with no father figure? It was a familiar story. Some might say Robbins was another statistic, but not Hal. He'd read Robbins from the start—knew he wasn't a killer. Hal hadn't given up on finding the truth. That was classic Hal. How had she ever let herself doubt him?

Never again.

"Okay," Robbins said.

"You'll be safe, I promise."

Robbins blinked, emotion in his eyes.

Hal joined them and put a hand on Robbins's shoulder. Robbins seemed to relax under the protective gesture. "You ready?" Hal asked him.

Robbins glanced at Hailey, who nodded. "He's ready," she said.

Hal pressed the intercom button and told O'Shea to bring them in.

The men weren't even all the way into the room when Robbins pointed out Gordon Price. "That's him."

"You're sure?" Hal asked.

"Positive."

Hal squeezed his shoulder. "That's all we need."

The marshall came to take Robbins back to his sister. As they started down the hall, Robbins turned back. "Thank you," he said to Hal.

"Thank you," Hal replied, smiling at him.

Hailey could feel Hal's pride at protecting James and Tawny Robbins. It was earned. Thank God for Hal.

"Time to tell Gordon Price what he's won. You want to be there?"

"Think I'll watch from here," she said.

Hal stepped into the interrogation room where Gordon Price stood with O'Shea. Hal was grinning.

O'Shea opened a manila folder and laid out photographs for Price.

"We know you killed these people," Hal said.

Price flipped the retainer in his mouth. He looked relaxed. Hailey settled against the two-way mirror, wishing she were in there. She wanted a piece of Price too. She glanced at the conference room where the girls were still sleeping. Not this time. Right now, she needed to be a mother. She'd have her turn later, in the interrogation room. For now, Hal and O'Shea could handle it.

Hal looked up at the mirror. He couldn't see her, but he was including her. Watch this, the look said. Then, he slid one final picture in front of Price. A photograph of Price's mother.

Price went pale. "What the hell you playing at?"

"Your mother's going to jail."

"My mother ain't done nothing."

"By helping you, she's been aiding and abetting a killer," O'Shea said.

"She's a receptionist at the law firm of Martin Abbott," Hal continued. "That's how you got his business cards. Carson called Abbott. Your mother takes the message, calls you. Then, you go out and take care of whoever it is."

"Ain't none of that true."

"We already talked to your mother," Hal said.

Hailey wasn't sure he actually had, but the grin was unnerving. It was working on Price.

"We have an eyewitness to Kenny Fiston's murder. The question is, do you want your mother to go to jail too?"

Price said nothing.

"We want the guy who hired you." Hal let it sit out there a minute. "You help us with that, we'll forget about your mother."

"And me?"

"Depends on how much we can prove."

Price chewed his lip. "If you get him for murder, I'll get a reduced sentence?"

"We can talk to the DA."

"I want it in writing first," Price said. "Then I'll talk."

"Got to give me something to take to the DA."

"Guy's name is Tom Rittenberg," Price said after a minute. "You get me a deal and leave my mama out of this—and I get you enough to pin him for all this … and more."

Hal's grin never wavered.

CHAPTER 34

Three weeks later

HAL SAT IN the back of the courtroom for Tom Rittenberg's preliminary hearing. The courtrooms were right off the marble foyer. Unlike the upstairs offices that had been remodeled with linoleum and cheap paper-thin walls, these rooms retained their original majesty.

Marble pillars marked the four corners of the room, crisscrossed by white veins that ran through the rich brown marble. Along the walls were black and white photographs of the judges who had doled out justice from the walnut bench. At the front, Ryaan Berry sat beside the DA. She would get the credit as lead investigator on bringing down this gun trade. This would be good for her career. Hal was glad for her.

The memory of Tom Rittenberg's face on the day of his arrest was still clear in Hal's mind.

"You are making a grave miscalculation," Rittenberg warned as Hal was cuffing him. "I'll have your badge for this."

Nope.

Turned out the miscalculation was on Rittenberg's end. Gordon Price had been on the bad side of a deal one too many times. To avoid being burned again, Price had been careful in his dealings with Tom Rittenberg and Harvey Rendell. "Can't trust white guys," Price told Hal.

Hal thought of Jim. "Some of them," he agreed.

Gordon Price had covered his ass big time. He had video of Rittenberg giving him instructions on taking out Dwayne Carson and Kenny Fiston—as well as whoever else was in the way. He also videoed conversations between Rittenberg and Rendell. All by using his Apple watch. Even Hal didn't know those things could do that.

Rittenberg had organized the whole enterprise— worked to get Wesson and Dennig on board to allow the guns to be stolen and sold on the streets. Then he laundered through a hedge fund.

Harvey Rendell managed and dispersed the earnings. The logistics of the hedge fund were remarkably simple. Hedge funds, Hal now knew, could buy anything.

In the end, if Rendell had lived, he might have gotten off with the lightest punishment. The DA would have prosecuted him for the insurance fraud and illegal distribution of stolen weapons, something akin to unregistered gun sales. Since Rendell never took possession or distributed the weapons, his punishment would have been an SEC issue. Not that it meant anything to Rendell now. He'd already gotten his punishment.

Gordon Price wouldn't get off easy either. They'd matched his tread to the prints at Hunters Point. Price had known he'd scratched himself on the night he shot Fiston and Robbins. He had been going back up there to clean up the evidence when he took shots at Hal. Price had trained in the Israeli shooting stance during an intense, 30-day military-style training course in Honduras a few years earlier.

Even if Price got a reduced sentence for helping bring in Tom Rittenberg, he'd killed two people, wounded another, and taken multiple shots at a police officer. He was going away for a long time.

It was still unclear whether Jim Wyatt would do any time. He had provided introductions to the right people in exchange for money, mostly in the form of illegal campaign funds—a little more than 6.4 million dollars in all. His attorneys were arguing that he made those introductions under duress, that Tom Rittenberg had Fredricks killed and then used that to threaten Jim and his family.

As far as Hal was concerned, whatever Jim Wyatt got for punishment, it wasn't enough.

His career was over. His wife was gone too. It turned out most of the Wyatts' money came from Liz's parents, and it was still held by her ninety-year-old father. Jim Wyatt would be living much more modestly from now on. There was something very satisfying about that outcome.

It also meant that Liz could help Hailey financially. Not that Hailey would ever ask. Hal was glad knowing that she wouldn't have to cover all their expenses on her own.

Hailey had skipped the hearing. She couldn't bring herself to sit on the side of the prosecution, and she wouldn't consider sitting on the side of the defense.

Roger had found one of Dee's prints inside Fredricks's coffin, proving that Dee had, in fact, exhumed his body some time ago in order to borrow his fingerprint. The crime scene team was doing a thorough search to confirm that Blake had helped. It was hard to imagine Dee could have done it on her own.

As the judge called for order, Hailey entered through one of the double doors in the back and slid in beside Hal. As she did, Tom Rittenberg eyed her. Hal willed Rittenberg to glance in his direction. He would have liked a chance to stare that man down, but Tom didn't look anywhere near Hal.

Ryaan Berry took the stand to tie the case against Rittenberg back to the guns they had confiscated. Rittenberg had avoided death at Blake's hand, but he wouldn't avoid time behind bars. O'Shea and Kong were working with Oakland PD to link Rittenberg to the death of Blake's family.

Hailey had requested the case be assigned to someone else. With Jim's involvement, the department would have probably made that call anyway. They certainly didn't want to lose the case because of an unnecessary conflict of interest.

Understanding what Hailey had gone through with John's death gave Hal a new appreciation for the complications of family and grief. It made him hope Blake finally found some peace. He was looking forward to working a regular old murder investigation. He suspected Hailey was too. O'Shea and Kong would do a good job. They already had some promising leads. It might take years to put it all together.

As the DA stood to make his closing remarks, Hailey and Hal left quietly. "Nice work," she said.

"You too." He paused, watching her sway from foot to foot, knowing her mind was already on the next meeting with a different DA, the one they'd selected over the past week. "You ready?"

She nodded, though she looked doubtful.

"You sure you don't want company?"

She hesitated and glanced down the hall behind her. "I think I have to do it alone."

He nodded, rubbed the scalp above his ear. "I understand."

"But I'd love to have someone waiting—say outside the DA's office at four o'clock?"

He smiled. "I'm your guy."

She exhaled. Her shoulders relaxed, letting him know what it meant. In these last few weeks, he had been baptized into a new space.

Family, he'd call it, if someone were looking for a label.

They'd become family.

Not in the way departments spoke of it as a recruiting tool, but in the subtle shift that happened between people who had survived hardships and held tight, instead of pushing away.

Hailey glanced at her watch. "I need to do one thing before the meeting. See you at four?"

"Four o'clock." He watched her go. She walked with strides that seemed too big for her short stature. Her hair bounced like little springs off her back as she went. She glanced back once, raised a hand, and smiled. What courage it took to face that part of her history.

The courtroom doors opened and the masses filed

out. As they drifted by—officers, reporters, the attorneys—Hal joined the stream.

The unmistakable high of closing a case surrounded him as the crowd ushered him back into the high marble foyer. He stepped onto the street and breathed the cool San Francisco air, the fog still low in the sky.

He read the familiar credo on the marble plaque.

"To the faithful and impartial enforcement of the laws with equal and exact justice to all."

Carson had walked right by that credo, just moments before he was killed. Hal wished they could have provided exact justice for Carson. There were always the ones that slipped through.

They weren't perfect.

He turned and looked back at the building.

Flaws and all, this was the place that felt most like home.

CHAPTER 35

HAILEY CAME OUT of the stairwell. Cameron and Jamie stood in the elevator lobby.

They didn't notice Hailey at first. Bent in, talking, Cameron held a hand across her middle.

Beneath it was a small rounded bump.

"Hi."

The two women smiled.

Hailey looked again at Cameron's middle, raising an eyebrow.

"I just came to meet with HR," Cameron confessed. "I had to let them know before someone figured it out."

HR would have put her on desk duty. It was the smart thing. Protect the baby. How many things changed with motherhood. "Congratulations," Hailey smiled.

Cameron's eyes grew teary and Hailey's with them. Cameron's boyfriend had been killed. The baby's father was gone. Her baby would never know his or her father.

How lucky Camilla and Ali were to have those years with their dad.

Hailey hugged Cameron. She didn't know how to put it into words. She was grateful for Cameron's strength, that her friend understood the intensity of the grief, how the ones left behind felt they were drowning inside themselves.

"I know," Hailey said. "It gets easier."

It did. That, at least, was true. Not better—just more distant, less intense.

"Rookie Club dinner tonight at six," Jamie reminded them as the two women stepped apart.

"You should come," Cameron said. "Please." She patted her rounded front. "Who knows how many more I'll make."

Drinks with Hal at four.

She would make dinner. In that moment, it was hard to remember how she had survived so long without them. They needed each other. She needed them.

How her life had changed in a year. John's death had led her to put all her faith in Jim. How badly she wanted to believe he was trustworthy—so much that she had ignored the signs. The signs Hal saw so clearly.

She had trusted the wrong grandparent. Liz was the one she should never have doubted, the one who loved Camilla and Ali as if they were her own.

The girls were with Liz now. She'd found the perfect four-bedroom house in Noe Valley. Away from the ritzy neighborhood where Jim had moved them, Liz seemed more relaxed, happier. She wore her hair down more. She dressed up less. Liz would tell Hailey to go to dinner with the club. She would insist on it. "Tommy's?"

Jamie laughed. "Where else would we go?"

"I'll be there," Hailey said. She meant it.

"I'm so glad," Cameron told her, still holding a hand on her belly. "I'll be reaching out for some advice too."

Hailey thought of all the things she had worried about as a new mother. How little of it mattered. Love them and keep them safe.

"You better," Hailey said. "I'm here any time."

*

Standing in the green marbled foyer, Hailey hesitated only a moment behind the fogged glass of the department doors that read "Internal Affairs." She stepped into the bustling department and walked past the secretary. People stared. There would be talk.

There already was.

She maneuvered around the green, steel desks to Bruce's office. He was crouched on the floor, loading books into a brown cardboard box. Other stacks of boxes sat in the center of the room. The walls were bare except for nails and the faint yellow lines where pictures had once hung.

"Last day?"

Bruce's lips curved into a smile, but there was something forlorn in his eyes, something that passed in a blink. The day would come when she could no longer remember those eyes.

"Last day."

He rubbed at his head, at the patch where his hair was cut shorter, where it was still growing back in.

From habit, Hailey stepped forward to touch it. Stopped when his eyes widened in surprise.

She stepped away. "You feel good?"

He stood slowly. "Better all the time."

After an awkward beat, she motioned to the boxes. "You're going to be great."

He grinned and it made her laugh. "A desk jockey for the FBI. Never thought I'd see the day."

They fell silent again.

The room still felt occupied. She saw the place where the Christmas banquet picture used to hang—the two of them standing carefully five or six people apart.

"Now I know who to call if I ever get myself in big trouble."

When his gaze returned to her, the expression was stoic, the strain of it impossible to miss. "Yes. Please call me first."

The familiar pull was still between them, but Hailey resisted it now. She didn't trust herself to hug him.

Instead, she said goodbye.

It wasn't as hard as she'd thought it would be. The more she had trusted Jim, the bigger the wedge between her and Hal. What she needed wasn't another man.

What she needed was her partner.

She needed Hal.

She had him back now. She wouldn't let anything come between them again.

Crossing the department, she walked slowly, confidently. She didn't pause until she pushed through the red door and into the stairwell. Relief and sorrow ran in simultaneous waves through her chest.

She stepped through the second set of doors and into the fresh air. Standing on the small cement patio, she squinted in the bright light and breathed cool air. Pushed her hair back and wiped her moist hands on the slacks of her suit.

She stood until she felt the pull to go back inside. It

was time to move forward. Upstairs in the DA's office, Martina Coelho awaited their appointment.

Getting this out in the open was important for all of them. One day Ali might remember. Even though Hailey prayed that day never came, she would have to be prepared for that.

Hal had helped her choose Martina Coelho. She had small children, a husband. With thoughts of Ali and Camilla, Hailey gripped the door handle and imagined—for the hundredth time—what she was about to tell Coelho and how she would say it.

How she would confess that her daughter had killed her husband.

Hailey stepped into the dim building, pausing to allow her eyes time to adjust to the darkness. Her gaze was drawn to the bench where Hal would be waiting when she was done telling the story of that night.

She patted her pocket for the photographs Liz had given her this morning. There were two—one of Ali and Camilla, taken by Liz only a month ago. The other was a family shot of the four of them at Christmas two years ago, just six weeks before John's death.

She entered the DA's office. Martina stood from her desk.

They would be fine. All they could do was move forward.

A little luck would help too.

She had earned some luck.

They all had.

AUTHOR'S NOTE

The first person I would like to thank is you—the reader. Thank you for reading this book and for following the Rookie Club stories. While we're at it, thank you for every book you've ever read. It is the greatest gift you can give an author like me. Without you, there would be no books, and what a terrible world that would be.

If you have enjoyed this book, please consider taking a moment to leave a review on Amazon or elsewhere. Reviews and recommendations are vital to authors. Every good review and every recommendation for one of my books helps me stay hunkered and warm in my basement, doing what I love best—writing dark, chilling stories.

To claim your free short story, to learn more about the Rookie Club or my writing, please visit me at www.daniellegirard.com.

Now, please turn the page for a preview of book three of the Rookie Club Series, Dark Passage.

CHAPTER 1

HEAVY BOOTS DRUMMED on the floor, partially drowned out by the rasp of zippers and the sticky rip of Velcro. Inside the Ops van, the officers pulled on jumpsuits and tightened bulletproof vests. For Special Ops Officer Cameron Cruz, the red light had a calming effect. The raid was minutes away. In these moments, the energy of the officers built a charge in the air that was almost visible.

Despite it, expressions were guarded, cool. Tension was at a peak. As soon as they started moving in, the jokes would begin. The pranks and stunts would come after, the rowdy celebration that followed a successful raid.

Cameron was the only woman, always a little on the outside, and yet, she loved it. The adrenaline, the strategy, every minute a test. Then, reliving each second when it was done. No one talked about that beforehand.

Superstition wasn't something any Special Ops member would admit to, but they all subscribed.

Tonight, they had a barricaded suspect. The red light protected their eyes, so they were ready for the darkness outside. Weapons loaded, Cameron smelled the acrid, grapefruit odor of sweat and the metallic scents of gun oil and ammunition. Already sweat ran along the line of her equipment belt and the weight cut into her hips. Two undershirts didn't prevent the familiar biting on her skin. The belt carried forty pounds of equipment, built for a man's hips, not hers. And even the extra-extra-small didn't hold the belt in place. Lately, though, it was getting easier. It had taken her until yesterday to figure out why.

"Four minutes," the sergeant called.

Silence buzzed inside the bus like the anticipation of tremors after an earthquake. Tonight, she would tell him. She surreptitiously crossed herself with a tiny motion of her index finger. It was a ritual for her. Everyone had one. She thought of Mama, Rosa, Diego, then of the unknown little person growing inside her.

The sergeant called the team's attention to a backlit board with a diagram that might have been for a complex football play. Cameron had intimate knowledge of the layout, as she had been on the reconnaissance team. On every job, the team was split into four duties: equipment; intelligence, who profiled the suspect; tactical, which coordinated the actual event; and reconnaissance. New officers began in equipment.

Reconnaissance was the fourth shop and the most dangerous. Not everyone was eligible for the recon team. Certainly they never risked the medics like Ambley. If something went wrong, medics were the last people the team could afford to lose.

"Lau, you're lead."

Ryan Lau's gaze swept across the team as he pulled his helmet over his black buzz cut. Lau was often lead. He was compact, maybe only five foot eight inches, but all wiry muscle, which made him easier to cover. The lead man was most at risk. He carried a fifty-pound ram to take out the door. If there was a shooter behind it, he depended on the team to cover him.

"Kessler does second, then Cruz." In many ways, Brian Kessler was Lau's opposite: taller and thick, built like a football player but also agile and quick. Sergeant Lavick went through the remaining list, eight in all. "Questions?"

Lavick ran his forearm across his face. He looked old. "Let's go, then. Gear on. We're moving in."

Cameron pulled the black helmet over her cropped blond hair. She patted her suit, fingered the reassuring bulge of her ammo. She signaled ready as the last of the weapons were checked, rechecked, and holstered. Hostile, agile, mobile was the recon credo. The door cracked open. The cool San Francisco night rolled into the van as the team moved out.

The perp was wanted for armed robbery. He had a weapons fetish and wasn't likely to go down without a fight. That's all she needed to know. Her job was to get him out. After that, he was someone else's problem.

The team stopped at the door, making their formation.

"Nuts to butts," Lau called back.

She tucked up against Kessler, felt Paules behind her.

She was grateful it wasn't Diego. This was no place for distractions. Diego was behind Paules along with Daley, Ballestrini and Ambley.

The line was perfectly still. Sergeant Lavick stood to the side, his hand on his watch. After a beat, his hand went up. A breath shot through the group. He showed five fingers, then four, then three, two, one. Go.

The ram struck the door. The cheap composite buckled in the center, tearing the lock from the jam. Lau dropped the ram and drew his weapon. The wave of officers streamed in like high tide. The first two went right, the next two left, splitting to the two sides of the place. She and Daley cleared the first room, full of gym equipment, and then moved into the bathroom. She swung around the door, used the barrel of her rifle to pull back the shower curtain. Clear.

The next door was closed. She and Daley hesitated. Standing clear of the doorway, they waited for the team to gather. This must be the room. Lau arrived followed by Kessler. Lau raised one finger and pointed to himself. He would take the door. Cameron pointed right, ready to move around the doorjamb, keeping her back to the wall. Buttonhooking, it was called. Daley pointed left. He would cross the door to the left. It would leave Cameron in the best position to shoot. Gun raised, her finger resting flat along the trigger ring, she nodded to go.

Lau threw the door open and rolled into the room followed by Daley. Cameron came behind, then Kessler. She kept her back to the frame of the door as she hooked around the doorway and into the room. Her back was safe, her gun aimed and ready.

A string of shots fired from the closet. The angle was steep; the shots made a line of dust as they pierced high on the wall behind them. The shooter was sitting on the floor. Cameron aimed low and shot back. Three quick shots, then she paused. There was no response.

Cameron kept her aim still on the closet, while Kessler, Daley, and Paules moved past her. Daley took left and Paules right, as Kessler reached for the door. He nodded back to Cameron. She nodded in return. *Just try it, you son of a bitch. I'm ready.* Kessler slid the door open. A Heckler & Koch MP5 machine gun fell to the floor with a clank. Kessler and Daley pulled the shooter out. Dead.

"Suspect is down," Lau reported into his radio. "I repeat, suspect is down."

Without looking at the perp's face, Cameron lowered her weapon and left the room. Diego stood in the doorway smiling. "Nice work, Officer Cruz."

"Well, thank you, Ramirez," she said, trying not to grin like a schoolgirl.

She followed him out of the house, itching to get him alone.

CHAPTER 2

DIEGO AND CAMERON were always careful to leave the station separately. Usually she went first, but tonight, he begged off drinks with the group. "Seeing my girl," he said without looking at her.

"When we going to meet this invisible chica?" Paules asked.

Diego shook his head.

"You afraid of a little competition?" Kessler joked.

"That's it," Diego responded. "You're so smooth, I'm afraid she'd fall for one of you bozos."

Cameron took her time, packing up her bag and listening to the male banter.

Sergeant Lavick came in and shed his coat. He stood in front of his locker and stared at the lock.

Paules and Lau stifled their laughter.

Lavick spun the knob a few times. "Sixteen." Cameron folded her belt into her locker. "Twenty-seven," she said.

Lavick frowned. "I know my own damn combination."

Lau burst out laughing. Lavick picked up a baseball

hat off the bench and flicked it at him like a Frisbee. "Watch it, Lau. Quarterlies are coming up."

Lavick turned to Cameron.

"Thirty-six," she whispered as her phone vibrated in her back pocket. Diego.

"You sure you don't want to join tonight?" Kessler asked, leaning against the locker beside hers.

"Not tonight."

She closed the locker and said good night. Only in the car did she read Diego's text.

PHNH in twenty.

Of course. She should have known they would go to the Potrero Hill Neighborhood House. It was one of Diego's favorite spots. During the day, it was a community center aimed at helping kids make good choices. It had been in use for more than fifty years. Diego had spent many afternoons there as a kid himself, before graduating and becoming a mentor. Now, he spent free afternoons at PHNH, talking with kids, helping with homework or playing basketball behind the house. At night, though, the center was closed, and the views of the city skyline were stunning. Tonight was the perfect night for it. No clouds and the temperature in the low seventies.

They might walk down the hill and have Cuban food at Fruitlandia. Maybe walk over to the park or climb the hill above the reservoir on the next block to get the extra twenty feet of view. The sun would set over the house, cutting down between the streets of the city and washing everything in pink and orange. And then, they would go home. Where in there did she tell him that he was going to be a father?

When she parked on De Haro, Diego was already on the porch, legs dangling over the banister exactly the way he told the kids they couldn't. He appeared lost in thought as she approached. He reached a hand back and helped her climb over the banister. She sat beside him, leaning into his warmth.

"Nice night," she said.

"Gorgeous." He smiled, but it faltered. Something in his brow was worried. He touched the hair along her face, slowly. Kissed her lips gently.

"What's wrong?"

He stroked her face, running his thumb along her jaw. "Nothing." He stared at the skyline and went quiet.

Normally, they would start in on the job, recount the moments from the day. He would talk about her kill shot. The banter before they got quieter, found the intimacy that they couldn't share at work.

Diego shook his head. "No, it's not nothing."

Cameron shifted away from him, waiting.

He didn't meet her eye as he spoke. "They're taking me undercover."

"What do you mean? Who?"

"ICE," he said. When she didn't respond, he added, "Immigration and Customs Enforcement."

She was in shock. "I know what ICE is."

"I offered to help with an ongoing investigation. Actually, I put my name in eight months ago. I got the call this morning."

"Where will you be?"

He looked at her without answering.

"You can't tell me?"

He held her gaze.

She thought about the baby, subconsciously crossed her arms. "How long?"

"Six weeks, maybe two months. It will seem like forever."

"It will." She thought about all the times her Papa had told her she shouldn't be training to be a police officer, when Mama pleaded with her to find a safe job. Telling him about the baby would be the same as asking him to stay. Two months from now she would be fifteen or sixteen weeks. It could wait. It would have to.

CHAPTER 3

Three months later

THIS WAS THE hardest part of the day at work, the time when she felt Diego's absence most profoundly. While it used to be a time of celebration, the job accomplished, now it reminded her that she was heading into another night when she couldn't see Diego, couldn't even talk to him. Cameron heaved her equipment bag back onto the top shelf of the storage room.

"Need some help getting it up there?" Daley joked.

"Mine's done, but you sure you can reach your spot? I can give you a boost," she joked back.

She'd originally been given a spot on the bottom shelf, but since she was one of the tallest members of the team, they eventually moved her to the top shelf.

Lau laughed out loud. "She's got a few inches on you, Daley."

"And on you," he sparred back.

She chuckled at them, more at ease in this environment than in any she'd ever known. As a kid, her brothers told her she could never be a cop. Not a girl, certainly not a gringa so unlike any of the police in her tiny hometown of Bleakwood, Texas. *Couldn't*, to her, meant *should*, and she'd been easily baited. What better way to make a stamp on the world than to make it safer?

Cameron rubbed her hand across her head. Tonight, she was ready to go home and get a shower. The changes in her body had pushed her to the outside of the group again. Sometimes, before Diego went undercover, she had gone along for the celebratory round of drinks. Careful to sit on the opposite side of the room from Diego, she'd listen as the men spun short tales into tall ones.

She was always the quiet one. Previous boyfriends had complained about her reticence. Women were supposed to ooze emotion, but that wasn't Cameron's style. No one had been worth talking to until Diego. He'd simply drawn her out, and it had felt as natural as exhaling.

Even after he went undercover, she still participated in some of the team nights out. She went to the bar and ordered a Coke. Mostly, she listened, laughed, and called out the really big lies. These men had no idea how far Cameron had come from the reticent girl she'd been. They called her the shyest tough girl on the force, but she was accustomed to feeling strange about her quiet nature. Being in the middle of the rambunctious group of men was no different from growing up the quiet, white girl in a raucous Mexican family.

"You coming out, Cruz?" Lau asked.

"Not tonight."

She caught Kessler eyeing her midsection and quickly pulled on her coat. She had to tell her sergeant. She'd been hoping to tell Diego first, to hold off until she'd heard from him. But, the bump was getting too obvious.

She grabbed her pack and said good night, heading to the sergeant's office before she chickened out again. As she passed the captain's office, she saw Sergeant Lavick sitting across from Captain Margaret Ahrens. Not wanting to interrupt, she kept walking, but Captain Ahrens caught her eye.

"You have a minute, Officer Cruz?" Captain Ahrens called out.

Cameron stopped in the doorway. The team had little interaction with Captain Ahrens. She was seldom in her office, as she coordinated the team's efforts with other departments. This meant she spent most of her time in the main station on Bryant. It felt especially strange since they were the only two women.

"That was nice work today," Sergeant Lavick said, taking off his glasses and rubbing the red marks on his nose with long, thin fingers. The skin on his knuckles suddenly seemed too loose, like an old man's. His face was thinner, too. Maybe he was sick.

"I heard you did very well," Captain Ahrens added. Even behind her desk, she was formidable. Taller than Cameron, she had the build of a basketball player.

"Thank you."

"Come on in," Ahrens said, motioning to the empty seat in front of her desk.

Ahren's office was largely sterile. Commendations and diplomas, as well as several pictures of Ahrens, including one with Michelle Obama, hung on the walls. But, the only personal picture was the one framed on her desk, an eight-by-ten of a large German shepherd. Cameron knew that dog was named Kleina, because the dog's tag hung from Ahrens' keychain.

"You okay?" Captain Ahrens asked.

Cameron didn't answer at first. It was now or never. She stepped into the office. "I'm going to need some time off."

Lavick put his glasses back on. "You mean vacation time?"

She considered telling them to forget it when she felt the strange gurgling of the baby moving. "More like leave."

"Medical leave?" Ahrens asked, folding her hands on her desk and leaning forward.

Cameron nodded.

"Are you all right?" Lavick asked.

"I'm fine. I have a—I'm—" Cameron hadn't said the words out loud, except to Rosa. Even Mama didn't know yet, although Cameron knew she had to tell her soon.

"Lavick," Ahrens interrupted. "Will you excuse us for a moment?"

Lavick frowned. "I should probably stay—"

"Please, Michael," Ahrens interjected. "I'll call you back in a few minutes. I would like to talk to Officer Cruz."

"Like woman to woman?" Lavick said, nodding.

Ahrens raised an eyebrow. "Sure."

Lavick got up and left.

"How far along are you?" Ahrens asked as soon as the door had clicked closed.

Cameron didn't blink. "Twenty-one weeks."

"Wow, you've kept it well concealed."

Cameron didn't answer. She felt huge.

"You're keeping it."

"There was never any question."

"And the father?" she asked.

"I think he'll be supportive."

Ahrens cocked her eyebrow again. "He doesn't know?"

"Not yet."

Ahrens was quiet before she said, "I have a son."

"I had no idea," Cameron responded as she scanned the room for some evidence of the child. There was none.

"We're not in touch," Ahrens added and Cameron didn't ask more. Ahrens opened her desk drawer and pulled out a notepad. "Twenty-one weeks," she said out loud. "You've got leave from the state—a portion of it paid and some unpaid. You'll be okay for money?" She asked this without looking up.

"Fine."

"You can take up to six months after the baby is born without jeopardizing your position. I'll get the paperwork started and get you in touch with the benefits group. They'll help arrange a desk position until you deliver."

Six months after the baby. A desk job until she delivered. That was twenty more weeks. She might be away for a year. In seven years, she'd never gone more than nine days without shooting. How could she last a year?

Outside Captain Ahrens' office, Lavick stood talking to Kessler. "Everything okay?" he asked.

"Fine."

He was heading toward Ahrens' office when he said, "Oh, you got a letter. It came in the department mail. It's on my desk. Go ahead and grab it."

Cameron went into his office and found the letter. On the front, in Diego's handwriting, it said her name and the words "Personal and Confidential." No postmark. No return address. It meant he was close. Maybe coming home. Thank God.

Kessler filled the doorway. His blonde hair was cropped short, his brown eyes wide. Women stared at him when they were out with the team and friends in the department had asked about him more than once. He was good looking, if in a Nebraska farm boy kind of way. "Hey." He glanced at the envelope, but she quickly folded it and put it in her jacket pocket.

"Hi, Brian."

"I thought you might want to see a movie this weekend," he said. "The new Bond is out."

"I'm going to have to pass. I've got company in town this weekend."

"Family?" he asked, hopefully.

She nodded.

"Maybe next weekend."

She thought about how the captain and sergeant would tell the others about her news. She was glad she wouldn't be here. "Good night, Brian."

"Good night, Cameron. Have a good one."

She hurried down the hallway and out the door. As soon as she was in the night air, she tore open the envelope. She flattened the note in her hand, wondering if he knew about the baby. She scanned the page and caught the words "love" and "miss."

She tried to calm herself and read the first line.

If you're reading this, it means I'm dead.

ABOUT THE AUTHOR

Danielle Girard is the bestselling author of *Chasing Darkness*, The Rookie Club series, and the Dr. Schwartzman Series—*Exhume*, *Excise*, E*xpose*, and *Expire,* featuring San Francisco medical examiner Dr. Annabelle Schwartzman. Danielle's books have won the Barry Award and the RT Reviewers' Choice Award, and two of her titles have been optioned for movies.

A graduate of Cornell University, Danielle received her MFA at Queens University in Charlotte, North Carolina. She, her husband, and their two children split their time between San Francisco and the Northern Rockies. Visit her at www.daniellegirard.com.

Made in the USA
Las Vegas, NV
18 February 2021

18069421R10229